The Cartel

*The shocking true story of the
rise of the Kinahan crime cartel and its
deadly feud with the Hutch gang*

STEPHEN BREEN
AND OWEN CONLON

PENGUIN

IRELAND

PENGUIN IRELAND

UK | USA | Canada | Ireland | Australia
India | New Zealand | South Africa

Penguin Ireland is part of the Penguin Random House group of companies
whose addresses can be found at global.penguinrandomhouse.com

First published 2017

001

Copyright © Stephen Breen and Owen Conlon, 2017

The moral right of the authors has been asserted

Set in 13.5/16 pt Garamond MT Std
Typeset by Jouve (UK), Milton Keynes
Printed in Great Britain by Clays Ltd, St Ives plc

A CIP catalogue record for this book is available from the British Library

ISBN: 978–1–844–88402–5

www.greenpenguin.co.uk

The Cartel

Before moving to Dublin in 2009 Stephen Breen worked in Northern Ireland – first for the *Belfast Telegraph* and then for seven years as the *Sunday Life's* crime correspondent, during which time he was twice named as Sunday Journalist of the Year. He is currently crime editor of the *Irish Sun* and has made regular appearances on RTÉ One's *Prime Time* to discuss crime issues.

Owen Conlon has been a journalist for over fifteen years and has covered crime, politics and international affairs. He started his career in national radio network INN before moving to Spain, where he worked as a freelance for several UK and Irish national dailies and RTÉ. He now works as an assistant news editor for the *Irish Sun*. As well as Spanish, he speaks Portuguese and French.

To all the innocent victims of gangland violence

cartel /kɑːˈtɛl/ › *noun* an association of manufacturers or suppliers with the purpose of maintaining prices at a high level and restricting competition i.e. 'the Colombian drug cartels'.

Contents

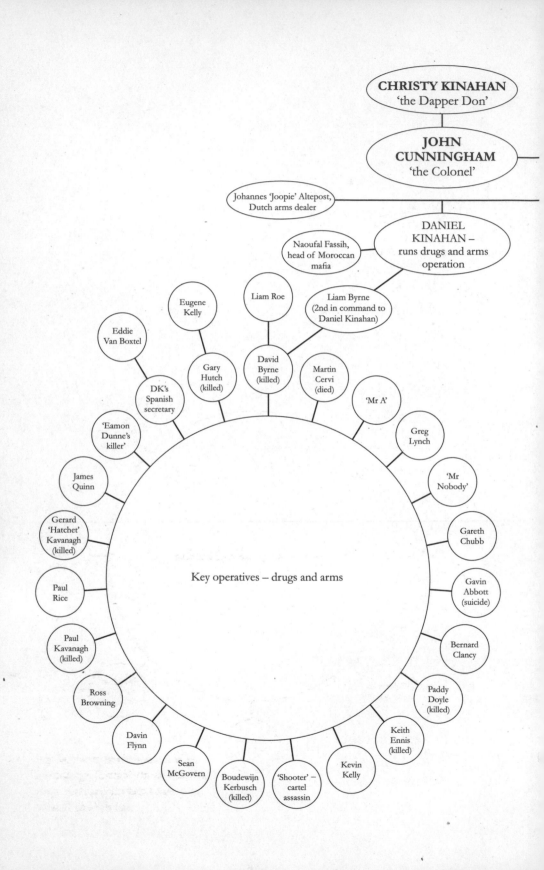

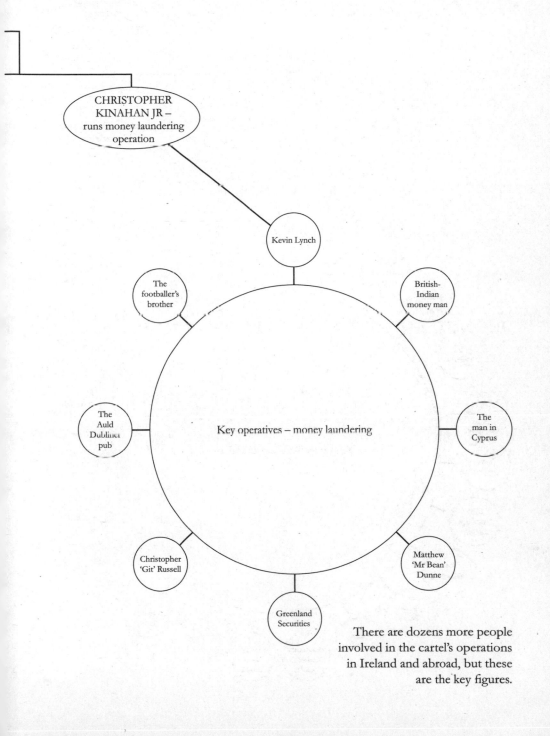

CHRISTOPHER
KINAHAN JR –
runs money laundering
operation

Kevin Lynch

The
footballer's
brother

British-
Indian
money man

The
Auld
Dubliner
pub

Key operatives – money laundering

The
man in
Cyprus

Christopher
'Git' Russell

Matthew
'Mr Bean'
Dunne

Greenland
Securities

There are dozens more people
involved in the cartel's operations
in Ireland and abroad, but these
are the key figures.

Prologue

The 999 call might well have been dismissed as a prank, were it not for its panicked tone and the fact that the man on the line identified himself instantly. John Glynn, Manager of the Regency Hotel in Drumcondra, on the northside of Dublin city, told the officer at the other end of the line that members of An Garda Síochána's Emergency Response Unit (ERU) were on his premises, and they were shooting people.

Patrol cars rushed to the hotel and came upon a scene of utter chaos. People were huddled outside the hotel in groups, still in shock. When uniformed cops went inside there was a strong smell of gunpowder in the lobby. A body lay flat on the floor against the reception desk, unmoving. The man's head and shoulders were turned at an awkward angle and blood oozed on to the floor from beneath the left side of his torso. Across from him gardaí found another man clutching his stomach and a third holding his thigh, both grimacing in pain.

The confrontation that had taken place just minutes beforehand, on 5 February 2016, was unprecedented in Irish history. Six armed men had arrived at a pre-boxing match weigh-in being held in broad daylight, looking for people to kill. Identifying their targets, they had opened fire inside a packed venue.

Three of the gunmen, who carried AK47 assault rifles, were disguised as members of the Garda's elite SWAT-like

ERU, prompting John Glynn's frantic call. Another man was dressed in drag, complete with make-up and a wig.

Ireland is a country which has dealt with large-scale terrorism in the past, but this invariably involved attacks on the security forces, particularly in Northern Ireland. It has also seen its fair share of gangland assassinations, but these were always carried out with as few witnesses around as possible. This was something else entirely.

One criminal gang, the Hutches, had launched a brazen military-style attack on a rival criminal group, the Kinahan cartel. The dead man, drug dealer David Byrne, was a senior figure within the latter outfit. One of the injured men, Sean McGovern, was a lower-ranking cartel member while the other, Aaron Bolger, was a hanger-on.

The real target, however, was Daniel Kinahan, the son of Christy Kinahan, and one of the leaders of the Kinahan drugs and arms cartel. When the gunmen entered the front door of the hotel, Daniel had been in the function room adjoining the lobby, watching the weigh-in take place.

As pandemonium broke out, the boxer and officials on stage and many of those watching from the floor ran for the fire exit immediately to the left of the raised area. Others, Daniel Kinahan amongst them, ran out a door directly behind it.

The heir apparent of the cartel was pushed outside by his bodyguard. They made their way up a staircase on to a flat roof and, jumping down, fled the scene on foot. The two men are believed by gardaí to have taken the first flight they could get, to reach safety in London.

No arrests were made by gardaí, the attackers having fled before the force's arrival. The getaway vehicle, a Ford Transit van, was later found burnt out in a nearby housing estate.

There was a general air of disbelief in the city following the attack, with the Taoiseach making statements aimed at calming an unnerved public. But if the authorities had been left stunned by what had happened, those who had found themselves under attack were stupefied.

For more than six years, the Kinahan cartel had been the undisputed top dog of Ireland's criminal world. It controlled the country's drugs and arms traffic and very little happened without its say-so, particularly if it would affect the gang's business interests.

The previous September, Gary Hutch, once a key member of the cartel, and an ally and personal friend of Daniel Kinahan, had been shot dead at his apartment in southern Spain.

Hutch had been accused of trying to kill his former boss, though he protested his innocence. That afternoon, Gary's associates had come for their revenge against the man who had ordered his murder. They had failed.

As Daniel Kinahan, Liam Byrne, brother of the dead man and a senior gang figure, and other members of the cartel gathered their wits, their shock turned to fury.

There would be hell to pay.

1. The Dapper Don

'When it came to the drugs importation business, he learned from his mistakes.'

Retired Assistant Garda Commissioner
Michael O'Sullivan

The young undercover officer posing as an electrician thought the man who had just opened the door of the apartment under surveillance in Fairview, north Dublin, was the target of the operation, but he could not be sure. The last photograph gardaí had of him dated back to 1979, an era when shaggy, long locks were all the rage. Seven years later, the man matched the description gardaí had been given, but he had shorter hair and seemed better groomed.

'Sorry, can you check to see if your lights are working, please, we've had some problems?' the cop asked him, remaining in character.

'Wha'?' replied the man in a strong Dublin accent, before quickly realizing he had a pretence of his own to maintain. Switching to an English drawl, he continued, 'I think the lights are fine, mate. I will check and let you know.'

The target closed the door and went back into the apartment. Mission accomplished, the undercover officer backed off. The Garda surveillance team, including current Garda Commissioner, Noirín O'Sullivan, continued to watch as a known drug addict visited the flat and handed over money for a small package.

As detectives were now satisfied their target, Christy Kinahan, was staying there, they obtained a search warrant the following day and swooped on the apartment.

When they burst in, Christy was eating a sandwich and almost choked when he saw the gardaí. An Algerian man, who detectives later discovered was named Rabah Serier, was also sitting in the living room.

While some officers began questioning Serier, others checked the bedroom. On the right-hand side of the bed they found a holdall. Inside was IR£117,000 worth of heroin. There was also a weighing scales, glucose, a mirror and razor blades, along with stolen cheque books, cheque cards and IR£2,275 in cash, all in a bundle at the bottom of the wardrobe.

The anonymous information gardaí had been given was correct. That summer in 1986, the Christy Kinahan they used to know as a chancer and a fraudster had moved into the far more profitable world of drugs.

Christopher Kinahan was born in Ealing, in London, in 1957 into a decent family and has two sisters. While he was still a child, they returned home to Dublin and settled in Phibsboro, north Dublin, where his father worked as a dairy firm manager. His parents, Daniel and Mary, were respectable people and their house at 13 Charleville Road had also been the childhood home of Taoiseach John A. Costello, the man who would go on to declare Ireland a Republic in 1948.

Christy was cut from different cloth. Though intelligent and devoted to his chosen sport of judo, he was a troublemaker in school and was kicked out of St Declan's College, in Cabra, on Dublin's northside. He was accepted at O'Connell's School on North Richmond Street, whose past pupils include James Joyce, Pat Kenny, actor Colm Meaney and his predecessor at 13 Charleville Road, John A. Costello. Once again, Christy would fall short of those who had gone before him.

Exempt from learning Irish due to his London upbringing, Christy failed his Leaving Certificate, finishing school with an E in maths, history and art. His only two passes came with Ds in English and – fittingly for a future international drug baron – geography.

After leaving school, Kinahan worked for a short period as a part-time taxi driver. He married his girlfriend, Jean Boylan, and the couple had two sons: Daniel, born on 25 June 1977, and Christopher Jr, born on 24 September 1980.

Christy soon abandoned his driving job and started concentrating all his efforts on crime. He focused on cheque fraud, distribution of stolen cheques, stealing cars and the odd burglary.

Christy's first conviction came in 1979 at the age of twenty-two for attempted car theft. He faced more charges for burglary and receiving stolen property over the next two years, but these were later struck out in court.

By the early eighties, Kinahan had taken his first steps towards becoming a household name in Ireland – for all the wrong reasons. He was familiar to gardaí, but more as a swindler than a serious criminal. However, he continued to network in dodgy circles – in both the north and south inner city – including those of Gerry 'the Monk' Hutch.

In 1983, Gerry Hutch was regarded as an up-and-coming criminal from the north inner-city area of Dublin. Like Kinahan, his early criminal career started with involvement in the stolen cheque trade. Through this common enterprise, he was introduced to Christy Kinahan and over the years the pair would forge a close friendship and working relationship.

That same year, Christy was arrested for cheque fraud. He received a IR£200 fine for this offence and was bound over to keep the peace for a year.

Despite being up to his neck in scams, a year later Kinahan set up a firm offering a 'sealed security card service' with another man, though it appears the company never actually traded.

By the middle of the decade, Christy was still primarily involved in theft and con jobs, but he could also see the enormous profits being made in the heroin trade. At the time, the Dunne family controlled the drugs scene in the capital and their network of dealers were selling openly in Dublin's inner-city flat complexes.

Widely regarded as the man who introduced heroin to Ireland, Larry Dunne was the country's first drugs godfather. By swamping inner-city communities with the drug, Dunne, who once paid IR£100,000 in cash for a house, led a champagne lifestyle. He was driven around Dublin in a limo as heroin took its stranglehold on entire communities, leading to the deaths of hundreds of people over the years.

The money the Dunnes were making from their drugs empire was huge and they flaunted it openly, moving to expensive areas on Dublin's southside, sending their children to private schools, taking expensive foreign holidays and eating at the city's best restaurants. None of these ostentatious displays of wealth escaped Christy's attention.

Christy left his wife, Jean, while his children were at a young age and began going out with a woman from Dublin's York Street area, near the St Stephen's Green shopping centre. His new partner knew some of those involved in the trade and Christy used her to gain himself an introduction. He approached local dealers in a bid to establish how they were operating, what contacts they were using and to offer his support in arranging shipments.

By the end of 1985 he was successful in gaining their trust and started dealing. Kinahan's outsider status enabled him to keep a low profile compared to many other criminals who the gardaí knew were actively involved in drugs.

As an experienced fraudster, Kinahan also maintained a smoother veneer than other nouveaux-riches working-class gangsters, such as the Dunnes. Christy was always well dressed and, due to his involvement in the stolen cheque trade, had often posed as a businessman. Earning a reputation as one of the capital's main fraudsters, he would later become known as the 'Dapper Don' because of his polished appearance and love of fine clothes.

Christy also operated from a small convenience store in Irishtown, in south Dublin. Although they couldn't prove it at the time, by the start of 1986 gardaí believed he used it as a front to launder the proceeds of stolen cheques.

He was under regular Garda surveillance but they did not have enough evidence to move against him. Some of the surveillance operations could actually be carried out from the back of Irishtown Garda Station, which overlooked his store.

Kinahan would motor around the city in a white Hiace van, frequently trailed by an undercover garda on a motorbike, posing as a courier. Around two months before gardaí swooped on the Fairview apartment, Christy had come to their attention as someone who might be involved in the drugs trade. They didn't think he was dealing from the van, but they wanted to keep tabs on his movements.

On one occasion, the cop followed Christy to the North

Circular Road. When Kinahan pulled up, the garda unhooked the motorbike's chain and pretended to work on it, as he subtly kept his mark under observation. As he knelt on the road, the garda also watched two men go into a nearby house. The pair looked suspicious and he watched as, sometime later, they came out the back door of the property carrying a fireplace, which they had clearly just stolen. Unable to blow his own cover, the garda discreetly informed his colleagues of the break-in and a squad car was sent to intercept the two scavengers. Meanwhile, the sporadic surveillance continued.

Timing was also on Christy's side as he sought to establish himself on the drugs scene. In May 1985, Larry Dunne was jailed for fourteen years after gardaí found IR£60,000 worth of heroin, cocaine and hash at his home. It was an ironic end for a man who boasted he would never be caught due to his motto: 'Larry doesn't carry.' Loud cheers came from the public gallery in 1985 as his sentence was announced. As he was being led away, Dunne reportedly told gardaí, 'If you think we're bad, wait 'til you see what's coming after us.' They would prove to be prophetic words. (Currently living in a modest house in south Dublin, the former heroin kingpin has consistently refused to comment on the devastating effect of drugs on Irish society, and on his family's role in bringing them into Ireland.)

Christy's next move was to rent a luxury apartment from a local couple at Crescent House, in Fairview, close to the upmarket area of Clontarf, in north Dublin. Complete with his fake English accent, he posed as a commercial traveller from London who made regular trips to Dublin.

'He was such a nice man,' explained a friend of the flat's landlord. 'He was very clean, courteous and the place was immaculate. He claimed he was a businessman, and there wasn't a hint of any trouble when he was staying there.'

On the surface, Christy was the perfect tenant – he was plausible, intelligent, articulate and drove a red sports car. In fact the apartment was being used as a safe house. The intention was to store the drugs there before bringing them to other distribution homes and locations across the city. Only a small number of people would have known the drugs had been stored there. The apartment was a world away from the flat complexes of the inner city and the kinds of places where heroin was usually stored.

The location was so unlikely that when gardaí received a tip-off about what was going on at the apartment, they initially had trouble believing it. Kinahan had barely hit their radar for drug dealing. The success of the bust on 14 September 1986 would change all that.

Once in custody, Christy held up his hands and admitted responsibility. Dropping his phoney English Home Counties twang, Christy said, 'I'm taking full responsibility for everything found – the gear, the cheques, everything.' However, he bizarrely denied having supplied the junkie who had just left the apartment, despite the fact detectives had watched Christy carry out the deal.

He admitted he had been dealing for about three months before the raid and, turning to the 'electrician' who had arrested him, said, 'I was told to watch out for you.'

Christy was held on remand after his arrest, and by the time his trial started in March 1987 Kinahan had changed his tune. The court heard he had rented the apartment, but was not living there. He claimed he had agreed to let Rabah Serier live there, but knew nothing about the drugs or Serier's involvement with them.

The middle-class suburb they were operating from was the ideal cover for their activities. It was notable that the heroin was not even hidden and was quite openly kept in a bag on the floor. The pair were cutting up and diluting the drug before wholesaling it to street dealers for between IR£300 and IR£500 a time.

During the trial, no explanation was offered for how Kinahan and Serier knew each other, but evidence was given that they had opened a joint bank account five weeks earlier, into which they had lodged IR£5,352. Serier's lawyer later suggested that this money was for the opening of a clothing business.

Caught red-handed, Kinahan pleaded guilty and settled on the wheeze that he himself was a heroin addict who was trying to turn his life around, and that he intended to enter a drug rehabilitation programme. Gardaí believed this to be a blatant lie.

Christy also stated that he was trying to better himself and was learning Arabic and French. Gardaí agreed, but were certain the Linguaphone tapes found at the apartment, which Christy was using to learn the languages, were part of a master plan aimed at furthering his drug-trafficking activities. Learning the languages would give him the tools to deal directly with organized criminal gangs all over Europe. Some of the biggest suppliers were in countries such as Morocco, and Kinahan's new skill would enable him to avoid the language barrier when it came to negotiating prices for shipments of drugs.

At Christy's sentencing hearing, his barrister said he had taken several courses while on remand and was continuing his French language studies.

Gardaí believed Kinahan's attempts to play the victim

card, portraying himself as a heroin addict, were his way of obtaining a lesser sentence from the courts. The ploy partially worked, as the trial judge declared that 'were it not for the circumstances', he would have jailed Christy for ten years. Instead, he got six.

However, the Dapper Don's efforts to hold on to the IR£2,275 in cash found at the apartment did not go as well. Opposing a subsequent application for its forfeiture, Kinahan said he had made the money from selling cars and had also been getting an enterprise grant from the State of IR£50 a week. The judge ignored his claims.

His co-defendant, the Algerian Rabah Serier, was something of a mystery man. Interpol had no record of him and gardaí had never come across him before either. He had married an Irish woman six years previously and the court heard the union was now in 'a spot of bother'.

One of Serier's brothers was a high-ranking Algerian police officer and his family had been genuinely shocked when he was arrested for drugs offences. After his arrest, another brother had flown to Ireland offering IR£10,000 in an attempt to have him bailed, but this was refused by the court.

At the trial Serier went for the religious angle. He had begun a hunger strike in jail, claiming he was a strict Muslim who was not being allowed to pray or access halal food behind bars. He too pleaded guilty and turned up for sentencing looking pale and drawn in a wheelchair. The tactic also succeeded to a degree, as Serier received a four-and-a-half-year jail term.

Michael O'Sullivan, the undercover 'electrician' who arrested Kinahan, became an Assistant Commissioner. He believes the relatively light sentences were a missed opportunity to end Kinahan's criminal career early:

Like many first business enterprises, there are always risks involved. But in heroin, the risks were huge. Anyone caught with the drug could face a lengthy prison sentence, thereby disrupting their activities and ability to accumulate profit. Kinahan knew nothing about heroin and, contrary to what many people believe, he wasn't using it. He wasn't a street criminal like many of the dealers at the time. The only people who knew about heroin at that time were the dealers and the users.

The only reason Christy Kinahan got involved in this trade is because he was a mercenary. He was an opportunist who saw there was money to be made. Well-known criminals at that time like the Dunne family didn't matter to him. Like any visionary businessman, he was a forward thinker and a planner. The only people who knew he was getting involved in heroin in 1986 were those who were close to him.

His first shipment was ultimately a disaster for Kinahan but because there was an Algerian national with him at the time it showed that he had already been building his international connections. He would also come to court with his books and read. Even then, he was already thinking of the future. But can you imagine if he had received twenty years? He probably wouldn't have been in business today. Heroin was absolutely devastating communities in Ireland at the time and a twenty-year sentence would have been deemed appropriate. If he had received twenty years, then he would have been coming out to a completely different society and one where he would have had no power.

Christy kept himself occupied during his six years in jail, using the time to study, but the way he was caught ate away at him. He was a man who bore grudges, both against those he blamed for his arrest and the cops who carried it out.

Eleven years after the bust at the Fairview apartment, then Detective Garda O'Sullivan was out for a run near his Dublin home when he noticed a white Ford Fiesta acting suspiciously. Manoeuvring himself so he could see the driver, he made out Kinahan's features behind the wheel. Detective O'Sullivan remained calm and he later told his colleagues what had happened. It was a forerunner of the sort of intimidation which Kinahan would try to impose on a much grander scale – particularly towards the gang member he had decided was responsible for his arrest.

Raymond Salinger had lived in London before and he hadn't particularly liked it. In fact, his first stay in the British capital in 1984 had ended abruptly after two months. The young Dubliner had been unable to find any work and, spending his days drinking and smoking cannabis, he could no longer stand the homesickness. So when Raymond with his wife, Paula, and their young daughter boarded a ferry bound for the UK again in the summer of 1987, it was not from choice. Salinger, then twenty-five years old, was fleeing for his life.

An occasional drug user and former drug dealer, Salinger was born into a family of eight brothers and four sisters on Kevin Street, in Dublin's south inner city, on 17 November 1962.

In his early teenage years, Salinger didn't have much interest in school and soon found himself in trouble with his parents. Easily influenced, he was engaging in antisocial behaviour, drinking and missing school.

Local gardaí soon noted him hanging around with minor criminals and he was stopped several times driving without insurance. When heroin hit Dublin in the late 1970s and early 1980s, it also hit Salinger too. Like many of his friends, he soon found himself experimenting with the drug. Once hooked, he turned to crime to feed his habit.

Raymond first came to the attention of gardaí as a seventeen-year-old. A file later sent to the DPP noted that he was considered to be 'associating with small-time criminals'. He started breaking into homes and stealing handbags. Then his dad, Martin, died.

As one former friend put it, 'With his father gone he had no one to keep him on the straight and narrow. His life became a mess after that, and his involvement in drugs and crime simply escalated.'

As the 1980s progressed, Raymond Salinger was regarded by gardaí as 'being involved in drugs'. But, on the numerous occasions he was stopped and searched, officers only recovered small amounts of cannabis and heroin. Salinger claimed they were for his own use, and he had no convictions for drugs.

But he would soon have far bigger concerns than searches by the gardaí. Having been identified by his neighbours as someone who was peddling cannabis to teenagers in the south inner city, it was only a matter of time before Salinger came to the attention of the members of the Concerned Parents Against Drugs (CPAD), the republican-dominated vigilante group.

The State was slow to respond to the negative impact of the drugs flooding working-class areas of Dublin. Many residents believed the gardaí weren't doing enough to arrest the drug dealers, and that's when the community responded. CPAD saw an opportunity to fill the vacuum, regularly marching on the homes of suspected dealers, demanding they leave the area immediately.

But there were concerns the response had been hijacked by republican paramilitaries. Very often, the protests descended into chaos, with fist fights between the dealers and the vigilantes. At the beginning of 1984, the CPAD group in the Crumlin and Kevin Street areas had compiled a list of targets. On it was the name of 21-year-old Raymond Salinger.

At first, Salinger and his friends had continued to sell small bags of heroin to users across the south inner city. But after his family were threatened by a senior republican figure in 1984, Salinger fled to London, hoping to create a new life for himself working on the city's building sites. Work was hard to come by, however, and Salinger lasted just two months before returning to Dublin.

The threat against him was still very much alive when he got back and Salinger knew that if he was to make himself less of a target, he would no longer be able to peddle drugs directly and would have to advance up the chain.

Using his connections, he was introduced to Christy Kinahan, who was five years his senior. It was at the same time that Christy was making his own moves in Dublin's underworld, graduating from fraud into drugs. Throughout 1985, gardaí believed Kinahan and a tight-knit group of associates were distributing cannabis across the south inner city to a regular customer base. Heroin, however, was a far more profitable drug and Salinger had experience in the trade.

Salinger was accepted into Kinahan's crew and became a trusted member. But when Christy was caught red-handed with drugs at his Fairview apartment in 1986, following the Garda surveillance operation, he decided he had been double-crossed by a member of his own gang.

Working through a number of suspects, Christy identified

the people in his inner circle who had knowledge of his shipment and, more importantly, knew the location of his flat. Eventually, he settled on his young friend and criminal associate Raymond Salinger.

Garda officers at the time had intelligence which suggested that '. . . Christopher Kinahan was convinced Salinger had given the gardaí information, which resulted in his arrest and conviction.'

Ostracized from Kinahan's inner circle, Salinger knew he was being blamed for what had happened. Despite pleading his innocence to some of Christy's closest associates, and despite there being no evidence to prove the young drug dealer was an informer, Salinger knew his new boss's mind was already made up.

Kinahan was in jail, but Salinger wasn't taking any chances. He escaped to the UK with his wife and daughter.

Arriving in London, he and his family were collected by the same friends he'd moved in with when he'd fled Dublin in 1984, that time under threat from the community activists. The exiled criminal had been diagnosed with asthma because of his smoking habit of forty cigarettes a day, but he continued to use cannabis, smoke heroin and drink heavily.

One friend said:

He was in London with a young family and he wasn't a single man any more. He was determined to do his best for his wife and daughter and would stay off the drugs any time he was in regular employment on the building sites around London but also in other UK cities. They found it hard adapting to life in London at the start but soon found their feet.

Raymond Salinger was not going back to Dublin any time soon — but he would discover that Christy Kinahan had a long memory.

Upon his release in 1992, Christy soon went back to his old ways. If you watch that year's episode of the popular RTÉ show *Reeling in the Years*, it features the usual range of nostalgic highlights to remind viewers how much has changed in this country and how much has stayed the same. Amid the footage of Annie Murphy's revelation of her affair with Bishop Casey, the horrific Yugoslav civil war and Michael Carruth's gold medal win in Barcelona, is an interview with Dr Eamon Keenan. He discusses how widespread rave culture, and the accompanying use of the drug Ecstasy, had become.

The popularity of Ecstasy meant that when Christy Kinahan walked out of jail in March of that year, a whole new world of opportunities had opened up for him. Drug use was no longer confined to heroin in poor working-class areas or cocaine in upper-class ones. Ecstasy was a drug that had reached all strata of Irish society, including small towns across the country where the worst the local drugs squad had previously had to deal with was a little cannabis. 'E' was being taken by adults and teenagers, from sinkhole estates to affluent suburbs. And even better from a drug trafficker's point of view, the new dance drugs could be synthesized far closer to the Irish market, eliminating the need for multi-stop transportation from abroad and the perils of dealing with rival gangs.

It was a market Christy was keen to exploit. To his old staples of heroin, cocaine and cannabis, he quickly added the new product and soon became involved in the Ecstasy trade through his contacts in Europe.

Christy also continued to network with other Dublin criminals. In June 1993, IR£16,000 worth of travellers' cheques were taken in a raid by armed robber Thomas 'Bomber' Clarke on the First National Building Society in Drumcondra, in Dublin. Once more, the police had been tipped off about Christy's possible involvement and mounted a surveillance operation.

A week after the raid, gardaí staked out a grotto near St James's Hospital, Dublin, and watched while Kinahan met with a man on a bicycle and handed him a bag, before they went their separate ways. Detectives pulled over the cyclist and found the travellers' cheques inside the holdall.

Kinahan was arrested and charged with possession of stolen cheques, and he was facing some serious jail time once more. He received bail, despite Garda objections, and, as he did not fancy heading back to Mountjoy Prison, he skipped to Holland. There, he returned to work as a drugs wholesaler, only this time on a bigger scale. The Dapper Don would also add a new interest to his CV – weapons.

Not long after this, Christy was caught in the Netherlands with a haul of Ecstasy, cocaine and weapons and was jailed for four years. He served just one year at Norgerhaven jail, in northern Holland. Christy again tried to make the most of the situation, hooking up behind bars with established Dutch criminals such as arms dealer Johannes 'Joopie' Altepost.

Following his release from prison, Kinahan continued his relationship with Altepost, who had extensive gun-running contacts in eastern Europe. Altepost was also a key target for law enforcement agencies across Europe.

Christy also established a relationship with a crooked Dutch lawyer who would prove very useful in building up a property portfolio for him in Belgium some years later.

Upon his release Kinahan was soon on the move again, this time to the upmarket town of Tamworth, outside Birmingham, in the UK. There, he busied himself making more criminal contacts.

Two of them were brothers, serious criminals from outside Birmingham. Others included Maurice Sines and James Crickmore, who earned a record fourteen-year ban from horse racing after they were found to be involved in a massive race-fixing scam.

For the sake of appearances, Christy was listed as the director of a tanning salon, along with the Dutch woman he had married in Surrey following the end of his marriage to Jean Boylan. His new wife would also later be named as the company secretary of a mortgage brokerage run by a British-Indian man who would go on to become a significant figure within the cartel.

Kinahan gradually solidified his network of contacts in Dublin's criminal underworld, including those associated with his old friend Gerry 'the Monk' Hutch.

In the intervening years while Kinahan had focused on the drugs trade, Hutch's speciality had become armed robberies. Hutch, who also had close links to the Provisional IRA, was regarded as the mastermind behind a IR£1.7 million heist from a Securicor cash-in-transit van in Fairview, north Dublin, on 26 January 1987. The veteran criminal, who claimed to have made his money through the property trade, was also suspected of orchestrating the theft of IR£3 million from the Brinks Allied depot in Clonshaugh, north Dublin, in 1995. Although not directly involved in the drugs trade, gardaí believed he turned a blind eye to Christy's operation.

Kinahan also built up a powerful list of contacts across

Europe, using them to arrange his shipments into Ireland. He used false passports to move over and back to Dublin from the Continent, to strike deals and drum up new customers.

Maintaining a low profile in his hideouts in Holland, Kinahan put his business plan into action. He started to put a team of trusted associates in place, including his young son Daniel, then in his late teens. Daniel was looking to his dad for inspiration and was also building up his own network.

The gang brought shipments of drugs and high-powered weapons into Ireland. Companies were established and premises sourced and rented in order to lend legitimacy. A few trial runs of genuine products would take place, to further beef up appearances, before the real merchandise would begin to flow through the secure system. Many of the warehouses would be used as bases to store his product. As his business plan took shape, Kinahan also established links with truck drivers and transport companies he could use to deliver his goods.

Following the murder of journalist Veronica Guerin on 26 June 1996, however, the State declared war on organized crime. The brazen murder of a young mother who had dared to question where drug traffickers, such as John Gilligan, were getting their money from caused genuine public outrage throughout the country.

Gilligan, then Ireland's top drug baron and one of its most notorious criminals, was making no attempt to hide his wealth, having bought an equestrian centre in Jessbrook, County Kildare with his illicit millions.* The pressure was

* John Gilligan would later be tried and acquitted of Guerin's murder, though he remains the chief suspect for ordering the contract hit. He was freed from custody on 15 October 2013, after serving twelve years of a

on the Government to respond. The establishment of the Criminal Assets Bureau (CAB) was their answer, aimed at hitting criminals where it hurt – in their pockets. The CAB, which was also adopted by other European countries, received powers to seize assets and to freeze the bank accounts of criminals who were benefiting from the proceeds of crime. Its staff are not just gardaí, they are tax officials, social welfare officers, customs officers, forensic accountants and other financial analysts. Christy's two associates from Birmingham would go on to become key targets of Britain's Serious Organized Crime Agency (SOCA), the UK's answer to Ireland's CAB.

Key members of the gang led by drugs kingpin John Gilligan went to ground amid the huge Garda crackdown.

The same could not be said of Christy Kinahan and his gang throughout 1996. Over the following months, the newly formed Garda National Drug Unit (GNDU) would receive intelligence that many of the drugs now coming into Ireland belonged to Christy Kinahan.

What they had come to call the Kinahan Organized Crime Group (KOCG) was officially open for business.

twenty-year sentence for possessing 20,000kg of cannabis. Gilligan now maintains a low profile after narrowly escaping two assassination attempts since his release from prison.

2. Building an Empire

'The Kinahans were bringing the stuff in and the
Hutches were helping them distribute. They
were the only show in town.'

Former Garda lead investigator

There were some familiar faces in the bar of the Valley Hotel
in Woodenbridge, County Wicklow when Michael Houlihan
and his wife walked in for an evening drink on the Sunday of
the All-Ireland football final in September 1996.

One of them was a prison officer, one of his work colleagues, who possibly should not have been there given
he was still supposed to be on shift. The two others with
him most certainly had no business to be in the pub. John
Cunningham and Eamon Daly were inmates in Shelton
Abbey, the open prison twenty minutes up the road, where
Houlihan worked as assistant governor.

Cunningham was serving a seventeen-year sentence for
kidnapping the wife of a wealthy banker. He had been
sentenced along with his older brother Mick and another
career criminal, Anthony Kelly. His drinking buddy, Eamon
Daly, was in the middle of a twelve-year stretch for armed
robbery.

The next day, the prison officer from the bar was suspended from duty, pending an investigation. Daly was sent

back to the harsher regime at Mountjoy Prison. But there were no consequences for Cunningham, because after being brought back to Shelton Abbey that night, he simply walked out the front gate the following morning.

It was the start of a new era for the 'Colonel', who had earned his nickname from the very abduction which had landed him in Shelton Abbey in the first place.

Cunningham had an impressive criminal résumé. Whereas Christy Kinahan made a conscious decision as an adult to devote himself to a life of crime, John Cunningham had never known any other way. He picked up his first conviction, for larceny, at the tender age of fourteen and never looked back. He hit the big time while acting as second-in-command to infamous criminal godfather Martin 'the General' Cahill during the meticulously planned IR£1.5 million O'Connor's jewellery heist in 1983.

Cunningham went on to take part in a string of armed robberies in the eighties, earning him hundreds of thousands of pounds, but he was not satisfied. He and his older brother Mick – who had also first been convicted at fourteen – were continually on the lookout for the one big score that would enable them to retire early, in their mid-thirties. They needed the money to maintain the lifestyle they had built up for themselves. The brothers were known for being somewhat flashy. They were particularly fond of expensive holidays abroad, visiting places like Barbados, and they also regularly hired boats to cruise the River Shannon.

In 1986, the siblings decided kidnapping was their ticket to a life of freedom. Abductions for ransom were in vogue in Ireland at the time, especially amongst paramilitaries. Cunningham and his brother Mick, desperate for a big payday, fancied their chances of pulling off their own score.

The brothers chose their target, Jennifer Guinness, after reading about the family in a magazine feature. Her husband, John, was a scion of the famous brewing dynasty and a merchant banker. Together with another convicted armed robber, Anthony Kelly, they forced their way into the family home in Howth, north County Dublin, and took Jennifer Guinness away at gunpoint. The gang demanded a IR£2 million ransom for her safe return.

The trio gave the impression they were paramilitaries and John was referred to throughout as 'Colonel', with Mick gaining the rank of 'Sergeant'.

An eight-day cat-and-mouse chase with gardaí ensued, before the gang were traced to a house in Ballsbridge, a suburb on the south side of the city.

Gardaí had nominated the brothers as suspects within forty-eight hours of the kidnapping taking place and were on the lookout for the pair. When John Cunningham was spotted driving a hired green Opel Kadett through Dublin city centre, the gardaí swung into action. The car was eventually located outside the house on Waterloo Road, Ballsbridge.

After an all-night siege, the brothers laid down their weapons and surrendered. The 'Colonel' later declared in custody, 'It was going to be the big one but it went wrong. We thought the family would not tell the police; we would collect and no one would ever know.' It was not an idle boast.

Unbeknownst to gardaí, IR£1 million in cash had been organized by the Guinness family, and was ready to be dropped off in three suitcases each containing almost STG£300,000 (worth almost IR£1 million at the time). The suitcases were to be deposited at an agreed location in Stillorgan, south Dublin, on the morning Jennifer Guinness was rescued.

Jennifer Guinness would later reveal how terrified she had been during the kidnapping, because she was convinced she was going to die. When news of her abduction broke on the radio, the Cunninghams became enraged and told her to get dressed, as they were going to take her to a wooded area to kill and bury her.

She said she had mentally rehearsed being executed and tried desperately to build a relationship with her kidnappers throughout her ordeal in an attempt to make it more difficult for them to murder her.

'I thought they would have to shoot me standing up, facing them,' she subsequently said. Referring to an interview given by Dutch industrialist Dr Tiede Herrema after he had been held hostage by the IRA a decade earlier, she added, 'I remember Dr Herrema saying: "Talk, talk, talk all the time."'

During the siege, the 'Colonel' discussed ending it all 'in a blaze of glory' with a grenade. It was here Jennifer Guinness's efforts to communicate with her captors helped to save her life. She was aware that Cunningham's wife was expecting a baby and made him promise he would name the child after her if she was a girl.

His wife's pregnancy was a crucial factor in making John Cunningham lay down his arms and surrender. Kelly, who had been captured by gardaí outside the house and was being used as liaison with the brothers, also referred to the baby, telling Cunningham, 'Remember the pud.'

The siblings eventually surrendered to gardaí in the early hours of the morning. Mick Cunningham ushered Jennifer Guinness out the front door with the words, 'Ladies first.' When the case came to trial in November 1986, John, seen as the ringleader, was jailed for seventeen years. His brother

Mick received a fourteen-year sentence, as did Kelly, who had been arrested trying to flee the house.

But just three months into his sentence, John Cunningham gave the authorities an early warning of his intentions. At 1.30 a.m. a warden doing his rounds at Limerick Prison spotted Cunningham trying to climb into the exercise yard through a hole in his cell wall. Gardaí and the army were rushed to what was supposedly one of the most secure facilities in the State. Amid fears a mass escape was being planned, the street outside was cordoned off.

Astonishingly, the hole had apparently been dug the previous afternoon when Cunningham had refused to go out into the yard for his daily exercise period.

After the failed escape attempt, there were calls for an urgent review of security at the prison, which held republican paramilitaries. Prison officers themselves admitted it was 'pure luck' the 'Colonel' had been caught, as there had been cutbacks in staffing levels.

John Cunningham served the first ten years of his time largely without further incident and was transferred to the laxer regime of the open prison at Shelton Abbey, County Wicklow in 1996 to see the rest of it out. With standard remission for good behaviour, he would have been free in another two years.

But then came the incident in the hotel bar in Wicklow. Cunningham's punishment would have involved a transfer back to the far stricter regime in Limerick Prison, meaning he would also miss the wedding of his adopted daughter, Caroline, a few weeks later.

The 'Colonel' decided he could not hack a return to hard time, even if it meant his non-attendance at the wedding ceremony. Gardaí maintained discreet surveillance on the church on the day and, unsurprisingly, Cunningham failed to show – something which left Caroline 'devastated', according to John's wife, Mary.

The gangster remained in regular contact with his spouse while on the run. She was remarkably open about her husband's intentions. 'He is adamant he will not go back,' she declared, two weeks after he'd fled. 'He has had a taste of freedom. He was getting out at the end of next year. I thought he was mad to escape.'

Using a fake passport, Cunningham made his way to Holland where he resolved to start over. He was soon joined by Mary and their daughter, who was in her early teens. He was helped somewhat in that Ireland had never bothered to issue an international warrant for his arrest following his escape.

Cunningham was now forty-five years old and there was little chance of a career change. Following his escape from Shelton Abbey, he relied on Ireland's then foremost drug baron, 'Factory John' Gilligan to help establish himself on the Dutch drugs scene. He quickly set up a drug supply line to Ireland, and within a short time he was making huge money. The 'Colonel' also used Gilligan to make more contacts for the purpose of importing cannabis into Ireland. (At the time, Gilligan's gang was one of the biggest importers of cannabis from Holland into Ireland.) The pair were working hand in glove but Gilligan was simply a means to an end, as Cunningham's loyalty was to Christy Kinahan.

Cunningham and Christy had forged a close friendship in the early 1980s when they first became known to each other because of Christy's involvement in cheque fraud. Cunningham's criminal links with Christy were strengthened by their shared time behind bars in the mid-1980s. Even when Cunningham was jailed for the Guinness kidnapping, the pair remained in close contact.

Following Gilligan's arrest in November 1996, Cunningham went into business big time with Kinahan. Christy needed someone as experienced as himself to help lay the foundations of the cartel, and Cunningham was the natural choice. With Kinahan still imprisoned in Norgerhaven jail in northern Holland, the 'Colonel' was given the role of arranging shipments of drugs and weapons to Ireland. He was the de facto leader in Kinahan's absence and was regarded as a trusted lieutenant. The contacts that had already been forged by Kinahan in Holland and the rest of Europe had simply been passed to Cunningham.

The Garda National Drug Unit (GNDU) was determined to put operations in place throughout 1997 in a bid to disrupt the Kinahan Organized Crime Group (KOCG), using intelligence from informers on the ground. Information came in from users, fellow gang members and from other criminal gangs involved in the drugs trade. These tip-offs were the key pillars of the case they were building against Christy's gang, as they needed to compile a picture of the gang's key players and their associates.

Top of the Kinahan tree alongside John Cunningham were Christy's two sons. Kinahan's bail hearing back in 1986 had been told that he had little contact with his ex-wife, Jean Boylan, and his young boys, Daniel and Christopher Jr, after he left her for another woman. But despite the lack of attention from Christy in their early years, both sons grew up eager to please the man who had abandoned them to concentrate on a life of crime. And when they were ready to join him, their father had the perfect roles mapped out for them.

Jeanette Cullen was one of several locals who gathered for the launch of a proposed IR£15 million redevelopment of the hundred-year-old Iveagh Markets in Dublin's south inner city by then Taoiseach, Bertie Ahern. Mrs Cullen laughed as she confirmed to the *Irish Times* she was a grandmother, something she did not like admitting as she was 'too young'. Pushing forward what was described as her 'shy' grandson, she said, 'Give him a plug.'

The paper noted the 'young businessman' Daniel Kinahan had only just set up a furniture restoration business a month beforehand. The firm went belly-up a year later, and with it went any pretence that the then 22-year-old would attempt a legitimate career. In reality Daniel had an even earlier start in criminality than his father and was involved in drug dealing from his late teens.

Daniel spent his childhood in the Oliver Bond flat complex in south inner-city Dublin, with his brother Christopher Jr, three years younger. Their mother, Jean Boylan, raised them alone after separating from their father, working hard as a cleaner to make ends meet. Ironically, one of her main jobs was at Harcourt Street Garda Station. One former resident from the area maintained that Daniel showed little interest in education. Although their father had been sent to prison when they were children, they maintained contact with him after his release. As they grew older, they continued their relationship with him despite their mother's objections.

In an interview with one of the authors, one former detective explained how a young Daniel Kinahan was determined to make a name for himself in Dublin's underworld scene. The officer explained:

> He had built up a group of loyal followers around him. These were people he could trust and people who would do anything to protect him. Nothing went on in the south

inner city, especially Oliver Bond, without his say-so. Everyone knew who his father was, and he used this to his advantage.

Daniel earned himself just a few relatively minor convictions from his activities. At twenty-two he narrowly escaped one conviction for violent disorder for taking part in an attack on off-duty gardaí at the greyhound track in Harold's Cross. The up-and-coming young thug was also caught driving without a licence. However, he avoided getting a serious rap sheet by ensuring his dirty work was farmed out to others. Gardaí who investigated him during the late nineties describe Daniel as 'aggressive' and say he would constantly look for confrontation during his dealings with police.

In one incident, he was spotted outside Kevin Street Garda Station and suspected of writing down the number plates of cars belonging to gardaí. When he was approached, he promptly ate the piece of paper.

While his older brother was put in charge of the 'hard' faction of their father's gang, Christy had different plans for Christopher Jr. Lacking his sibling's thuggish side, the younger boy was instead chosen to head up the money-laundering end of the Kinahan empire.

No opportunity to learn was passed up – having heard that a programme about washing dirty cash was airing on UTV one evening, Daniel rang Chris Jr and told him to watch it. Certainly, the younger Kinahan did not seem to fancy himself as a hard man like his older brother. His only conviction was for a public order offence in Dublin in 2001, when he was twenty-one.

Growing up in Oliver Bond, Christopher Jr was always

close to his brother. Throughout his childhood years, he showed more of an interest in education. Into his twenties, he kept in the background, as his brother was given a senior role within the gang.

A senior garda who investigated both brothers at length confirmed they are quite different characters. He explained:

> Daniel is arrogant, reckless and acts on impulse . . . His brother is much quieter and keeps in the background. Christopher isn't like many of the other gang members, who are notorious womanizers and would think nothing of sleeping with countless women at all times. Family is important to them but they operate on zero family values.

Other sources said that while Daniel would make a point of seeking confrontation during searches of his mother's flat, Christopher Jr would be courteous towards gardaí, 'very quiet' and behave 'like a gent'.

That said, officers were alarmed when they learned that Christopher Jr had obtained a temporary clerical position in the Irish civil service in 2001, where he would have access to the addresses of driving licence holders, including gardaí. To their relief, he did not stay in the job long.

The Dapper Don continued to build his foundation of key players, using his elder son to recruit likely candidates. Apart from his loyal supporters based in the south inner-city stronghold of the Oliver Bond Estate, Daniel Kinahan had also forged links with young criminals from the north inner city. One of these was Gary Hutch, Gerry 'the Monk' Hutch's nephew.

Born on 29 September 1981, into a family of one brother and one sister, Gary Hutch was a career criminal from the age of sixteen, linked to a gang involved in the stolen car trade.

His father, Patsy, was a younger brother of Gerry 'the Monk' Hutch and Gary wasted no time in following in his uncle's criminal footsteps. At a time of life when most teenagers were preparing to sit their Leaving Certificate to end their secondary school education he was a small but important part of the Kinahan–Hutch cannabis importation business. He had responsibility for distributing the Kinahan cartel's drugs around the north inner-city area.

Around the same time, petty criminal Martin Cervi was progressing through the ranks and had come to Christy's attention.

Born on 6 September 1976, Martin Cervi lived with his father, Gerard, at Russell Avenue, East Wall, in north inner-city Dublin. Growing up in the 1980s, Cervi was a popular child in the area and had many friends, not just from his native East Wall, but also from the nearby areas of Bally-bough, Summerhill and Fairview.

At the beginning of his teenage years, Cervi had little interest in school and aspired to become a top-flight foot-baller in the UK. One former resident from East Wall explained:

> He was a decent lad in his early teenage years. He was very polite and would always be willing to help his neighbours, especially the elderly residents. He was always playing foot-ball in the street and running around until all hours, convinced he could make it as footballer when he was older.

Cervi's hopes of a career as a professional footballer were doomed, however, as soon as he was introduced to the young Gary Hutch from Champions Avenue, also in Dublin's north inner city.

Although five years Gary's senior, Cervi was in awe of his

young friend's infamous uncle, Gerry 'the Monk' Hutch. By 1987, Gerry Hutch was an established armed robber and had already earned legendary status in his native north Dublin for leading the IR£1.7 million robbery of the Securicor van in Marino – the biggest robbery of its kind in Ireland up until that point, and with all those behind it getting clean away. In his teenage days, Hutch had been involved in the Bugsy Malone gang, a group of inner-city kids who specialized in car thefts or small-scale bank robberies, where they would nimbly vault over counters and grab cash. Progressing to a higher level, he was, by 1987, considered the number one mastermind of armed robberies in the State. His gang was one of the three biggest heist outfits in the city and the 'Monk' was treated with respect by other criminals accordingly. Although non-political, Hutch had also forged close links with members of the Provisional IRA, who would receive payments from his heists. It was people like Gerry Hutch who were the local heroes when Martin Cervi was growing up.

Cervi was just one of many young men in the north inner city who idolized the criminal and were determined to follow in his footsteps. But Martin's opportunity wouldn't be provided through armed robberies, it would come through the drugs trade – at the time a step into the unknown.

No longer interested in school or a possible career in football, the impressionable young man committed his first offence when he was eighteen. The incident related to the theft of a car from O'Connell Street. Cervi and some other young up-and-coming criminals in the area were trying to make a name for themselves in the criminal underworld and were linked to a spate of thefts.

Progressing to burglaries, Cervi was also identified by

gardaí in 1995 as the ringleader of a group of young thieves who had been raiding homes across south Dublin.

Gary Hutch was too young to join the gang but he had been earmarked for a future role by older criminals in the area. Although he had yet to reach his mid-teens, Gary was well known in the area for his role in stealing cars. He was someone who was respected by Cervi, and the pair had become good friends.

On 19 November 1996, Cervi earned his first conviction for the theft of a car and was bound over to keep the peace for a year. The young criminal, who by this stage was coming under the guidance of senior figures in the Hutch gang, stole the car from a local family in the north inner city before crashing it. One former officer explained:

> Cervi just loved Gerry Hutch and loved hearing stories about him. He was only a young lad but he was someone who was identified as a potential serious gangland figure in the future. It wouldn't be long for that theory to be confirmed.

The same year he would also earn another conviction for criminal damage when he was charged with damaging a car in a failed theft. He received a suspended sentence and was fined IR£100.

Shortly after his first appearance in court, and with his reputation on the streets as someone who could be trusted, Cervi was introduced to another young criminal – Daniel Kinahan, who was already following in his father's footsteps.

Desperate to start earning money, Cervi knew there was no future in stolen cars or petty crime. He wanted to hit the big time and the only way to do this was through the drugs trade. As a regular cannabis user, he could see the wealth that many of the dealers in his area, including people he had gone to school with, were now enjoying. Tired of being on the outside, Cervi knew there was only one criminal gang who could introduce him to the world of drug importation – the Kinahans.

By the start of 1997, Christy Kinahan was well on the way to establishing himself as one of the main importers of drugs into Ireland. Having earned the trust of Daniel Kinahan, Cervi was later introduced to Christy, with the pair immediately hitting it off. Kinahan, impressed by Martin's willingness to learn, noticed the potential in his young protégé and, despite being just twenty years old, and from a different part of the city, the Dapper Don would soon bring Cervi into his group of trusted associates.

According to a report later compiled by gardaí on Cervi, he remained tight with Christy Kinahan after joining the gang. 'He was especially close to Christopher Kinahan Senior,' the report concluded. 'Christopher Kinahan saw him as almost like another son.'

Before accepting Cervi into the fold, however, the head of the Kinahan organization had sought advice from his contacts in the Hutch gang, exploiting the links he had fostered over the previous two decades. Both gangs were working closely together in criminality. Many in the gardaí saw them as one huge gang, operating in tandem for the sole purpose of making cash. The reports that came back were all positive. Cervi was someone the gangs could do business with and, more importantly, he was someone they could trust. That trust would soon be put to the test.

Up until that point, Cervi's criminal CV contained relatively minor offences. He had stolen two cars, been linked to a spate of burglaries and been found guilty of criminal damage. His only previous involvement in the drugs trade as he entered his twenty-first year was distributing small deals of cannabis to users across the north inner city. But when he started playing with the big boys, his criminal enterprises would quickly become a lot more serious.

In the summer of 1997, undercover officers from the Garda National Drug Unit (GNDU) were attempting to infiltrate Dublin's drugs gangs. They received intelligence that three young men from the west of the capital had forged an alliance with Daniel Kinahan. One of the three men also had close links to up-and-coming cartel members Gary Hutch and Martin Cervi.

A former investigator explained:

> The Kinahans and the Hutches were working hand in glove at the time. The Kinahans were bringing the stuff in and the Hutches were helping them distribute. It was a win-win situation for all of them. They were the two biggest gangs in the country and it was in their interests to work together. They were the only show in town. People like John Gilligan were on the way out.

The closeness with which both sides were working at that stage would go a long way to explaining the bitterness of the feud which would follow. The three men's role, gardaí believed, was to store drugs shipments smuggled into Ireland before distributing the product, primarily on the north side of the River Liffey. Operating from a garage in the Phibsboro area of the capital, the dealers were under surveillance.

The garage, detectives believed, was the gang's distribution centre and their preferred mode of transport was high-powered motorbikes. Fast and easy to use, the machines were better equipped to escape the fleet of Garda cars.

By the middle of 1997, business was booming. That year Cervi was arrested for selling drugs to an undercover officer at the Olympic Ballroom but only received a suspended sentence. It was a minor blip. Now firmly established within the cartel, he and Hutch were soon given a licence to recruit others for the gang's drugs distribution network. Those selected included people the pair had grown up with, from the north inner city, and others who were willing to transport drugs for a decent payment. Additional candidates were addicts or those who owed debts to the gang.

Hutch and Cervi were on the ground, helping to maintain the distribution network, while the overall boss, Christy Kinahan, and his close associate John Cunningham continued to arrange for the drugs and arms shipments to be sent to Ireland. However, a few months later, the gang would suffer its first setback. It would be the first of many.

In October 1997, Kinahan slipped back to Dublin to attend his father's funeral. Outside St Fintan's cemetery in Sutton, Detective Inspector Brian Sutton and Sergeant Brendan Burke were waiting for him, to execute the bench warrant for his arrest for skipping bail on the stolen travellers' cheque charges back in 1993. 'We can do this the easy way or the hard way,' Christy was told. The fugitive nodded his assent and went inside to pay his respects. A short time later he re-emerged, his wrists held out and ready to be cuffed.

Criminals have various ways of dealing with police interrogation and by now Kinahan had adopted a nonsensical approach. While in custody, he responded to questions with meaningless rhymes he had apparently just made up and quotes from the medieval Italian political philosopher

Niccolò Machiavelli, who is most famous for coining the phrase 'the end justifies the means'.

However, one of the officers questioning him was under-cover 'electrician' Detective Michael O'Sullivan who had brought Christy down in 1986 and Kinahan could not resist a chance to try to get one over on him.

'You think you're so smart, but I followed you one day,' he told him.

The detective answered, 'I know you did. I saw you and I saw the car you were driving. I said to myself, "I think that's Christy Kinahan," and I let my colleagues know.'

At the trial, Christy pleaded guilty and threw himself on the mercy of the court. Given his previous heroin conviction, he could have received up to fourteen years in prison but, once more, luck was on his side. The sentencing judge said he felt in a quandary because he had only been given a 'thumbnail sketch' of Kinahan's activities, despite being told of the Dapper Don's drug-dealing past, both in Ireland and in the Netherlands. The judge handed down a four-year term, something which now-retired Assistant Commissioner O'Sullivan feels was another lost opportunity.

He says:

> We had two chances to put him away for a long time but we failed. He had moved to Holland because this is where the action was and this is where the crème de la crème of the world's organized crime gangs had gathered. It was the hub of organized crime in Europe and if you wanted to make the right connections, then this was the place to be ... Christy was also lucky in the sense that he got into the heroin trade at the right time but he also got out of Ireland at the right time.

Behind bars once more, Kinahan did all he could to shorten his already relatively light four-year sentence. Even though he had fled the country while on bail for possessing the stolen travellers' cheques, he wrote to the Department of Justice demanding temporary release after serving less than half of his time.

When his request was ignored, Kinahan wrote directly to then Justice Minister, John O'Donoghue, outlining his concerns. Christy's legal team went all the way to the Supreme Court before his request was rejected.

Despite Christy's arrest, it was business as usual for the cartel and for the GNDU, pursuing its fight against them. On 11 November 1997, detectives launched 'Operation Gemini' after receiving intelligence that three members of the Kinahan gang had masterminded a shipment of cannabis and amphetamines from Holland.

The three gang members, Patrick Ralph, Christopher Burke and Maurice O'Riordan, were immediately placed under surveillance and their movements were tracked. During the surveillance operation, investigators traced the suspects to a house on Pineview Road in Tallaght, south-west Dublin. Keeping a vigilant eye on the premises, which had been trading under the name 'Jackson Nurseries', the detectives watched as the gang members met with other associates and went about their daily business.

Two days later, the surveillance team from the GNDU swooped. During the search, gardaí recovered 150 potted plants. Hidden inside the soil of the plants were 300kg of cannabis and 1kg of amphetamines, worth IR£3 million. Sitting alongside the plants were three men in their twenties, who were all arrested.

O'Riordan, whose father was a garda, was considered the

most significant arrest, as he had been a long-term target because of his connection to Gary Hutch and Martin Cervi. He knew Kinahan but his main link in this operation was his close friend Cervi.

As the search of the property continued throughout the day, officers standing guard outside noticed a car and motorcycle travelling in convoy towards them. Belatedly noticing the Garda presence at the building, the drivers of both vehicles attempted to leave, but were stopped by detectives. Gardaí then struck lucky for the second time that afternoon, recovering 400kg of cannabis resin which was concealed inside the boot of the car.

Earlier that morning, gardaí had recorded the motorcycle rider, Eugene Kelly, from the Dorset Street area of Dublin's north inner city and another close associate of Gary Hutch and Cervi, meeting with Patrick Ralph. Kelly's arrest would, once again, demonstrate the trust and co-operation between the capital's gangs in the north and south inner-city areas.

By the end of the day, five men in the pay of the Kinahan gang and a significant amount of drugs, worth almost €6 million in today's market, had been taken out of business.

According to one ex-detective, Operation Gemini reflected the cartel's growing influence on the drugs market:

This particular criminal enterprise was the one that proved the Kinahan gang was now operating on the big stage. The degree of sophistication and logistics involved in arranging such a shipment meant that it could have only been co-ordinated by a gang who had the expertise and were clearly well organized. There was no doubt Operation Gemini had caused disruption to the gang but it also brought home the reality that the Kinahan gang were serious players in the illicit drugs trade.

Gardaí later established the drugs had been sourced in Amsterdam by second-in-command John Cunningham and sent to Ireland with false paperwork, claiming the shipment was from a legitimate florist in Holland. In a file sent to the DPP, gardaí explained:

> We suspect the importation of these drugs into Ireland was organized by the Kinahan Organized Crime Group and that at this time Eugene Kelly and Patrick Ralph were facilitators and organizers at the Irish end of this organized crime group.
>
> We suspect Eugene Kelly was the main organizer for the Kinahan gang in Ireland at that time and he was directly involved in the collection and redistribution of these drugs on their arrival in Ireland.

The massive drugs haul was found on the same day as a Bruni automatic pistol, a black revolver and a quantity of ammunition were found in Martin Cervi's grandmother's house.

At the start of November 1997, Martin Cervi had been approached by Daniel Kinahan. Daniel was still eager to prove to his father that he could step up to the plate, and he asked Martin to help him store weapons and drugs that were coming in on a major shipment.

Keen to prove his loyalty, Cervi had accepted the offer immediately. Awaiting further instructions over the next two weeks, he was ordered to keep a low profile and not to come to the attention of gardaí.

On the morning of 12 November 1997, the young

gangster in the making got the call he had been waiting for. He was now entering the big league of crime. His previous history as a petty car thief and burglar would soon be a thing of the past.

Travelling to Tallaght, he'd met with the three other members of the Kinahan gang. Once there, he'd been given a bag and ordered to 'keep it safe'. Showing no signs of nerves, Martin Cervi returned to his grandmother Sadie's home at Church Road, in East Wall, which had been unoccupied since her death on 23 July 1997.

A subsequent Garda investigation established that, using a set of spare keys, he entered unobtrusively and climbed up to the attic. He emptied the contents of the holdall, hiding the Bruni automatic pistol, a black revolver and a large quantity of ammunition in the attic. The young criminal also concealed IR£24,000 in cash. When he was finished Cervi left the house and used a telephone box to inform his boss that the package had been delivered.

Satisfied with his day's work, Martin Cervi had considered himself a fully fledged member of the Kinahan Organized Crime Group. However, his mission for his new employers would soon end in disaster as, following the IR£3 million drugs seizure in Tallaght, officers from Store Street Garda Station stormed the property on Church Road, and another property on Russell Avenue, both in East Wall, in follow-up searches. Gardaí suspected the weapons had come into Ireland in the same shipment before being separated from the drugs.

Unable to find any drugs or money in the Russell Avenue property, detectives struck gold with the search of Cervi's grandmother's house. Luckily for him, he wasn't present when his former home was raided.

Hours after the search, Cervi's father, Gerard, and brother, Derek, were both arrested. Denying any knowledge of the weapons and cash, the gardaí would later accept the father and son's version of events and they were released without charge.

As the investigation continued, detectives established that Martin Cervi, who had by now gone into hiding, had 'access to the house and had possession of keys on a number of occasions'.

It wasn't long before gardaí identified him as their number one suspect. As one investigator would later claim, 'We suspect that Martin Cervi was the owner of these firearms and cash and that he concealed them in an attic of a property on Church Road.'

After the raid, Cervi realized the gardaí must have an informer in the gang. His next move was to arrange a meeting with his boss, Daniel Kinahan. Cervi knew the gardaí were still looking for him and he feared that he might be sent to prison for a fifteen-year sentence on firearms offences. He also spoke with senior members of the Hutch gang, who advised him to leave Ireland. Cervi's first major job for the Kinahan gang had ultimately ended in failure, but his loyalty was appreciated. There would be other opportunities for him and new avenues he could explore.

Just one week after the seizures, Cervi was heading for new pastures. His destination was Amsterdam, where he would join forces with John Cunningham. Although Cervi escaped justice, his friends were not so lucky.

In January 2000, O'Riordan would receive a seven-year jail term and Burke a four-year sentence after pleading guilty to possession of cannabis resin. However, there was widespread public outrage when both sentences were suspended.

The Director of Public Prosecutions appealed the sentences to the Court of Criminal Appeal on the grounds they were 'unduly lenient'. The court agreed, and replaced the suspended sentences with four years for O'Riordan and two for Burke.

Ralph, who was the third man in the house, went down for six years, while motorcyclist Kelly was handed an eight-year term for his role as a ringleader. The driver of the car, Michael Maguire, was sentenced to four years after the court heard he was an 'absolute failure in life'. He later abandoned crime after his release from prison and has kept a low profile.

Once their sentences had been completed, the five criminals cut their ties with the Kinahan gang and they went their separate ways. Meanwhile, the property used to store the drugs had been targeted in an arson attack by vigilantes and, on top of his time in jail, Burke also received threats from republican paramilitaries because of his involvement.

This was of little interest to Christy and Cunningham, however, who went back to business as usual, with the Dapper Don continuing to run his side of the business from prison.

Although the seizures on 13 November 1997 were a huge setback for the cartel, they immediately got to work on their next shipments in a bid to recoup the profits they had lost.

There was a steady stream of young men from the north and south inner city ready to join the cartel's ranks. Daniel Kinahan ordered Gary Hutch and Cervi to organize the recruitment of more 'foot soldiers', especially from outside Dublin, focusing on those involved in the transport and haulage business.

By 1998, the gang were considered one of the most

sophisticated and ruthless criminal outfits in Ireland. As they continued to flood Ireland with drugs throughout the year, gardaí hit the jackpot just before Christmas of that year with an arms seizure which would eventually bring down John Cunningham.

Kinahan was furious and decided he had an informer in his ranks. Someone would have to pay with their life.

3. The Quiet Man

'This man looks like everybody's favourite neighbour but don't be deceived by his friendly face and tidy appearance.'

Prosecutor Frits Posthumus

In December 1998, a forklift driver accidentally dropped a crate of pitta bread in a cold room in a warehouse in Castleblayney, County Monaghan. When he checked what damage had been done, he saw the crate had partially burst open. What was inside ensured gardaí were immediately called. When the cops arrived, they discovered 800kg of cannabis, 15 Intratec 9mm fully automatic pistols and silencers, 10 Smith and Wesson semi-automatic 9mm pistols and 400 cartridges of ammo inside.

The haul, which was concealed in a delivery originating in Holland, was so significant that gardaí initially believed it was bound for a splinter republican group. It would eventually be valued at more than €15 million.

Following the paper trail, Dutch investigators mounted a surveillance operation on a bar owned by a man named Peter Lingg. Lingg had already raised red flags due to the amount of foreign exchange transactions he was making.

Reports revealed frequent visits to the bar by a slight, grey-haired man. When gardaí were shown the photographs by Dutch police, they could not keep the smiles off their faces – the 'Colonel' had been found.

When Christy was jailed for handling the stolen travellers' cheques following the visit back to Dublin for his father's funeral in October 1997, his partner, John 'the Colonel' Cunningham, continued on by himself. He was the caretaker boss until Kinahan's return.

Over the next two years, gardaí and international police forces aware of the cartel's activities abroad would continue to monitor their senior players, such as Christy, his son Daniel and John Cunningham, and continue to cultivate informers. For every shipment that was intercepted, investigators knew there would be others that would slip through the net.

During the late 1990s, Cunningham, who was obsessed with guns, busied himself making new alliances with some of Europe's most dangerous criminals. Cunningham also fostered his own criminal contacts. However, he wasn't embarking on a solo path. Everything he did was for the cartel.

Cunningham's primary focus was Holland and his role was also to visit the secret labs making Ecstasy tablets to supply to countries across the Continent. In addition, he was sourcing weapons from eastern Europe via Christy's old pal from Norgerhaven jail, Johannes 'Joopie' Altepost. Cunningham and Kinahan were by now making serious profits.

The cartel's clandestine labs were equipped with tablet-making machines, and each tablet cost IR£1 to produce and would be sold on to other criminal gangs for IR£4. By the time it was being hawked around the pubs and clubs of Ireland, an Ecstasy pill could go for between IR£10 to IR£15, depending on the location.

Due to the chance event in the Monaghan warehouse, Cunningham was put under surveillance. He was tailed and his phones, along with a phone box near his home, were tapped. Dutch police listened in as he made contact with his Irish business partners, organizing deals and arranging shipments.

Many of his calls were to Christy in Portlaoise Prison, one of the most secure jails in western Europe. The pair would converse entirely in a form of code, referring to amphetamines as 'wallpaper' and cannabis as 'bread'. Cunningham also regularly called Daniel Kinahan.

Undeterred, Dutch police called in the cryptographers from their country's military. Once they became involved the 'Colonel' was living on borrowed time and the 'code' was soon broken.

What proved more troublesome to the cryptographers was unravelling the rhyming slang and strong Dublin accents of the two kingpins. Two members of the Garda National Drug Unit (GNDU) had to be sent to Holland to assist their Dutch colleagues in its comprehension. In one instance, the gardaí had to explain to their hosts what 'going for a Jimmy Riddle' meant. On another occasion, the visiting gardaí educated the Dutch police on what Cunningham meant when he spoke about having his 'knob polished'.

In one of their calls Cunningham was also told about the imminent arrival of a promising young gangster – Martin Cervi. Cervi had been sent, with a glowing endorsement from Christy Kinahan, to assist Cunningham in forging contacts with drugs syndicates from Holland, South America, Turkey, Russia and the Far East. Although ordered to welcome Cervi into the fold, the veteran criminal would, over the course of the next three years, remain distrustful of his new associate. Despite his paranoia, however, the pair would build relations with some of Europe's biggest drugs and weapons importation gangs.

With the scale of their operation it was inevitable that Cunningham and the rest of the cartel would come to the attention of the local authorities. In 1999, Cervi was arrested in possession of a handgun by Dutch police while in the company of John Cunningham. Cervi claimed he had bought it while drunk in a bar, after he had been mugged at knife-point in Amsterdam. He was later sentenced to eighty hours' community service by a Dutch court.

By the time police began carrying out surveillance on the 'Colonel', code-named 'the Irishman', and his associates in September 1999, they discovered his drug profits were accounting for 60 per cent of all Irish punt to guilder currency exchanges in all of Holland.

Cunningham had hooked up with Peter Lingg because, as a fugitive using two false British passports, he did not have a permit to reside in Holland. He would meet Lingg up to twice a week and hand over holdalls stuffed with around IR£35,000 (€44,000) in cash for the Dutchman to convert to guilders.

While Lingg trooped off to different bureaux de change, Cunningham would wait in his car or go for a coffee in a nearby hotel. It was an arrangement which worked well for both crooks – Cunningham is believed to have laundered up to IR£6 million (€7.6 million) in this way, with Lingg getting a 1 per cent commission on each transaction, netting him IR£60,000 (€76,000).

Cunningham needed all this cash because of the expensive lifestyle he and his family were leading. Although he was keeping his head down, and paying for everything with cash where possible, he was still racking up living expenses of almost

€7,000 a month. These included rent on a luxury house with an indoor swimming pool in the town of Weteringbrug, outside Amsterdam, and on an apartment, closer to the city, in the southern suburb of Amstelveen. The money also went on designer watches and weekend breaks. Meanwhile his daughter was attending a €3,000-a-year private school which catered for the children of diplomats and top international executives.

Mary, his wife, had stood by him during his lengthy spell behind bars in Ireland, and Cunningham was determined to reward her. He had once organized for a diamond ring worth IR£7,000 to be delivered to her by a British drug trafficker. It was her Christmas present.

According to surveillance reports from Dutch police, Mary, who denied all knowledge of her husband's gun- and drug-running operations, spent her time 'out shopping and spending money like water'. The hold his wife had over Cunningham was obvious in conversations recorded by the authorities on the couple's house phone. After being tailed to motorway lay-bys, where he collected holdalls packed with cash and returned similar ones filled with Ecstasy, the 'Colonel' would always call home and be told, 'Get back in time for dinner.'

Through all the surveillance, Cunningham's suspicious nature shone through. Cervi had grown close to the Kinahans but Cunningham still had a deep distrust of people he had been introduced to. It was obvious from the eavesdropping that Cunningham was wary of Cervi. He was recorded telling another gang member back in Ireland, 'I just don't trust that new man. There's just something about him.'

One of the reasons may have been Cervi's habit of splashing the spoils of his earnings in his spare time, by treating friends from Dublin to luxury meals at some of Amsterdam's finest restaurants. Pictures taken between 1997 and 2000 showed him smoking joints with other members of the Hutch gang. On another occasion, he was snapped posing happily with a 9mm handgun at a Dutch firing range. The young gangster was learning skills he would soon be show-casing on Irish soil but his flashiness would have been anathema to the eternally cagey 'Colonel'.

Despite Cunningham's reservations, Cervi knew that if he returned to Dublin he could be arrested and charged over the weapons seizure in 1997, so he was staying put. Martin was having fun but he had also risen through the ranks of a major criminal outfit. He had gone from transporting can-nabis to storing weapons for the gang in a short space of time. He was also undertaking firearms classes and was determined to do anything for the cartel.

As one former garda explained:

> He [Cervi] was still in his twenties but he was still associat-ing with people who were extremely dangerous and who were at the top of the pile when it came to Ireland and crime. There was nothing he would not have done for his associ-ates. People like Gary Hutch were looking up to him in those days and were hoping that they too could follow in his footsteps. He was a vicious wee bastard and that's why he was welcomed with open arms into Ireland's criminal elite.

The authorities watched as Cunningham visited a couple of the clandestine Ecstasy labs he was maintaining in Amsterdam. And, though he was unsure of Cervi, he still ordered him to go and bag the drugs and organize their transportation to Ireland.

Unaware his code had been broken, over time Cunningham gave the whole operation away. Gardaí and their European counterparts were careful to carry out seizures across Ireland, the North, France and Belgium, all specifically designed to avoid exposing the source of their information.

Cunningham, convinced he had an informant in his ranks, was enraged. 'Shit happens, but Jesus Christ, you can't get kicked in the balls this often,' he fumed down the line to one contact.

A fifteen-man Dutch police team kept round-the-clock watch over the Irishman for six months. Eventually it became clear Cunningham knew he was being watched. 'I get a bad feeling,' he confided down the line to another gang member. 'They operate in groups of five or six. One will drop back and another will pick you up. Like that, you know.'

The cops' hand was finally forced in March 2000, when gardaí listened to Cunningham tell Martin Cervi, 'I'm telling you, there's someone on me.' The Dutch team was immediately ordered to pull back, after which Cunningham remarked that he was 'clear'.

The next day, armed police swooped, catching their quarry with a loaded Browning pistol in his belt and an extra magazine in his pocket, along with a fake UK passport and a driving licence in the name of John Hayton. Cunningham, who was loading up yet another drugs and weapons consignment, was caught red-handed.

At his Weteringbrug home, police found 100,500 Ecstasy pills and over 50kg of speed. The drugs were hidden in flower boxes in a cupboard beside his swimming pool, ready to be shipped to Ireland. But more shocking to investigators was a secret ledger they also seized which revealed Cunningham had imported €31m worth of cannabis and Ecstasy into Ireland in the months before his arrest. His wife Mary was also arrested but later released as part of the investigation.

When Dutch cops raided the apartment in Amstelveen he

was using as a storage facility for drugs and weapons, they discovered two Intratec machine guns, a Steyr assault rifle (as favoured by NATO forces) and nine handguns. Two of the few items seized from him, which were eventually returned, were a couple of books he had bought to educate himself on the merchandise he was selling. One was *Modern Handguns* by Robert Adam. The second, *Jane's Infantry Weapons*, even had bullet holes in it.

The task of unravelling the web and eventually prosecuting Cunningham, however, was made easier by his failure to insulate himself from risk. The 'Colonel' had been collecting money from his Irish customers via hauliers travelling to the Continent. The Irish punts were then changed into Dutch guilders and used to pay for drugs and arms in the Netherlands, with the consignments going back to Dublin the same way. However, Cunningham had also been using Lingg to organize the shipments in which he was concealing his wares. When the catastrophic accident in Monaghan occurred, a paper trail led directly back to the 'Colonel' in the Netherlands.

Cervi, left at a loose end in Holland after Cunningham's arrest, eventually made the decision to return to Ireland to face the music. In May 2000, just days after landing on Irish soil, the Kinahan gang member handed himself in to gardaí at Store Street Garda Station, Dublin.

Questioned about the guns and cash discovered in his family home in 1997, investigators would later report how he 'made no comment in relation to either the firearms or cash during his detention'.

Released without charge, due to lack of evidence, investigators still suspected the young criminal of having major links to key figures within the Hutch and Kinahan gangs.

According to another security briefing document, investigators in Dublin and Amsterdam:

> ... suspect that Martin Cervi plays a part in the Kinahan Organized Crime Gang but he is not a direct organizer of activities of the gang. Rather, he is a facilitator in relation to enforcement for their activities and he sources his illegal drugs and firearms from this organized gang. We suspect that Martin Cervi is a close associate of John Cunningham, and Gary Hutch.

Back on home soil and a free man, Martin Cervi was soon back in business once again. Working for both the Kinahan and Hutch gangs, who were close allies, the former car thief put his experience in Holland to good use by arranging shipments of Ecstasy from the contacts he had made there thanks to his mentor, John Cunningham.

At the same time, gardaí believed he was working with the Hutch gang in arranging shipments of illegal cigarettes through Dublin Port. Although a major target for the GNDU, Cervi managed to avoid arrest.

What started as a normal day for Christy Kinahan in the high-security Portlaoise Prison, on 10 March 2000, soon turned into a nightmare when he received the telephone call informing him his partner-in-crime and the man who had been leading his organization in his absence had been arrested.

Cunningham's detention was a massive blow to the cartel. Investigators were now aware that Kinahan PLC was in a very healthy state and earning vast profits.

Working closely alongside the Dutch police, the gardaí continued their investigation and received another breakthrough when a tip-off led to them swooping on properties in the Harold's Cross area of Dublin, in Dun Laoghaire and Glenageary (both in south Dublin), and in Balbriggan and Swords (in north County Dublin).

During the searches, on 13 March 2000, 20kg of cannabis resin and 1,000 Ecstasy tablets, worth a total of €210,000, were recovered. One of those properties searched during the operation belonged to Christopher Casserly, from Beaumont in Dublin. According to a Dutch police file obtained by the authors, Casserly was 'sourcing his drugs from John Cunningham'. He was another supplier who was primarily providing drugs to gangs in west Dublin, organizing a system of 'couriers and modes of transport'. The report concluded: 'We suspect these drugs are directly linked to the Kinahan Organized Crime Gang.'

Spooked by the searches, Casserly later fled Ireland, cutting all ties with his associates in the process. A warrant was issued for his arrest and remains in place. Gardaí suspect he could be living in the UK under a new identity.

Three of Casserly's associates weren't as lucky as him, and soon found themselves before the courts for their role in the huge drugs importation network: 26-year-old Mark Hall, from Garristown in County Dublin, 31-year-old Steven Martin and 23-year-old Helen Lynch, both from County Meath, were considered as lower-level members of the gang.

Hall was jailed for four years and his associates were each sentenced to eighteen months, after pleading guilty at Dublin Circuit Court to possessing the cannabis and Ecstasy. During the trial, Judge Elizabeth Dunne accused Hall of being 'more involved' in the enterprise, with Martin and Lynch branded 'foot soldiers'.

In her address to the court, the senior judge commented that the three of them must have been 'heaven sent' for the people running the criminal operation, as they were of general previous good character. It was a more frequent occurrence to see foot soldiers appear in court, rather than the criminals running the operation, but the judge made the point that the three defendants could have refused to become involved.

The court also heard details of the payments made to the trio for their role in the smuggling operation, with Hall, for example, receiving IR£500 per week for storing and delivering the drugs. Detective Garda Paul Doran also told the trial how Hall was 'almost relieved' after his arrest but was 'afraid' to name the person he was working for.

After completing their sentences, the trio distanced themselves from the gang and left their brief flirtation with the world of drugs in the past.

For investigating Gardaí, the arrests showed the Kinahan network had become adept at using people previously unknown to them who had no criminal record. It was a trend that would continue over the coming years.

Furious about the losses, Christy Kinahan was convinced somebody was 'ratting' to gardaí. He started looking for the culprit and soon decided that it was Kieran Smyth from Ravensdale, outside Dundalk in County Louth.

As part of their investigation into the shipment, detectives had established that the transport company used to bring the drugs into Ireland, Westlodge Freight, was owned by Smyth. Following the huge seizure, 39-year-old Smyth went to ground and tried to distance himself from the gang. Later charged with possessing drugs with intent to supply, Smyth was released on bail.

Convinced Kieran Smyth was the informer, Kinahan ordered his execution. On 10 February 2001, Smyth, who remained living at home in Ravensdale, was found shot dead in a cattle pen, located five miles from Ashbourne village.

His murder, just a few days after the start of John Cunningham's trial in Amsterdam, was a reminder of the consequences anyone suspected of informing on the gang's criminal enterprises would face.

John Cunningham went on trial on 6 February 2001, charged with smuggling drugs and weapons. He was subsequently found guilty by an Amsterdam court of sending more than IR£6m worth of guns and drugs back to Ireland and given an 'unusually long' nine-year sentence, later reduced to seven years on appeal.

In his summing up, Dutch public prosecutor Frits Post-humus noted, 'This man looks like everybody's favourite neighbour, but don't be deceived by his friendly face and tidy appearance.'

Cunningham's trial was told about his four main contacts in Ireland. Three of them were Christy and Daniel Kinahan and Cunningham's old boozing buddy from Shelton Abbey Prison, armed robber Eamon Daly.

Daniel's name also cropped up during the trial of 'Joopie' Altepost, who was charged with supplying drugs to both him and Cunningham. When cops raided the shaven-headed mobster's home in the southern town of Oss in June 1999, they found used Aer Lingus airline tickets, boarding passes and a key card for a Dublin hotel.

'Joopie' had travelled over to Ireland to see Daniel Kina-han and visited Christy in prison to discuss business. Altepost went down for four years for his role in the operation, while Lingg received a comparatively light two-year sentence.

During the Cunningham trial, judges also listened as a

prosecutor outlined how, despite the 'Colonel' regularly worrying aloud about being caught by police, he would not entertain any similar fears amongst his subordinates. In the moments before his arrest, the gang had been under surveillance and their every move was being recorded. Police had observed Cunningham pass an Israeli Uzi sub-machine gun and a semi-automatic pistol to an Irish truck driver. The man was then instructed to take the guns back to Ireland and deliver them to a criminal associate of Cunningham's. When the driver said he was nervous, and that he feared they were being watched by cops, Cunningham replied, 'You said you would do it, so you have to now.'

Before his arrest the 'Colonel' was successful in stashing the estimated €10 million he made from his Dutch operations out of reach of the authorities. The only assets they could seize from him at his trial were about €67,000 worth of goods and cash found at his house.

As the trial ended, it wasn't just the Irish and Dutch police forces who were beginning to take notice. Authorities around the rest of Europe, particularly in Spain, were also keeping a watchful eye on the cartel because of the gang's growing list of international contacts.

Once freed from Portlaoise Prison in 2001, Christy Kinahan decided to head for foreign shores again. The Dapper Don had taken six courses while in jail, including legal studies and languages. Towards the end of his sentence he changed his mind about early release and opted to stay inside to complete an environmental science degree via the Open University.

But this was not evidence of a reformed character turning over a new leaf. Gardaí believe all the education Christy undertook while in jail was aimed at improving his ability to

run an international drug-smuggling business. His Supreme
Court case heard he was contemptuous of probation services
and 'indicated that he did not need to work with them on his
offending behaviour'.

After his convictions in Ireland and Europe for drugs
offences, Christy was concerned that gardaí would be keeping even more of an eye on him and his activities on his
release. His old Garda nemesis commented, 'Kinahan was
furious that he would now be a permanent fixture on the
gardaí's watchlist and he couldn't cope with the pressure.'

Christy based himself in Belgium and continued to move
freely to Spain and Holland, to arrange drugs and arms shipments. He also travelled to Cyprus to launder his profits. But
the head of the cartel still kept a close eye on what was happening in Dublin.

It was known that 23-year-old Daniel was acting as Christy's deputy in Dublin, overseeing the sale of drugs his father
was importing into the country. By this stage, he had moved
into his own flat in the Oliver Bond complex and it was occasionally searched by detectives, seeking to disrupt the cartel's
activities.

During one raid, cops burst in on him and his then girlfriend in bed. Detectives handed over a search warrant and
proceeded to rummage through the house, looking for evidence. When one female detective began to search near the
girlfriend's side of the bed, the young gangster told her, 'If
you go near her, I'll kill you.'

Given the nature of who they were dealing with, the threat
was taken seriously. Events two years later would prove the
gang seldom made idle threats.

4. Best Served Cold

'It is now believed this murder was carried out as a
result of an incident in 1986 where one Christopher
Kinahan was found in possession of a large amount
of heroin and was convicted and sentenced to six
years' imprisonment.'

Internal Garda report

While Christopher Jr had been earmarked for the 'softer' side of
his father's operations by Christy, he still had to learn the ropes
of the business. Another massive shipment of drugs and arms
was in the pipeline and gardaí suspected Junior had been given
responsibility for organizing it. It was a big responsibility and
Christy's younger son ordered his associates within the Hutch
gang to find him a suitable candidate. Professional courier David
Dempsey ticked all the right boxes for their transport needs.

It was yet another indication of how closely the two gangs
worked together at that time, with the Hutches dealing
directly with Junior himself, as the now 21-year-old sought
to fully earn his spurs.

Everything was set for another successful operation – but
it all went wrong.

Despite the obvious setbacks for the gang at the start of the
new century, it was business as usual throughout the course

of 2001. The following year, however, gardaí would once again receive an insight into the Kinahan gang's sophisticated smuggling operations when they swooped on a van in the Clonshaugh area of Dublin.

Acting on yet another tip-off, gardaí had put a surveillance operation in place to monitor David Dempsey on the morning of 16 August 2002. Dempsey, a van courier from Coolock, north Dublin, was observed passing his van to another man outside the Poitín Stil pub on the Naas Road. When the man returned with the vehicle, Dempsey got in and drove off.

As he made his way along Clonshaugh Avenue, armed detectives pounced. Inside the Ford Transit van they found 500kg of cannabis. Following his arrest, detectives searched Dempsey's home in Belcamp Lane, in north Dublin, where they made another discovery. Hidden in his attic and underneath his bed were bags containing another 430kg of cannabis, making the total estimated value of the drugs' haul €12 million.

When gardaí recovered firearms hidden in another part of the attic, they could prove once again that the gang's contacts weren't just shipping drugs to the cartel. The weapons cargo included a Czech-made Skorpion machine pistol, nine rounds of ammunition and three magazine clips for a 9mm handgun.

At his trial, on 27 March 2003, Dempsey received an eight-year sentence, after he pleaded guilty to possessing drugs with intent to supply and to possession of firearms.

During the hearing Detective Sergeant Greg Sheehan, who had been investigating the Kinahan gang since 1997, told the court gardaí had intelligence Dempsey had been delivering and storing drugs in the months before his arrest and was paid per drop.

Judge Desmond Hogan commented:

> Not only is the value considerable but it does appear to me that while he might not have been a major player he was actively engaging in the distribution of drugs as a business for himself. It also appeared he was trusted by the major players because as well as the massive quantity of drugs, he was also employed to store a number of guns and ammunition of serious proportion. This proved he was involved to quite an extent.

Dempsey's barrister, George Birmingham, also explained to the court how his client's job as a courier made him 'appeal' to major players in the drug industry, who, he said, were 'not nice people'. The court was also told how a fire at the suspect's home in the months after his arrest was being treated as suspicious by gardaí.

Three days after Dempsey's arrest, the gardaí's ongoing investigation in August 2002 brought them to a remote part of the Dublin Mountains. Their target was an equestrian centre. The business was registered as a livery service and had thirty horses in its stables, including jump horses. However, acting on another tip-off from someone inside the Kinahan organization, detectives raided the stables and uncovered €6m worth of cannabis, two firearms and ammunition.

A man was later charged with possessing drugs with intent to supply and possession of firearms. In their file to the Director of Public Prosecutions, gardaí claimed:

> We suspect that these drugs, firearms and ammunition originated from the Kinahan Organized Crime Group and that this location was being used as a distribution and storage centre for the sale and supply of illegal drugs.

Gardaí would also allege how another man arrested at the site, who cannot be named for legal reasons, was a 'close associate of Christopher Kinahan Snr' and was a 'facilitator in the importation of illegal drugs and firearms into Ireland'.

The man took responsibility for the drugs and weapons and was the only person to be charged in connection with the haul. When he failed to show up at his court date, gardaí initially believed he had been accused of being an informer, executed and dumped in a shallow grave. However, in late 2016, they received information that he was living in England under an assumed name. He has since been extradited back to Ireland and is facing charges.

In the months that followed the raid on the stables, Christy Kinahan and his associates were still the number one target for the Garda National Drug Unit (GNDU). Dozens of other gangs had been bringing drugs into Ireland, but the Kinahan gang were operating at a different level.

Garda sources had indicated that Martin Cervi, Christy's 'third son', was adopting the same modus operandi as his bosses. The former burglar now had a team of young men ferrying his drugs to his associates across the city. Raking in the cash, Cervi would often spend large spells away from his hometown, soaking up the sun in Spain's Costa del Sol and visiting with Kinahan associates. He kept his distance from key players, however, as he didn't want to be seen in public with them.

Gardaí also received intelligence that Cervi was working on his own shipments without the knowledge of his associates in the Kinahan gang. He would operate by offering young addicts from his local area the chance to earn much-needed cash. Obtaining illegal passports for his employees,

Cervi would order the young men to travel to Bolivia, in central South America, with suitcases lined with lead to avoid Customs' scanners. The drug mules would meet with Cervi's South American contacts, established during his time in Holland, and then pack their lead-lined suitcases with cocaine, before flying back to the UK and Ireland. To try to avoid detection, Cervi was bringing in smaller shipments and the people he used were not on the Garda files.

Around the same time, detectives were also told that the young drug dealer was using vulnerable pensioners to deliver his drugs.

One investigator revealed:

He wasn't just sending people to South America – he was using all sorts of people in Ireland. For him, pensioners would rarely be stopped by the gardaí. They were told not to ask any questions and in return they would be rewarded for simply delivering a package. He was extremely manipulative and had people from all walks of life working for him and often without the knowledge of the Kinahan or Hutch groups.

As the months went by, the Celtic Tiger was starting to roar and, with the economy booming, so too was the demand for cocaine and other synthetic drugs. According to sources, Martin realized that there was money to be made from the selling of Ecstasy and cocaine. Previously involved in distributing cannabis, he was now involved in the selling of more Class A drugs.

Cervi expanded his drug-dealing activities, making even more money for himself and for his already wealthy associates in the Kinahan gang. In one incident, he was suspected of buying one kilo of cocaine for €50,000, before selling it on the street for €70,000. He was making a €20,000 profit for every kilo he sold.

Continuing to flood the capital with cocaine from South America, cannabis from Morocco and highly potent Ecstasy from the Netherlands, Cervi focused all of his energies on the drugs trade. He was regarded as having a fascination with weapons, namely handguns, but he opted to keep away from the weapons importation and storage business.

His experience with firearms, however, was put to use around Christmas 2002, when his associates in the Kinahan gang requested his services. Cervi's mission was to source weapons for a hit from the extensive contacts he had made across Dublin. He was also given another role – to source the gang's getaway car.

Martin duly obliged and an Audi A4 Quattro was stolen from a house in Leopardstown, south County Dublin, four days before the gang's planned attack on 28 January 2003.

Once again, Cervi's involvement with the Kinahan gang was about to reach a whole new level.

For fourteen years, Raymond Salinger made secret visits to Ireland to see family and friends. After fleeing from Christy Kinahan in 1987, Salinger was making sure that they never set eyes on each other again. However, when his wife was diagnosed with cancer in November 2001, the builder, now aged thirty-nine, made the decision to return to Ireland and to his old haunt, the Coombe.

When the family returned, in January 2002, the Dublin that he had once known had changed. Salinger was no longer involved in crime and he intended to avoid the dangerous young criminals who were controlling the drugs trade in the south inner city.

Maintaining a low profile, and with Christy Kinahan now relocated abroad, Raymond was determined to get his life back on track and stay on the straight and narrow. Many of his old associates from the 1980s were either dead or in prison. For Salinger, there was no going back.

A year after the family returned, Paula lost her battle with cancer. Salinger moved in with his daughter, Danielle, in Eugene Street, in the south inner city but struggled to cope with his wife's loss. Over the course of the next five months, he filled his days by working from time to time on the building sites popping up across the capital thanks to the early advances of the Celtic Tiger. His nights were often spent enjoying a few drinks in the capital's many pubs.

By January 2003, Salinger had been back in Dublin for just over a year and was beginning to feel safe. After all, it had been fifteen years since his last association, or indeed contact, with Christy Kinahan.

On a bitter winter's morning on 28 January 2003, Salinger headed off to work on a building site in the city centre. Returning home that evening, he decided to go to his local pub, Farrells, on New Street, in the south inner city.

As one native who knew him from the time said:

> He certainly didn't look as if he was under any type of threat because his involvement in drugs was such a long time ago. He was an easy target. It would have been so easy for anyone to follow him because he did the same thing every single week.

Unbeknownst to Salinger, however, his every move was being watched by a group of young criminals loyal to Kinahan and his elder son, Daniel. From his luxury apartment in Spain, Kinahan had discovered Salinger had been back in

Dublin for some time. Although focused on building his huge drugs empire, Kinahan was determined to settle an old score.

At 9.15 p.m. that evening, Raymond Salinger entered the pub after walking the short distance from his home. January is traditionally a quiet month in Dublin pubs, but it was unusually busy, with between twenty-five and thirty-five customers there to watch the Premiership football game between Leeds United and Chelsea. The Farrells' darts team was also practising before their game with another pub from nearby Kilmainham.

Walking to the bar, Salinger ordered his usual pint of Guinness, sat down on a stool and began chatting to other customers. After half an hour, he went to use the toilet and returned to his seat to finish his drink.

Before he could lift the glass to his mouth, he was shot four times in the chest, at point-blank range by a masked man. As the gunman fled, Salinger stumbled from the counter before collapsing at the rear of the pub, terrified customers rushing to his aid. He was dead before he reached hospital.

One witness later told gardaí:

I could see the bloke had a small black gun in his right hand. He was manoeuvring it around to point it towards Raymond. Then I heard 'bang, bang' and then I think another bang. Raymond fell back on to the bar and then fell forward on to the ground. The lad who had shot Raymond ran out the front door of the pub.

Another witness recalled:

Before I took a sip of my pint I heard the sound of what sounded like a pellet gun, then a further two shots. I didn't think it was that loud. Then suddenly the man who was beside me was slouched over. I turned, lifted my hands and touched off a man with a gun wearing a balaclava. He was standing about three feet behind the man who was shot. His arm was outstretched and he had a gun which I can't describe.

Other customers told how a second gunman, also masked, had entered the pub with the killer, and stood calmly at the door waiting for him. One local woman put her own life on the line by chasing after the two criminals when they left. She saw them drive off in a long black saloon, breaking the lights.

'I saw the gunman get into the car and he seemed almost casual,' said another customer. 'The car was black in colour and looked new.'

Just three minutes after the shooting, Fr Brian O'Ceileachain was also driving his car when he saw the gunman run from the pub. He would later tell gardaí:

When I stopped my car, I was about two feet from the rear of this car. I suddenly saw two people coming out the doorway of the pub which is lit and which was to my right-hand side. They were fast and co-ordinated. Their faces were covered. I saw both people get into the rear of the car. I watched this car speed off across the junction against the red light.

Around the same time, Detectives Dermot McDermott and Alan Waters were on patrol in the Robert Street area when they noticed a black Audi car driving towards them. Shortly afterwards, word came through the gardaí's radio system that a large dark car had just been involved in a gun attack at Farrells pub.

Both officers searched the area, but could find no trace of the vehicle. Next morning, however, a black Audi was discovered, partially burnt out, at the Marmion Court flats complex, off Blackhall Street, in the north inner city.

As investigators began looking into the murder, they received information linking the victim to Christy Kinahan. Gardaí also established that two senior members of the Kinahan gang were also in the bar at the time of the shooting, apparently 'pinpointing Salinger and monitoring his movements'.

According to one file on the case:

As a result of enquiries, coupled with confidential information received from a number of reliable sources, it is now believed this murder was carried out as a result of an incident which occurred in 1986 where one Christopher Kinahan, 56 Crescent View, Fairview, was found in possession of a large amount of heroin and was convicted and sentenced to six years' imprisonment.

It is believed that Christopher Kinahan was convinced that Raymond Salinger had given the gardaí information which resulted in his arrest and conviction. Raymond Salinger did go to England shortly after the conviction of Kinahan.

The aforementioned Christopher Kinahan is at present residing on the Continent, basing himself between Amsterdam and Málaga. It is believed by gardaí that he is one of the leading players in the importation of cocaine and cannabis to Ireland and the UK. The key members of this network in Dublin are his sons, Daniel and Christopher, Matthew Dunne, and three other men.

The late Christopher Hutch, who's suspected of dying from an overdose of cocaine on 30 March 2003, was also one of his leading henchmen. All of the above mentioned are serious players in the criminal fraternity in the Dublin area.

Matthew Dunne, who the Kinahans nicknamed 'Mr Bean', ran several businesses involved in laundering the gang's drug money. He was a key member of the cartel and Christopher Kinahan Jr was best man at his wedding.

Christopher 'Bouncer' Hutch, the son of Gerry 'the Monk' Hutch's brother Eddie, was a close associate of Martin Cervi. He was also used by the Kinahan gang to distribute cannabis in the north inner city. Gerry Hutch turned a blind eye to his nephew's involvement in the drugs trade.

Once the victim's links with Christy had been established, gardaí arrested his two enforcers who were present in the pub. Both men refused to co-operate but detectives had another promising avenue of investigation.

A damaged copy of the *Irish Daily Star* newspaper was recovered from the front passenger seat of the partially torched Audi. A fingerprint from a man's left thumb was harvested from the newspaper, which had been used to try to burn the vehicle out.

As the investigation into the brutal killing was ongoing, Cervi tried to disguise his drug-dealing activities by applying to work as a legitimate taxi driver. But his attempts to hide his real work failed when the Garda Carriage Office rejected his application.

Furious over the decision, Cervi then made an appeal to Dublin District Court in a bid to reverse the ruling. During his appeal, on 5 March 2003, the court was told how he was currently completing an ECDL (European Computer Driving Licence) course. However, the court also heard details of the discovery of the firearms at Martin's grandmother's home in 1997, and of his conviction in Holland for possessing a firearm.

Detective Sergeant Greg Sheehan, who had been involved in investigating the Kinahan gang in 1997, further revealed details of Martin's links to John Cunningham in Holland and his disappearance from the country after the Cunningham weapons seizure in 2000.

In his defence, Cervi's solicitor, Michael Staines, told the court how his client wanted to 'better himself' and had put his past 'behind him'. As part of his appeal, Cervi again claimed he had bought the weapon in Holland for his own defence after he was mugged at knifepoint.

Following statements to the court from the State and from Cervi's defence team, Judge Seán MacBride accepted the gardaí's concerns and upheld the original ruling denying his application for a taxi licence, before adding, 'If the gardaí were satisfied in the future that he had cut all ties with people of dubious repute he could re-apply.'

Shortly after the court's decision, the criminal had more pressing concerns to contend with. He was arrested for the murder of Raymond Salinger by Detective Sergeant Michael O'Brien on 2 April 2003, after a warrant was issued by Detective Superintendent P. J. Browne. The murder suspect was taken from his new home in 53A Seville Place, in Dublin's north inner city, and brought to Kevin Street Garda Station for questioning.

During the course of eight interviews about the murder, Cervi repeatedly replied 'nothing to say' when asked about his possible involvement in the killing. He would maintain the same stance when an officer from the Garda Technical Bureau, Detective Garda John Sweetman, was brought in for the last interview.

Throughout the questioning, Detective Garda Sweetman presented Cervi with the evidence of the fingerprint they had found on the newspaper in the gang's getaway car, which irrevocably linked Martin to the crime. The detective explained:

> Yesterday I received a set of finger/palm prints endorsed as having been taken from you by Detective Garda Ken Donnelly during your detention at Kevin Street Garda Station. I have compared your fingerprints with a thumbprint found on the part of the *Irish Daily Star* newspaper.
>
> I have identified the thumb mark as having been made by your left thumb and I am satisfied beyond doubt that the thumb mark on the newspaper was made by you. Again that's the piece of newspaper there. What do you have to say?

Just as he had done with his previous answers, Cervi replied, 'I've nothing to say.'

In a file later sent to the Director of Public Prosecutions, investigators claimed they were 'satisfied' as a 'result of enquiries and confidential information received Martin Cervi and his associates were involved in the murder of Raymond Salinger'.

They continued:

> The only factual evidence against Martin Cervi is the finding of his thumbprint. This newspaper was set on fire with the intention of burning and destroying this and any evidence within [the car]. Bearing in mind that this item is a moveable object, it no doubt links Martin Cervi to the shooting dead of Raymond Salinger. It should also be borne in mind the motive for this murder and the close association between Christopher Kinahan and Martin Cervi.

He [Cervi] declined to give any explanation as to why his thumbprint would be on the newspaper. We recommend that strong consideration be given to a charge of murder or a lesser charge of being an accessory.

However, for Raymond Salinger and his family, especially for his mother, Elizabeth, who passed away on 14 May 2014, there would be no justice. At 11.50 p.m. on 3 April 2003, and despite his fingerprint being found inside the car used in the Salinger killing, Martin Cervi walked free and the DPP later decided that no charges should be brought.

It would be the last time Cervi would face any serious charges over his work within the Kinahan Organized Crime Group.

Christy Kinahan had just ordered what was believed to be his second murder and he had got away with it. He would wait only a year before killing again.

Throughout 2003, Christy was running large amounts of drugs and arms into Ireland and the UK from Spain. His Dutch cannabis business used a local businessman who was ostensibly running a seafood importation business. He was sending empty trucks to Ireland to return to the Netherlands laden with Irish oysters, mussels and prawns.

In reality, the lorries belonging to 58-year-old Boudewijn Kerbusch were also packed with hash as they travelled towards Dublin. The operation was going well until 650kg of cannabis was intercepted by Customs in Newcastle-upon-Tyne in the UK, in the summer of 2004. The drugs were worth €1.5 million and their final destination was Dublin.

Kerbusch fell under suspicion, with the Kinahans believing he was a police informer. At 8.15 a.m. on 29 October

2004, he was out walking his dog in a green area behind his house in the southern Dutch town of Oss when a stolen grey Audi pulled up alongside. A gunman fired a number of shots out the window, killing Kerbusch instantly.

Twenty-five police officers were assigned to the case and a reconstruction of the murder featured on the Dutch version of the TV show *Crimewatch*. The appeal led to dozens of calls from the public. Cops were aware Kerbusch's death was probably linked to the cannabis seizure, but were having difficulty establishing who had ordered the hit.

The case was shelved by Dutch police the following February – just three months later. Garda intelligence subsequently determined the cartel was most likely responsible for the assassination.

Drugs were not the only pie in which the cartel had a finger. Daniel Kinahan was still posing as a furniture restorer when he cropped up in a major police investigation in the UK. British police were probing an alleged race-fixing ring, in May 2004.

Gambling on racing had long been a major strategy for gangsters to launder their drug money and was a favoured tactic of deposed drug baron John Gilligan. By betting on the favourites, criminals can ensure they statistically lose only around 10 per cent of their money and have a betting slip handy if the authorities ever query the source of their large amounts of cash. It makes it more difficult to prove in court that they are not merely the most astute bettors in the land.

The City of London police had received information, however, that the Kinahans planned to eliminate even the slightest chance of losing their money. They believed Christy was attempting to bribe or coerce jockeys to lose races – with the Dapper Don having placed a sizeable bet on the surprise 'result' shortly beforehand.

British investigators watched with interest as Daniel Kinahan flew into Leeds Bradford Airport from the Costa del Sol, on 26 May 2004, and met with another Irishman, Philip Sherkle. Previously arrested following a Garda operation in 2002, Sherkle was a long-time associate of Daniel's and lived in Tamworth, the town Christy had moved to in the mid-nineties. Sherkle was one of four men arrested when gardaí seized half a tonne of hash and three automatic weapons with silencers in Rathcoole, in Dublin. A file was sent to the DPP, but Sherkle was never charged. By 2004, he was described as working as a barman in Tamworth.

When the race-fixing case came to court in 2007, it heard Sherkle and Kinahan had driven south to a hotel in Newmarket, where they checked in under false names. The court was told that Daniel, Sherkle, Miles Rodgers and another man were then spotted driving towards Irish jockey Kieren Fallon's home in Newmarket, in the early hours of the morning. They turned back when they spotted a police tail.

Evidence was given of phone intercepts from one of the accused, Yorkshire businessman Miles Rodgers. Rodgers was a racehorse owner and trainer who would be banned from the sport for life by the British Horseracing Authority over his role in the affair. The trainer was charged as part of the probe and jurors heard that he had referred to Kinahan as a formidable character called 'D'.

Rodgers told an unidentified associate that while he had met many 'menacing' people in the course of his business, they paled beside 'D'. He said he was 'only a little fella, but you know when you've been spoken to'. Daniel Kinahan was not charged in the case, during which he was referred to as 'an Irish businessman'.

The trial heard the foursome were on their way to confront Fallon because their 'bet to lose' syndicate had lost €231,000 when he had won one of his races at Newbury, on 15 May 2004.

Irish jockey Kieren Fallon and all the other defendants were eventually acquitted of all charges, in what was labelled the 'trial of the century'. After its conclusion, the judge severely criticized the way both police and prosecutors had brought their case.

The cartel's intimidation attempt had failed in this instance but it was a favoured tactic of Daniel's. He was aware of the power he had, and he wielded it with relish. Just like a character in his favourite *Godfather* movies, other criminals would approach him, asking him to sort out problems, eager for his assent. One such case was when he was asked to put the squeeze on a former Ireland Under-21 soccer international who was not paying his gambling debts.

The ex-pro had never made it to senior international level, spending his career playing for several lower-league English clubs instead. Nonetheless, he had apparently fallen victim to 'the footballers' disease' and owed STG£6,500 to a dodgy bookmaker in London.

'Now he's claiming he doesn't even know me and he's suing me and I have to appear in court,' whined the bookie to Daniel down the phone.

'Give me his name and the area where he lives,' Daniel answered. 'If you tell me the exact area where he lives, I probably have some friends who can go and see him. Send me a text with that and where he hangs out and I'll call someone later.'

The police cannot be sure what happened next, but it was presumed the recalcitrant sportsman changed his attitude.

The scale of the drugs seizures highlighted the extent to which the Kinahan gang was operating in Ireland by the mid-2000s. Although gardaí were working closely with the Dutch and Spanish authorities, the consensus in Dublin was that more needed to be done – especially on the Costa del Sol where Christy Kinahan, his sons and senior members of the gang were based.

The idea for a new offensive would soon present itself, thanks to the Kinahan gang's newest member.

5. A Safe Pair of Hands

'There were a hell of a lot more talented players in Ballymun than me. Most of them ended up in Mountjoy and I knew I had to get out.'

Eddie Van Boxtel

Gino Lawless's testimonial on 30 July 1994 was going better than expected for the home fans, when disaster struck early in the second half. Dundalk United were 2–1 up on the previous season's English Premier League champions Manchester United, in front of a packed Oriel Park, and had been more than holding their own. But when a panicked defence took down Paul Ince as the Manchester United midfielder surged into the box, the home support feared the worst. Eric Cantona stepped forward to claim the penalty. Up until that point in his career, the French striker had never missed from the spot and the odds were heavily against the goalkeeper he faced.

Eddie Van Boxtel, however, grabbed himself the next day's headlines and a mention in Cantona's autobiography when he correctly dived left and palmed the shot away. Manchester United would eventually run out 4–2 winners, but it did little to dampen the fresh-faced keeper's joy, describing the save afterwards as 'every schoolboy's dream'.

Then just twenty-one, Van Boxtel was one of the stars

of Ireland's domestic football leagues. Originally from Bally-mun, a tough working-class area of Dublin, he had appeared to be on his way to fulfilling his childhood ambition of becoming a professional footballer when, aged fifteen, he moved to the north of England and signed for Leeds United.

Speaking about his move to England in an interview with a local paper, he revealed:

> I didn't want the opportunity to slip by in case another one didn't come along. There were a hell of a lot more talented players in Ballymun than me but they just thought it was better to rob than to play football. Most of them ended up in Mountjoy and I knew I had to get out.

Van Boxtel had had a chequered childhood himself. At the age of just thirteen he had been identified by local gardaí as a suspect for a number of break-ins at factories and for general vandalism in the area, but he was never brought before the courts.

Moving to Leeds was the first step on his championship dream, but it soon turned into a nightmare when he got involved in a few arguments with the youth team managers. Van Boxtel returned home after a year, with his contract terminated. 'I was just a kid with a lot of growing up to do then,' he would later admit.

Fathering his second child at the age of seventeen, Van Boxtel, who rarely attended school when he was growing up, was unemployed over the next three years before finding work as a taxi driver. At twenty, he returned to playing football when he was signed by Dundalk.

Van Boxtel, who would go on to be named 'Player of the Year' for Dundalk in the 1994/1995 season, embarked on a career that saw him turn out for Galway United, Drogheda

United, Monaghan United and Bray Wanderers. A tribute website was also launched online in his honour in 2002.

Back playing the game that he loved, he even had hopes of being spotted by a UK scout for a second time. 'It's a dream that hasn't died and won't until the day I finally say I'm not good enough,' he said. 'That'll be the day I'm too old to play.' Despite a series of star performances over the years at a professional and semi-professional level for his various clubs, the goalkeeper retired from Ireland's professional league at the age of thirty-five.

Van Boxtel was back living in his native Ballymun, again working as a taxi driver and playing part-time football at an amateur level. He also coached local children from his area, all desperate to make it as professional players. Unfortunately for him, the telephone call that he had been waiting for, after his disastrous spell in England, never materialized. But he did receive one approach in the summer of 2005 that would see him signing up with a much less savoury outfit.

Growing up in Ballymun, Van Boxtel had kept in contact with many of his old associates, some of whom were now involved in the capital's booming drugs trade. Van Boxtel's vice was gambling and he was betting heavily on football, greyhounds and horses. According to sources, he had enjoyed a few wins but also many heavy losses – yet he couldn't stop. Every penny he earned from taxi driving went to bookmakers.

Desperate to make more cash to feed his gambling addiction, Van Boxtel was soon hiding packages of drugs in his taxi and ferrying them across Dublin for the Kinahan cartel.

It was a busy time for the gang. With Christy forging close links with criminal gangs in the UK, Holland and Spain, Daniel Kinahan was reaching out to gangs based outside

Dublin. Organized gangs in Limerick, including the McCarthy-Dundon faction, and others in Sligo were just some of the criminals using the Kinahan gang to source their drugs.

The McCarthy-Dundons were an up-and-coming Traveller gang who would go on to form one faction in the Limerick feud which saw up to twenty people die. But though they could claim almost complete control of their city's gangland scene, they lacked the sophistication to build up the international contacts available to the cartel.

Due to the heavy Garda presence in the capital, the Kinahans were using drivers like Van Boxtel to get their drugs around Dublin, while storing them in areas outside the city.

At the beginning of December 2005, gardaí received confidential information that the Kinahan gang had sourced a property in Windgates, Maynooth, County Kildare. They were using it as a base for storing drugs before they were distributed across Dublin. Having identified the building, detectives put together another surveillance operation.

As their clandestine observations continued, gardaí recorded Martin Walsh, a convicted armed robber, bringing boxes of creatine, a mixing agent for cocaine, into the building. Satisfied the property was being used to store drugs, gardaí swooped on the morning of 20 December 2005.

During the search, officers recovered €560,000 worth of cocaine. Another man was also arrested but later released. In their submissions to the court during Walsh's trial, a detective said, 'I suspect this location was being used as a processing area for the mixing and distribution of illegal drugs imported into Ireland by the Kinahan Organized Crime Group. When caught, they were acting on behalf of this gang.'

Walsh, from Rowlagh Gardens in Clondalkin, west Dublin,

was jailed for ten years on 12 October 2009, for his role in the smuggling plot. Walsh told gardaí that his involvement had 'destroyed everything I worked for, for that scum'. He was another example of the 'foot soldiers', used by the Kinahan gang since the turn of the century, who had ended up in prison. Walsh would also lose €107,500 to the Criminal Assets Bureau after the State ruled that he had profited from drug dealing.

Van Boxtel was unaware of it, but he was heading down a similarly dangerous road.

Earning the Kinahan gang's trust, and that of the Hutch gang operating alongside them, Van Boxtel was promoted to a more sophisticated criminal enterprise at the beginning of June 2006.

From their base in Spain, the cartel had masterminded an elaborate plot to ship tonnes of drugs – cannabis resin, cocaine and heroin – and some firearms, including machine guns, to Ireland and the UK.

The illegal enterprise started with the Spanish woman who acted as Daniel Kinahan's secretary/personal assistant registering herself as the director of a bogus food exportation company 'Foods Almacen General'. Officially trading from 30 September 2006, the firm's office, containing computers, telephones, business cards, printers and a fax machine, was opened in Estepona, Spain.

Once the set-up was completed, the Irish end of the drug-smuggling operation swung into action. A heroin addict selected by Van Boxtel, and with the initials 'MK', was paid €300 to apply for a passport. Known as 'fraudulently obtained genuine passports', the scam works by an individual completing a passport application form containing their own personal details, and with their image which is then officially stamped by the gardaí. Once the Garda stamp is obtained, the images are switched and the application form is then sent to the passport office in Dublin, containing the photographs of the cartel gang member. The signature of the garda who signed the back of the original images is also forged on to the back of the gang member's images along with their own fake Garda stamp.

Approved, the passport is sent to the applicant's own address. It is then handed over to the gang member, enabling them to move freely around Europe.

MK's legal passport, containing the photograph of the gang member, was duly posted out to him, as per his application details. He then delivered it to the gangster and collected his €300 fee.

To open a bank account, you need a passport and a utility bill. The criminal next rented an apartment to get a utility bill and then, armed with the passport ID and proof of address, an industrial unit in Dunboyne, County Meath was registered as the location of 'MK Foods' and a bank account was opened.

Paperwork later recovered by officers from the Garda National Drug Unit (GNDU) – renamed the Drugs and Organised Crime Bureau in March 2015 – discovered that sixteen containers of 'pasta' had been shipped to MK Foods between 13 October 2006 and 14 September 2007. Investigators established that the shipping costs of the containers were paid for by Foods Almacen General, based in Estepona, Spain.

The Foods Almacen General supply chain wasn't the only major drug-smuggling operation under way at that time. Kinahan's secretary was kept busy registering a second fictitious food exportation business in August 2007. It was called 'Euro Express Foods', based in Murcia, in the south-eastern region of Spain.

Back in Ireland, Van Boxtel was given the task of finding another suitable candidate for a second passport application. Following orders, he paid a west Dublin man named Thomas Stokes €300 to apply for the travel documents. The Garda's National Bureau of Criminal Investigation launched a major investigation into this illegal scam. They established that the cartel was using homeless people to apply for the travel documents.

Once obtained, Thomas Stokes' passport was then delivered to a member of the cartel. As in the previous drug-smuggling operation, the gang member rented another apartment, was soon receiving electricity bills and opened a bank account.

Using the fake passport as his identification, the criminal registered the firm 'TS Foods' at Companies House in Dublin before renting an industrial unit from an unsuspecting landlord at the Orion Business Centre in Ballycoolin, Blanchardstown, west Dublin.

The unit was fitted with advertising boards, computers, phones and business cards, all in an attempt to provide it with the cover of legitimacy. Officially fully operational and trading, it also employed a managing director who would make frequent trips to the office. That man was Eddie Van Boxtel.

As part of their investigations into the cartel, investigators would later establish that six containers of 'Romero pasta' and 'spaghetti' were shipped to TS Foods from Euro Express Foods, Spain between 26 October 2007 and 18 January 2008. According to the paperwork recovered, the total number of containers shipped to Ireland was twenty-two. Detectives estimated the cartel had sent 22 tonnes of cannabis resin, worth €132 million, during that approximately 3-month period.

One investigator explained:

> This figure is just a conservative estimate. They could literally have packed those containers with all kinds of drugs and guns. Whatever was popular at the time would have been in those containers. People also have to realize that the guns used in the feud today would have been coming in on those type of shipments.
>
> This was a well-organized and well-planned drugs importation business, showing the sophisticated nature of the cartel. Every angle had been covered and every avenue explored. There may have been one legitimate container imported just as a dry run before the drugs landed on Irish shores.

However, as the gang continued to plot more shipments at the turn of the year, they were about to be dealt a significant blow.

The Garda National Drug Unit (GNDU) received a tip-off the cartel was bringing drugs into the country disguised as shipments of pasta. On the morning of 6 February 2008, officers from the GNDU, under 'Operation Perch', along with their Garda colleagues from Naas and Newbridge, made their move. They had received specific intelligence that a drugs transfer was to take place later that morning.

Taking up their position at 6.20 a.m., at Toughers Garage on the road from Naas to Newbridge, undercover officers watched as a silver Ford Transit van, driven by Van Boxtel, and a black Audi A6, whose driver was 42-year-old lorry driver Vincent Percival, drove into the facility.

Percival was a low-key member of the gang. He was used by them because he was a truck driver and had plenty of storage at his home. He was also someone who had never appeared on the Garda radar in the past.

Minutes later, a second Ford Transit van, driven by Martin O'Connor, and a black Ford Fiesta, driven by a long-term GNDU target named Fran Delaney, arrived and parked at the rear of the garage. O'Connor, a 54-year-old man from North Great Charles Street in Dublin's north inner city, had a string of minor convictions. O'Connor was another man who was used by the gang because he was willing to store drugs in return for cash.

A short time later, the Fiesta left the garage and was closely followed by O'Connor and Percival in the van. O'Connor drove for two miles, before leaving his vehicle off the N7 road. Van Boxtel waited to see if anyone was following them before going to collect the empty van.

Picked up in the Fiesta, O'Connor was then driven back to the garage where he stopped and had breakfast. Van Boxtel, his every move under observation by the undercover officers, collected O'Connor's van from the N7 road and drove off. His associate Percival was following closely behind him.

Travelling to Percival's home in Clongorey, Newbridge, County Kildare, they reversed O'Connor's van to the rear of the bungalow before loading a pallet of drugs into the vehicle.

The van was then driven to the same location where it had been parked earlier, and Van Boxtel left the keys. The former footballer was collected by Percival, before being taken back to the garage where they also had breakfast.

At 7.02 a.m., O'Connor was driven back to his van, now full of drugs, by Delaney in the Fiesta. The pair then drove along the N7 in the direction of Dublin city centre. Watched closely by the GNDU team, O'Connor's van followed the Fiesta, both keeping in the same lane.

Gardaí decided to move in at 7.15 a.m. They stopped both vehicles, and O'Connor and Delaney were arrested by Detective Garda Martin Long and Detective Sergeant Greg Sheehan. Inside the back of O'Connor's van detectives found 500kg of cannabis resin, valued at €3.5 million. Unaware of the two arrests, Van Boxtel and Percival were stopped as they left the garage at 7.45 a.m., by Detective Garda Ronan Cowley and David Kennedy.

While the pair were being questioned at Newbridge Garda Station, officers obtained a warrant to search Percival's house and arrived there at 8.20 a.m. The isolated bungalow had a garage at the rear of the property and was surrounded with CCTV cameras. It was well away from prying eyes.

Unfortunately for Percival, the CCTV cameras acted against him, as the two gang members had been recorded loading boxes into O'Connor's van. Inside the garage, detectives recovered a large number of cardboard boxes and two pallets. The boxes contained 1,000kg of cannabis, worth €7 million. The cartel's business venture was now at an end.

During questioning, Van Boxtel admitted to detectives that he had already earned €10,000 from drug drops. He explained how he had been approached by a passenger in his taxi and offered the chance to 'earn extra money' by delivering the illegal substances.

According to sources, Van Boxtel had known Daniel Kinahan but wasn't a high-ranking member of the gang. Like many of the gang's associates, the footballer had been approached because he was regarded as someone they could trust. Sources are also adamant that Christy Kinahan would have known of the illegal enterprise because it was through his contacts the arrangements had been made.

At the same time, investigators were also searching the 44-year-old's home on Sillogue Avenue, Ballymun. Inside they found business cards, detailing the address and contact details for TS Foods.

Gardaí also contacted an estate agent whose number was found in a text message on Van Boxtel's mobile phone. The agent confirmed that a 'Thomas Stokes' had rented an industrial unit at the Orion Business Centre in Ballycoolin, Blanchardstown, west Dublin. Obtaining another warrant, investigators then swooped on the premises, where they recovered the empty 'Romero pasta' boxes, covered in Van Boxtel's fingerprints.

They discovered paperwork outlining how six previous shipments of containers had been sent to Ireland. As the investigation continued, investigators also established how the Spanish bank accounts which paid for the containers to be sent to TS Foods were also the same accounts that had sent sixteen containers to MK Foods the previous year.

When officers searched the MK Foods office in Dunboyne, it was empty. One officer explained:

> Detectives spoke to some other businesses in the area at the time but they were unable to help. They simply hadn't seen anyone coming to MK Foods and the office might never have been used during the day. These criminals would have been very aware of shielding their identities from potential witnesses.

As their interrogations concluded, the four-man gang were all charged with possessing cannabis with intent to supply. Their work for the cartel was at an end.

As the investigation dug deeper, detectives uncovered how Daniel Kinahan's secretary had played a key role in organizing the venture. However, with the Spanish authorities unable to charge her because of lack of evidence, she was free to continue working inside one of Europe's most dangerous drug gangs.

The frightening extent of the cartel's global drugs and weapons network also emerged one month after the seizures in Newbridge, County Kildare. Officers from the Metropolitan Police in London recovered three sub-machine guns, four handguns, four silencers and eight boxes of ammunition hidden inside pasta boxes sent from Euro Express Foods, on 11 March 2008, to property developer Neil Williams. He would subsequently receive a five-year sentence at Kingston Crown Court in London, for possessing the weapons. Williams was a close associate of an Englishman involved in a relationship with Daniel Kinahan's Spanish personal assistant.

As the person who established Euro Express Foods, Daniel's personal assistant was identified as a chief suspect in 'assisting' Van Boxtel's criminal enterprise, providing logistical support from the Spanish side.

Her role within the criminal organization was also explained when the file outlined:

> She's suspected of having set up a number of companies for the Kinahan Organized Crime Gang for the purpose of the importation of illegal drugs and firearms into the UK and Ireland, as well as for the purposes of money laundering the

proceeds of this criminal activity. She is the personal assistant of Daniel Kinahan. Her companies were set up to facilitate the illegal operations of the Kinahan Organized Crime Gang.

As investigations continued, Van Boxtel was identified by gardaí as:

[Someone who had] no recorded convictions but who associated with a number of known criminals. They established that his bogus company 'TS Foods' was set up to import the cannabis into Ireland and the fingerprints of the former footballer were found at the premises in Ballycoolin.

One former GNDU officer stated that Van Boxtel acted as a 'middleman between the gang, by bringing drugs into the country and [liaising with] the distribution man, Percival. He is a vital cog in the organization.'

O'Connor was regarded as a 'mule' who had been employed to do a 'drugs run', while Percival was identified as having 'storage supplies' at his home for 'some time'.

Delaney, who was born in 1972 and is also from north Dublin, had been monitored by the GNDU for a 'number of years' because of his links to major criminal organizations across Dublin, including the Hutch gang. One source explained:

Delaney associates with and is part of a criminal organization in the north Dublin area that are involved in the wholesale distribution of controlled drugs. He rarely handles the drugs himself but on this occasion he was present to oversee the transfer of the drugs. He's also the subject of an investigation by the Criminal Assets Bureau.

With the evidence stacked against them, a week after their arrest the four criminals appeared at Naas District Court on the drugs charges. Van Boxtel, O'Connor and Delaney made no application for bail and were remanded in custody. Percival, however, was remanded in custody with consent to bail of €10,000 after providing an independent surety of €250,000.

At a court hearing the following month, both Percival and O'Connor pleaded guilty to the drugs offences. The pair, regarded as lower-ranking members of the gang, were sentenced on 29 July 2009 at Naas Circuit Court for their role in the international drug-smuggling operation. As €7m worth of drugs had been found in Percival's home, he was the only member of the gang to be sentenced for the full haul of a fourteen-year term, though two years were suspended. (Gardaí learned that behind bars Percival distanced himself from the cartel and became a model prisoner. He was released in early 2016 because of a health problem and has abandoned crime.) O'Connor got a ten-year sentence. O'Connor appealed the severity of his sentence and he received a fourteen-year sentence, with five suspended, on 14 June 2010.

Van Boxtel, who had received bail one month after his initial arrest, was due to appear in court on 16 July 2008 for another hearing as the case progressed. Each case was being treated separately and the former goalkeeper was due in court to enter his plea on the matter. When he failed to appear a bench warrant was issued for his arrest but at that stage Van Boxtel was on his way out of Ireland.

At the same time, Delaney had also failed to appear at his hearing, and a warrant was also issued for his arrest.

Months later, detectives received information Van Boxtel was staying at one of the cartel's safe houses in Liverpool, in the north-west of England. However, the criminal was soon on the move and made his way to Amsterdam where he would spend the next five years living alongside the cartel's associates. According to sources, he was helping them with other shipments but quickly found himself out of favour and was increasingly isolated. He was viewed as a spent force and no longer of any use to them.

During his exile, Van Boxtel, now going by the name Thomas Anthony Fitzgerald, completely changed his appearance. He covered a tattoo of his wife's name on his shoulder with a Celtic cross tattoo, grew a beard, changed his hair style and lost weight.

The fugitive was also joined in the Dutch capital by Delaney. In the summer of 2013, Delaney was spotted drinking in an Irish pub in The Hague by two members of the gardaí who walked in. Immediately identifying him, they were powerless to act without having a European Arrest Warrant. Noticing the detectives, Delaney fled and remains at large to this day.

As autumn approached in 2013, Van Boxtel, who was now with a new partner, was becoming increasingly restless and homesick in Amsterdam. In August 2013, the one-time professional footballer made the decision to return to Ireland.

The Van Boxtel who had fled Ireland in 2008 had completely transformed when he returned five years later. Staying away from his native Ballymun and avoiding his old associates, 'Thomas Anthony Fitzgerald' settled into life in Ronanstown, west Dublin, with his new girlfriend, who was pregnant. Maintaining a low profile, his only visits would be to a local pub and to bookmakers.

Still obsessed with football, and still unemployed, he enjoyed placing bets on English Premiership games. Gradually becoming at ease with his new sense of freedom at being back in Dublin, and continuing to evade gardaí, the man who had once saved a penalty from Eric Cantona made the decision to stay in Ireland throughout the course of 2014.

His faith in his new identity would prove to be his downfall, however, after detectives received intelligence he was back in the capital and living under a different name in west Dublin. As had been the case in February 2008, Van Boxtel was unaware that he was, once again, under the spotlight of gardaí.

Although his appearance had been completely altered, detectives believed the man they were monitoring was the same man who had vanished six years ago. Concerned their target could disappear for a second time, investigators swooped on 28 February 2014.

Hauled in for questioning, Van Boxtel made desperate attempts to convince detectives they had captured the wrong man. Producing a driving licence in the name of Thomas Fitzgerald, Van Boxtel continued to deny his real identity. He had changed so much in six years that detectives were unsure if they had the right man.

One officer explains:

His driving licence was very professional and he was very calm about the arrest. He had covered the tattoo of his former partner's name with another piece of body art and he did this as part of his cover story to pass himself off as someone else. He was very arrogant about his new identity but when the fingerprints were put to him he knew he was on the losing side.

He had probably slipped into Ireland during his absence because he still had connections but people can only run for so long. It had taken a long time but he was finally caught.

If he'd stayed away from Ireland, he might still be a free man today.

At the same time, gardaí also searched the house he had been staying in and recovered a photocopy of a passport in the name of Mark Kenny. Detectives believe Van Boxtel was using the identification document to secure cash transfers from associates of the cartel in Holland.

Remanded in custody, Van Boxtel was once again charged with possessing €3.5m worth of cannabis and on a count of possessing drugs with intent to supply. Despite numerous attempts to receive bail at various hearings at the High Court, Van Boxtel remained in prison until his trial was due to commence at Naas Circuit Court in November 2014. At one bail hearing, Detective Sergeant Greg Sheehan told the court Van Boxtel was a 'flight risk' and had 'fake documents'.

During his time spent on remand at Dublin's Cloverhill Prison, the ex-professional footballer attempted to impress a senior cartel figure by attacking a prison officer. The only thing it earned him was a transfer to the medium-security Midlands Prison.

Van Boxtel was due to stand trial on 7 November 2014, but detectives from Operation Perch were left disappointed when a retrial was ordered. The trial had collapsed because a member of the jury panel had unwittingly noticed Van Boxtel in handcuffs when he was being brought into the court.

Rescheduled for January 2015, investigators waited anxiously for Van Boxtel's appearance in court. On the morning of 20 January 2015, the former teenage football star pleaded guilty to possession of €3.5m worth of cannabis, along with a charge of possession with intent to supply.

Almost seven years after Van Boxtel and his associates

had masterminded a €10.5 million drugs shipment into Ireland, the Kinahan gang member received a ten-year sentence, with the last two-and-a-half years suspended.

Although one member of the gang from that day on 6 February 2008 remains at large, the unravelling of the huge drugs importation network would lead to the birth of 'Operation Shovel', the major offensive against the Kinahan cartel on Spanish soil.

Meanwhile, gardaí were battling to deal with another cartel member – who was more difficult to catch than a gullible former footballer.

6. Criminal Heavyweight

'It's gone too far; I can't get out.'

Mr A

In the year 2001, gardaí scored a major victory in their constant see-saw battle against Ireland's drug gangs. The country had been left stunned when journalist Veronica Guerin was murdered five years earlier on the orders of John Gilligan. But in March 2001, Gilligan's crumbling reign ended when he was sentenced to twenty-eight years for importing large amounts of cannabis resin. The sentence was later reduced by eight years on appeal, but the implication was clear: as far as drug trafficking was concerned, Gilligan was a busted flush.

Senior cops were under no illusions about the temporary nature of their victory. The amount of money to be made in the drug trade meant other figures would quickly take Gilligan's place. Since the journalist's murder he had been gradually ceding turf in Dublin to other criminal outfits, including the Kinahans and the Hutches.

The following September, gardaí pulled over a car driven by an up-and-coming young gangster who must be referred to as Mr A for legal reasons. The tax disc of the car bore a different registration to the vehicle itself. The car was searched and nothing was found, but gardaí noted that the young criminal was 'obnoxious and aggressive' to them throughout.

'I'm going to be the next John Gilligan and youse are going to be busy then,' he told them. It was a promise he would do his best to keep over the next decade and a half.

But there has always been something a bit ridiculous about Mr A, possibly because of his habit of wearing a wig around Dublin to disguise himself. It was something that continued into his dealings with gardaí. Mr A was fond of making smart remarks to cops or attempting to flee for no discernible reason when stopped and searched. Senior detectives who have been investigating him for some years, however, will tell you that behind the foolish facade lies a very violent and dangerous criminal.

One senior garda commented:

> He's reckless. If you were selling drugs and you wouldn't sell for him and his gang, he'd cut you up. They were cutting up people for just €200 or €300. If they couldn't get at them, they'd get at their family.

Mr A was just sixteen years old when he gained his first conviction before the District Children's Court for 'indictable general comments'. He was bound over to keep the peace for six months, but less than a year later he was back up before the District Children's Court again on the same charges. This first conviction began a cycle of suspended or light sentences for road traffic and public order offences until he landed himself his first serious stretch in Mountjoy Prison. (He would be convicted for endangerment in 2002, after driving his car at a garda to try to help a man in custody to escape, and would earn himself a two-year sentence.)

By his early twenties, he was part of a gang of young hoods heavily involved in drugs and other criminality. Gardaí began to keep a special eye on the group and, in July 2000, they pulled over a car some of them were travelling in. Inside were several of the gang, including Mr A, who had clearly been in a fight.

Three of the young gang in the car would go on to establish themselves in the cartel. Others, like David Byrne and Declan Gavin, would die violently, their murders kicking off major gangland feuds.

Gavin was just two weeks shy of his twenty-first birthday when he was stabbed to death outside an Abrakebabra take-away, in Crumlin, in August 2001. Brian Rattigan, a former drug-dealing associate, was shouting about the victim being a 'rat' as he killed him after a night's drinking.

The previous year, Gavin had escaped prosecution following the seizure of large amounts of cocaine and Ecstasy by gardaí. On the second occasion, Gavin was dozing in an adjacent bedroom when gardaí raided a hotel room in the Holiday Inn on Pearse Street, Dublin, and found two others cutting up the cocaine with coffee grinders. Both men were jailed for their role, but although there were drugs in Gavin's room, he was not physically holding them, so the case against him progressed more slowly. For this reason, he was branded a 'tout', even though the DPP would later direct charges against him and he was due to be tried in October 2001. Despite this, after the arrests two separate groups formed – one supporting Gavin, the other behind Rattigan and his brother Joey.

Brian Rattigan had made only a cursory attempt to hide his identity when he carried out Gavin's murder. He went into hiding afterwards and was not arrested until a month later, on 4 September. Under questioning, he denied being present on the night of the murder. He claimed that gardaí had planted his bloodied handprint, which had been recovered from the window of the Abrakebabra outlet. When he was told witnesses had placed him at the scene, Rattigan responded they would 'never say it' if it ever came to court.

Retaliation from the other side came seven months later, with Mr A at the forefront of it. The following St Patrick's night, two gunmen burst into Brian Rattigan's home. Rattigan was shot at point-blank range in the chest, but remarkably survived, albeit with the loss of a kidney and his spleen.

On the way out, one of the gunmen had deliberately pulled up his balaclava and stared at Rattigan's girlfriend, Natasha McEnroe. She told cops she had shouted, 'Come back here, you bastard ...' at the departing criminal, who simply laughed at her in response.

Gardaí subsequently learned the gunman's accomplice had been a feared criminal associate, Paddy Doyle. Despite recommendations from gardaí, nobody was ever charged in connection with the incident.

However, the stage had been set for what turned into the bloodiest criminal feud ever seen in Ireland. By the time the Crumlin-Drimnagh feud (as it became known because the protagonists were largely based in this area of south Dublin) petered out, sixteen young men were dead. There had also been dozens of attempted hits, pipe-bomb attacks, stabbings and beatings. The feud tied up thousands of Garda hours as detectives attempted to curb the slaughter, while the army bomb squad was also regularly called out to defuse the devices left outside homes and under cars.

Mr A was at the very heart of the war. Gardaí believe he personally ordered two of the most shocking murders which illustrated just how ruthless gangland could be.

In November 2005, Darren Geoghegan and Gavin Byrne were shot dead as they sat in the front seats of a Lexus in a middle-class housing estate in Firhouse, south Dublin. It was obvious to detectives from the off that the two criminals had known and trusted their killer, as both men had been shot twice in the back of the head by someone who was sitting in the back seat.

Geoghegan and Byrne were senior members of the Crumlin faction and their killing puzzled the rival Rattigan side, as they had not been responsible. Subsequent investigations convinced gardaí that one of their own side was the real culprit. They believed Paddy Doyle had been commissioned to carry out the hit in an internal row over money.

As the feud dragged on throughout the mid-2000s, Mr A refocused on business. He turned his mind to the bigger task of drug importation and left subordinates to maintain hostilities.

Holland was the principal go-to spot for Irish criminals looking to purchase drug shipments to move home. As well as Christy Kinahan and John Cunningham, the presence in the Netherlands of other Dublin drug traffickers – including George 'the Penguin' Mitchell and Peter 'Fatso' Mitchell (no relation) – made it easier for the likes of Mr A to get their hands on large quantities of cocaine and heroin to supply the Irish market. Mr A also had the advantage of knowing Daniel Kinahan, who he would have grown up nearby in inner-city Dublin. He duly travelled over to the Netherlands to organize a shipment with his cartel associates, which he planned to sell off for a hefty profit back in Dublin.

Unbeknownst to the gangster, he was being watched by Dutch police who had been tipped off by gardaí. Mr A was arrested following a raid on an apartment in a Dutch city. Inside police found several kilos of cocaine and a number of handguns. Three other Irish people, a man and two women, were also lifted. Two of these Mr A planned to have carry the drugs and weapons home. They were due to travel from the enormous Europoort facility via the north-eastern English port of Hull.

The cautious approach taken by the Dutch police, however, eventually allowed Mr A to wriggle out of the charges. When the apartment was raided, he was in the foyer of the building. The Dutch police were aware of his violent reputation and feared a shoot-out if he was taken inside the apartment so they arrested him in the lobby. This decision had serious consequences four months down the line when the gangster was freed from custody, after convincing judges the drugs and guns did not belong to him. Gardaí were incredulous, as was the local public prosecutor's office. Mr A had slipped through the net once more.

The Dutch operation had come just a week after gardaí made a huge €11 million seizure of heroin, a sub-machine gun and thousands of rounds of ammunition at an apartment complex in Clondalkin, in west Dublin. Gardaí established some of the drugs belonged to Mr A. The others were the property of other dealers in the city who had agreed to store their merchandise at the apartment because it was the home of an addict who owed them thousands, due to a serious cocaine habit.

Some of the drugs belonged to Karl Breen, who ran the locally-based D22 gang. At the time, Breen was awaiting trial for stabbing his friend Martin McLaughlin to death during a boozy row at the Croke Park Jury's Inn in the early hours of the previous New Year's Day. His manslaughter conviction subsequently saw him nicknamed the 'Champagne Killer' after it emerged he had spent the evening downing expensive glasses of Moët.

The feud was ongoing and gardaí had an active policy of stopping and searching members of both gangs when they were spotted, in case they were on their way to carry out more murders. Often, searches of cars in which Mr A was travelling would reveal hammers, sometimes wrapped in plastic, in the boot or under one of the front seats.

The gangster would rarely co-operate with gardaí on these occasions, even if he had nothing to hide. He would sometimes attempt to flee only to be caught after a high-speed chase. Gardaí were confident he had nothing on him on most of these incidents and was merely bolting for the hell of it. Other times, he would refuse to be searched on the spot, resulting in his arrest and transport to the nearest Garda station so that a search could be carried out. It would turn up nothing. On the face of it, it seemed a bigger waste of his own time than that of the gardaí, but Mr A continued to act this way regardless.

In one incident, he pulled the SIM card out of his phone as gardaí questioned him and tried to swallow it. In another, he ate the top-up slip for his mobile phone in front of officers, telling them it was 'to stop youse checking my phone'.

By 2007, the Crumlin side were winning their war against Brian Rattigan's side, largely because their nemesis had been behind bars on remand for Declan Gavin's murder since 2003. Several top associates of Rattigan, including Gary Bryan, Shay O'Byrne and Anthony Cannon, were all now dead. However, a new threat, in the form of the INLA, had entered the fray.

The republican terrorist group had long funded its activities, both north and south of the border, through drug dealing and now its Dublin leader, Declan 'Whacker' Duffy, had his eyes on Mr A's turf. From Armagh, Duffy had joined the INLA as a thirteen-year-old, following the shooting dead of his older brother by the British Army in 1987. He was just eighteen when he was part of a three-man paramilitary team which murdered British Army recruitment officer, Sergeant Michael Newman, in Derby, England, in 1992.

Throughout the nineties, the INLA was up to its neck in drug dealing and extortion. In 2001, Duffy had been given a nine-year sentence for leading the INLA gang involved in the 'Ballymount Bloodbath' two years earlier. On 6 October 1999, four criminals had called to the premises of a Walkinstown warehouse looking for IR£600 compensation from the businessman who owned it, John Creed. They believed a member of Creed's family had carried out an arson attack on their van and, armed with knuckledusters, a machete and a sword, were determined to make him pay up.

However, Creed had contacted the INLA, several of whom (including Duffy) were lying in wait in the shadows, some armed. The would-be debt collectors were stripped naked, bound and tortured and were told they had twenty-four hours to leave the country. Events then spiralled out of control when twelve more of the criminal gang arrived to rescue their colleagues. In the ensuing melee, INLA man Patrick 'Bo' Campbell was stabbed to death. Duffy went down for false imprisonment and arms possession. But no sooner had he been released, in February 2007, than he began to eye up Mr A's operation for potential extortion.

In late 2007, gardaí seized a gun from a man who was walking up a city-centre street in Dublin. The weapon was destined to be used in an INLA assassination attempt against Mr A and he was warned his life was in danger. He temporarily left the city, but continued to move between Dublin, Birmingham, Holland and Spain, using a bulletproof vest any time he was home. Like most of his contemporaries, Mr A was buying his drugs from the Kinahans and would meet with them when in Spain.

Despite the serious threats against him, Mr A continued to act in the same hot-headed way of old, even though it was affecting his own gang's unity at a time when he needed it most. After a fight between Mr A and his own younger brother in a nightclub in central Dublin, cartel member Liam Roe sided with the younger sibling. Roe told gardaí he was 'no longer an associate' of Mr A's Garda files reveal.

Shortly before that, Mr A had ambushed and battered a man with a baseball bat simply because the man had previously gone out with his then girlfriend. There seemed to be a never-ending string of violent incidents involving the gangster, mainly drink-related.

In May 2008, he had to be separated from a man in a wheelchair after pouring a drink over him, again in a nightclub in central Dublin. Roe, who had by then reconciled his differences with his violent associate, was forced to intervene and carry the drenched victim upstairs.

The attempts on Mr A's life continued and, soon afterwards, a lone masked gunman entered a pub he frequented, looking to kill him. His brother was there but the main target was not, so the gunman left. The following day, gunmen walked into a bookies Mr A was known to use, but again missed him. As might be expected, the gangster was in fear for his life. Most times he was stopped and searched by gardaí, he was found to be wearing a bulletproof vest.

Mr A was dividing his time between Dublin, Holland and Spain and was regularly out of the country. During another brief visit home in September 2008, he was spotted on Grafton Street in the city centre and again patted down.

In his pockets were €35, his passport and a scrap of paper bearing the address of a man in Ballyfermot. Asked about this, he told cops the man was 'just an old friend'.

'Have to catch up, you know how it is,' he smirked.

But as the conversation continued, he became more serious, admitting he was 'paranoid' about his safety and saying he knew of at least ten people who wanted him dead.

'All the gardaí are pulling back, nowhere to be seen,' he said. Referring to notorious gangster Martin 'the General' Cahill who was shot dead by the IRA in August 1994, he added, 'Isn't that what happened to Cahill? Look what happened to him.'

Senior gardaí say the gangster has expressed regret over his life of crime. A mere three years into the feud in 2004, he told one experienced officer that he felt trapped in the spiral of violence and had no choice but to continue. 'It's gone too far; I can't get out,' Mr A said.

While Rattigan's power had been greatly diminished by his incarceration while awaiting trial for Declan Gavin's murder, and by the deaths of his senior associates, he remained a force to be reckoned with. At the beginning of 2009, there were a rash of false bomb reports to gardaí as an apparent means of testing response times and to simply waste their time.

There were over thirty of these incidents during the first four months of the year alone, many of which required the deployment of the army bomb squad. Occasionally, however, the threats were real. In one incident, a viable device was left under the car of the blameless relative of a friend of Mr A.

Three weeks later, another innocent person – this time the mother of David and Liam Byrne – was targeted in an identical incident at the Byrne family home in Crumlin. The Byrnes were major members of the cartel and Liam, whose nickname is 'Bugsy', was in regular contact with Daniel by phone, occasionally travelling over to speak with him in person. They were furious that their mother had been drawn into the feud.

The incensed brothers turned up at the scene and clashed with gardaí in irate exchanges when they were told they would have to stay away from the house until the all-clear was given.

It is an offence to refuse to give your name and address to a garda if asked, so cops regularly do it to annoy criminals. The gangsters know they must comply or face arrest, even though both parties are often on first-name terms. On this occasion, Mr A was asked for his details and angrily went through the motions. He then ranted about the Rattigan gang: 'Why are they wasting police time? They don't have the guts to shoot someone. Wasting taxpayers' money.'

Throughout 2009 there had by now been a rash of attacks by both sides on innocent family members' homes, as each gang recognized this as the other's weak spot.

By the end of the year, Mr A had had enough. He told Liam Byrne, in a phone call home from Spain, that he wanted to strike a deal with Rattigan. He wanted them to agree to leave relatives' homes alone, particularly his mother's home, which had also been targeted.

'We're out of that situation,' he told Byrne. 'If he wants to pay for my mother's house and your mother's house, then I'll do the same.' A similar call took place the next day, with the transcript of the tap reading: 'Mr A says this is his thing, they shouldn't involve their mothers.'

His plea for a truce had little effect and the family home would be fire-bombed twice the following year.

While Mr A was worried about his mother, others close to him were also suffering because of his activities. Cops learned that one such individual had undergone rehabilitation, costing €30,000, for addiction to the cocaine he was most probably supplying.

By 2008, Mr A had established his main base on the Costa del Sol, in Spain. Over there, he was a much smaller fish in a considerably larger pond. Mr A had been a loyal associate of Daniel Kinahan and knew Christopher Jr from mixing in the same Dublin circles. He might have expected to be part of the inner circle in Estepona.

Initially, he was. Mr A was employed as a driver and a bodyguard by the cartel's top echelon and underwent firearms and anti-surveillance training along with Daniel and other gang members.

Along with Gary Hutch, he was sent on drug runs to collect narcotics and weaponry from secret locations in Portugal. Another job of his was to procure arms for other members of the gang.

Mr A also seemed to get on with the Dapper Don in the beginning. Christy had had a serious falling out with former Martin Cahill henchman Martin 'the Viper' Foley in the early 1990s, over a debt of IR£100,000. In 2008, he decided to act upon it and exact his revenge. A young associate of Mr A's was tasked with the job.

After getting to know Foley and befriending him, the young criminal shot 'the Viper' four times in the chest as he drove away from the Carlisle Gym in Kimmage, south Dublin. It was the fourth attempt on Foley's life – and the fourth time he survived.

But while Mr A was being treated relatively well by Daniel

he was soon being treated with extreme disdain by the father. Christy handed him a series of menial tasks to do.

It was clear Christy and John Cunningham did not trust the man, probably because of his notoriously erratic behaviour. The importance of saying nothing on the phone had been drilled into all the gang repeatedly. Mr A, however, was prone to the occasional, potentially serious, slip.

In December 2009, he rang Gary Hutch, with whom he would chat several times a day. Asking where Hutch was, Mr A mentioned that he had something for him 'in his pocket'. Ignoring Hutch's reply that he would see him in a couple of minutes, Mr A continued, 'Now, it's not that big.'

'I can fucking imagine,' answered Hutch.

'No, seriously, it's not that big.'

'It'll work, though, right?' asked Hutch.

'Yeah, probably. It'll probably just spit out one bullet and that'll be it.'

'Hang up the phone,' came the immediate reply.

And the line went dead.

In another taped conversation with an unknown Spanish-based associate, Mr A chatted with the man who asked him repeatedly if he would be back before the morning.

'We're on the way back but . . . we're about fifty from Algeria and I don't think we'll arrive until four in the morning.'

The Spanish detectives concluded he was on his way back from a drug-smuggling trip, but without knowing further details, there was nothing they could do.

Indiscretions aside, Mr A and Gary Hutch appeared quite close. They regularly spent evenings together smoking cannabis at the apartment they shared near Marbella or going out on the town. Mr A also offered to intercede on behalf of Hutch's younger brother Derek, known as 'Del Boy'. He was awaiting trial for armed robbery and feared being attacked by members of the Real IRA outfit, led by Alan Ryan, while he was stuck behind bars. Mr A was recorded saying he knew a 'kangaroo' (screw) at Portlaoise Prison, but whatever transpired did not appear on subsequent phone taps.

Mr A regularly moved between Dublin and his foreign boltholes of Birmingham and Amsterdam. He returned home frequently and could not resist reminding gardaí of his position within the city's underworld.

In one incident, Mr A and David Byrne were stopped in a car on Dame Street in the city centre. As usual, gardaí took their time in searching the vehicle and all its occupants. This irritated Mr A, who urged them to get on with it. The man who had once promised to become the next John Gilligan said he wanted the search over quickly as he was awaiting a phone call from the fallen drug baron from behind bars in Portlaoise Prison. Cops took his claims with a pinch of salt, particularly when he said a prison official was allowing Gilligan to use his phone.

Eventually, Mr A's habit of getting into rows proved his undoing. On a visit home he got into a pub brawl during which he threw a beer bottle at one former associate and slapped a woman in the face. The incident developed into a mass brawl and spilled out on to the street outside. When gardaí were called, many of those involved refused to co-operate.

Unfortunately for Mr A, the entire incident had been caught on the pub's CCTV. Detectives called to his home two days later, only to be told he had left the country. Tracked down to Holland, he was extradited back home some months later.

Mr A continued to throw his weight around in jail while

he awaited trial, telling one inmate who had been his driver at the height of the feud with Rattigan, 'I haven't forgotten about that sixty grand you owe me.' The man, who was due for release, went into hiding once freed. Other threats did not work out so well. Mr A's attempt to intimidate another criminal from Ballyfermot ended with him receiving what was described to gardaí as 'a serious hiding' in the exercise yard at Cloverhill Prison.

Mr A was convicted of violent disorder and given a jail sentence. And there may yet be other consequences as a result of the incident in the pub. The woman Mr A slapped is the former partner of a psychotic individual currently serving a lengthy sentence for attacking a man with a meat cleaver. The criminal, who has previously been involved in plots to kill gardaí, a lawyer and journalists, told gardaí in interviews months after the melee that Mr A was lucky he had made it out of the country afterwards. He added, 'This is not the end of it.'

The threat has so far come to nothing, primarily because the man behind it is in prison. Mr A has a long-standing role within the cartel, but this might not be enough to save him from the other criminal's vengeance if it came to it. As others have learned, past friendships have counted for nothing when the cartel decided they were more trouble than they were worth.

7. A Pan-European Problem

'Patrick told me he wished he could start his life
again and do it all differently.'

Paddy Doyle's father, Donal

The battle between the authorities and the country's biggest
crime gang continued throughout the mid-2000s. Concerned at
the alarming number of drugs on Irish streets, gardaí were also
worried about the number of weapons, including many from
eastern Europe, that were readily available to criminal gangs.

Persisting in their offensive against the Kinahan gang, investigators received further intelligence that guns were being
stored at a house in Oak Way, Clondalkin, in west Dublin. It
was the home of Keith Ennis, a major gangland figure at the
time, who ran his own drug-dealing network in west Dublin.
Before swooping on his home on 26 October 2007, Ennis was
stopped in Dublin city centre by officers from Pearse Street
Garda Station and found to have €23,000 on him.

Once Ennis was in custody, gardaí raided his house and
found a Glock handgun and €3,000 worth of cocaine. Two
days later, officers – who had received further information
weapons were being stored at an industrial unit – launched a
separate search. Inside Unit 10 of Hillcrest Industrial Estate,
officers recovered two full-length barrel shotguns, a sawn-off
shotgun, another Glock and 9kg of cocaine, worth €500,000.

Also recovered were mixing agents for cocaine, compression machines and the paraphernalia used, according to one detective, in the 'mixing and packaging of illegal drugs'. The detective explained:

> We suspected this location was being used as a processing area for the mixing and distribution of illegal drugs imported into Ireland by the Kinahan gang. These drugs and guns were under the control of this gang.

Keith Ennis was considered by gardaí to be 'one of the main Irish-based connections to the Kinahan gang and that he organized and controlled a large portion of their activities in Ireland'. Ennis was charged with possessing drugs with intent to supply, and possessing firearms.

He received bail and, desperate to avoid prison, he later fled to Holland. Convinced he would be killed because he was suspected of being an informer, he arranged his own funeral. His prophecy would be fulfilled when his dismembered body was recovered from a suitcase in a canal in Amsterdam on 24 February 2009. Two men have been charged in connection with the killing and are awaiting trial in Holland.

That same autumn of 2007, gardaí received an unexpected boost. Christy's younger son, Christopher Jr, had been in a relationship with Georgina Corish for some time and, in September, the couple married in Dublin. Corish was from a decent family and was also reared in the south inner-city area of Dublin. She had known Christopher Jr from a young age.

The reception was held at a five-star hotel in Wicklow, which the gang had booked using a cash deposit, to avoid leaving a credit-card trail. Unfortunately for them, gardaí got wind of what was happening. When they confirmed the name of the groom, they mounted a full surveillance operation.

Christopher Jr's wedding reception helped them to piece together the make-up and layout of the gang. Although the focus of the surveillance operation was Kinahan Senior, the wedding also provided investigators with the opportunity to record details of Kinahan's associates. The surveillance initiative was predominantly orchestrated to provide detectives with a clear picture of those known to have links with the Kinahan cartel, but who were flying under the radar.

Christy had by then ended the relationship with his second wife and begun another with a third woman, also Dutch, but of Turkish descent. Amongst the wedding guests, however, gardaí were interested to see his second wife's British-Indian boss from the mortgage brokerage. This individual would later follow Christy to southern Spain and set up a firm to help the Dapper Don launder his money, through the purchase and sale of commodities online. The mortgage broker's presence at the wedding was indication enough to watching gardaí of his importance within the cartel.

Others present included Kevin Lynch, a convicted armed robber from Ballyfermot, who had also clearly become a leading figure in the cartel. Gardaí also monitored several other gang members whose invitation indicated they might rank higher within the organization than the detectives had previously suspected.

One of Christy's associates who was not there was John Cunningham, his long-time partner. After serving a total of six years in prison, the 'Colonel' had been released in 2006. Cunningham did four years of his seven-year term in Holland before being sent back home to see out the rest of the

Jennifer Guinness kidnapping sentence, from which he had escaped in 1996. Despite having absconded from Shelton Abbey, his remission was not affected and he was only imprisoned for the final two years he was due to serve anyway. Cunningham only served a year and three months of that and upon his release, in February 2007, the 'Colonel' had joined his wife and daughter in southern Spain.

That same year, Cunningham was observed travelling with Christy to Hong Kong. Investigators believed the pair were planning to look at other possible business ventures, as new ways of laundering cash. When Cunningham had hooked up with Kinahan again, gardaí knew it wouldn't take long for such a career criminal to get back to his old ways. Investigators also gained intelligence in 2007 that the 'Colonel' was sending cannabis shipments to a Cork-based drug baron.

Cunningham and Kinahan had proved themselves virtually interchangeable in the past, one taking over when the other went behind bars. Soon after his move to Spain, the Spanish investigators had come to view Cunningham as Christy's most trusted man in the operation, outside of his two sons, and just below him in the drug-smuggling pecking order. Phone taps revealed how the 'Colonel' would give orders to Daniel and he would have to follow them. One junior member of the gang was recorded telling another how Daniel had said 'his father and John are his new bosses and anything they ask him to do, he has to do it'.

Christy held regular meetings with Cunningham, usually on the fairways of the luxury golf course where both were members and could discuss business, far away from prying ears. Indeed, so close were the pair that Christy had agreed to act as guarantor on a loan taken out by one of the gang's front firms, Pearlsea 1 SL. It was to purchase Cunningham's luxury villa in Estepona, on the Costa del Sol, in the summer of 2006 while he was still in jail in Ireland. Just like all of Cunningham's other assets, the property was held in someone else's name.

The mere fact Christy had allowed his name to be involved in the transaction at all revealed the strength of their relationship. The Spanish police files noted, 'The close bond between Cunningham and the Kinahans has ensured they took part in the matter to avoid John's name appearing in any legal paperwork.'

Certainly, the 'Colonel' was back living the good life he so enjoyed, despite not having any visible, legitimate means of maintaining it. He drove a BMW X5 and a Corvette C6 sports car and spent most of his days working on his golf handicap.

His home, the purchase of which Christy had stuck out his neck for, was worth over €644,000. Though he lived there with his wife and daughter, Cunningham ran all the bills for it through Pearlsea 1 SL, to maintain the front of deniability.

The rest of his money was funnelled to bank accounts abroad or invested in property in Spain and Cyprus over the course of several years. Cunningham deferred to Kinahan's expertise when it came to money laundering, ploughing some of his money into the same villas in the Mediterranean resort of Paralimni, in Cyprus, that the Dapper Don had selected.

Kinahan had been legally resident in Cyprus since 2007, despite spending most of his time in Belgium and Spain. But in 2008, Christy received a serious setback when he was informed that the Belgian authorities had opened a money-laundering investigation against him. Having residency in

Cyprus allowed Christy to keep his money in a recognized money-laundering haven which had the major advantage of lying within the Eurozone. Cyprus has been a source of concern to its EU neighbours for decades. In February 2016, a Dutch MP publicly hit out at the island's failure to deal with illicit bank accounts owned by the Russian mafia. This was just three years after the EU anti-laundering body MONEY-VAL had identified 'serious deficiencies' in Cyprus during bailout talks in 2013.

'Operation Excalibur', the Belgian probe into his money-laundering activities, had uncovered a sizeable network of Cypriot firms through which Kinahan had been passing money, in order to also buy real estate across Belgium. The courts froze his considerable assets in Belgium – including a former casino called Fantasy in the old town of Antwerp, which cost him €1 million. After the Belgian courts seized the ex-casino, it fell into disrepair and was occupied by squatters. They nearly blew the whole place up in January 2013 when one of them had a row with his girlfriend and tried to turn the gas on, to kill himself.

Christy also lost a €600,000 villa and an apartment in Brasschaat, a nearby affluent town. During a search of one of the properties in May 2008, cops found €54,000 worth of cash in €50 bills. Many of the notes bore heavy traces of cocaine and of a common cocaine bulking substitute, lidocaine. Dr Crista Van Haeren, of Belgium's National Institute of Criminalistics and Criminology, testified both substances showed up 'in amounts far exceeding normal contamination'.

Christy would later be convicted and handed a four-year sentence in September 2009.

Kinahan lost €2.5m worth of property in the Belgian swoops in Antwerp and Brasschaat, when the court ruled they were the proceeds of crime. Both the cash and the properties were impounded and the latter were auctioned off after Kinahan was found guilty.

By then Christy had decided to move to southern Spain. He already had properties there and his sons, Daniel and Christopher Jr, and their families had lived in the area for several years. He reluctantly hired two Belgium-based North African criminals to drive his personal possessions to the Costa del Sol.

There are several other reasons why a drug trafficker would seek to base himself in Spain. It is the main entry point into Europe for both cocaine and cannabis and has been the base of dozens of international criminal organizations for decades, with local authorities only able to monitor so many of them. The average 325 days of sunshine per year probably does not hurt either.

Christy found himself two homes: the first was a €6 million white-washed villa near the seafront in San Pedro de Alcántara, with high gates and conifer trees to keep curious passers-by away; and the second was in a luxury apartment block in Torre Bermeja, Estepona.

The Kinahan gang had also established their own gym in an industrial estate outside Marbella in 2007, where members could hang out, practise kickboxing or other disciplines, and hold business meetings. It also served as a drop-off point for cash and a place to stash mobile phones.

As might be expected, there is a certain hierarchy in criminal circles. Once the Kinahans had established themselves on the Costa del Sol, the word went out that it was their patch and only those close to the cartel were allowed there. Garda intelligence reports indicated riff-raff such as the violent and troublesome McCarthy-Dundons, for example, were told they were not welcome. One of the most ruthless crime gangs in Ireland, they were responsible for the murder of innocent businessman Roy Collins. The gang was later dismantled after its leader, Wayne Dundon, was jailed for the killing. The Kinahans banished the Limerick gangsters to Alicante for their visits to Spain.

Former associates of John Gilligan were warned off too. There was one occasion when an organized Traveller gang from the Midlands, who had close connections to Gilligan, were desperately trying to meet with Christy Kinahan, with a view to arranging shipments of cocaine into Ireland. The request was made by a Gilligan associate from west Dublin but Kinahan refused to deal with the gang, giving no explanation for the knockback.

By 2008, a lot had changed in Christy's world and the cartel had grown much more extensive. Like Salinger, it meant the recruitment of some individuals who Kinahan would subsequently decide he could no longer trust. Paddy Doyle would eventually turn out to be one of these figures.

Doyle had established his reputation as a cold-blooded assassin beyond any doubt by carrying out the clinical killings of Darren Geoghegan and Gavin Byrne in November 2005 during the Crumlin-Drimnagh feud. Doyle had gone to ground in the aftermath of the double murder.

Two days afterwards, he had been called into action again. This time the target was Noel Roche, a leading member of the Rattigan faction. Roche's brother John had already been murdered in Kilmainham earlier that year.

On the night of 15 November 2005, Noel Roche was attending a Phil Collins concert at the Point Depot (now the 3Arena), a large concert venue near Dublin Port. For some bizarre reason, Collins is hugely popular with Dublin criminals of a certain age. It is believed Roche was spotted at the concert by someone loyal to Mr A.

At 9.30 p.m. that night, Roche received a phone call. He suddenly told his girlfriend that he had to leave the venue and sent his driver off to pick up their Ford Mondeo car. The pair were apparently unaware that they were followed from the Point by two men in a Fiat Punto.

Roche dropped his girlfriend off at her home in Coolock and was being driven back into the city when a stolen blue Peugeot 307 containing Doyle appeared behind them. A 21-year-old gangster named Craig White was at the wheel.

A desperate chase ensued before White managed to pull up alongside Roche's car near the Yacht pub on the Clontarf Road. Doyle fired four shots through the tinted passenger-side window at him. Roche was hit once in the face and twice in the chest and died instantly.

Satisfied Roche was dead, White and Doyle drove off and dumped the Peugeot on nearby Furry Park Road, in Killester. A local woman was drawn to her front window by the sound of the car driving by at high speed and saw two men running away from the vehicle.

Unfortunately for them, Doyle and White were in such a hurry they failed to burn out the car. Gardaí later found the can of petrol, which did not ignite, inside the vehicle. They also found a paper bag bearing White's fingerprints and containing the Glock semi-automatic pistol used to shoot Roche, a balaclava, a tea towel and a pair of gloves.

More gloves containing White's DNA were discovered further along Furry Park Road. White would subsequently be jailed for life. Meanwhile, Doyle knew he was a marked man. The shooting of Noel Roche was Doyle's third murder inside forty-eight hours and there was simply no way he could stay in the country.

If gardaí did not catch up with him, the Rattigan side eventually would. He left Dublin for the UK and made his way onwards to Spain, where he again hooked up with Mr A, who was dividing his time between the Costa del Sol, Holland and Dublin.

It was like old times again for Doyle, who was also palling around with Gary Hutch. The trio would regularly work out together at a local gym and spend their evenings socializing in upmarket Puerto Banús. The triple murderer had come a long way from when he used to hang around Dublin with his criminal associate Mr A and the other young hoods.

Doyle was also heavily involved in drug trafficking and had been offering himself around as muscle. He was working for the Kinahans at the time but had also offered his services to the McCarthy-Dundon gang in Limerick. As he was 6ft 3ins, addicted to steroids and had a propensity for violence from a young age, Doyle was used to getting his way when dealing with his fellow Irish criminals. During one trip to Amsterdam, he gave a Finglas gangster named Michael 'Roly' Cronin a severe beating after they had a falling out. Doyle also had a habit of getting involved in rows in nightclubs, and reportedly attacked a Russian mafioso in a club on the Costa del Sol.

On 4 February 2008, Doyle, Hutch and Mr A were driving back from the cartel's gym to Doyle's house in a BMW X5 SUV. Doyle and Hutch were living together in the Bel Air estate and were a familiar sight to locals, who regularly saw them take a narrow, curved alleyway which led into the estate from a nearby dual carriageway.

Other people were also aware of their routine. When the

SUV, driven by Hutch, emerged from the alleyway that morning on to the residential Mejorana Street, there was a car waiting for them. It pulled up opposite and a gunman fired five shots into the passenger-side windscreen and window of the BMW.

Hutch drove the SUV into a lamp post on the corner, jumped out and ran for his life. Mr A, who was in the back seat, did likewise. Remarkably, Doyle was not hit and sprinted off in the other direction, back down the alleyway from which they had just emerged.

The gunman was only a few feet behind him, however, and began firing after Doyle as he ran. A forensic re-enactment carried out by Spanish police in the days following the shooting showed that the towering Dubliner had managed to make it halfway down the lane before he fell to his knees. Doyle was then finished off, with two bullets to the back of the head.

A post-mortem would later reveal the 27-year-old had been hit with thirteen rounds. He had so many wounds the autopsy took two days to complete. Hutch later handed himself in to police and was freed after being questioned by detectives investigating the case. Mr A got out of Spain as quickly as he could, probably to Holland.

'They all think they're big men until they come out here and then . . .' shrugged a forensic detective to one of the authors at the scene the day after the killing. According to his father, Donal, however, Doyle was wracked by doubts and fears.

In an interview with the *Irish Daily Star Sunday* following the killing, Donal Doyle said his son:

> . . . wished he could start his life over, that's the hardest thing. Patrick told me he wished he could start his life again

and do it all differently. He said, 'I'd give anything to be able to go out, do a week's work and come home and have my dinner.' But he had got in too deep and didn't know how to get out.

Doyle's second thoughts about his chosen career were no doubt influenced by the fact that he had two young children.

Gardaí and Spanish police would later discover that Doyle – and Mr A – were not the only cartel members who had regrets about the path they had set out upon.

Various theories were investigated by the Policía Nacional, in conjunction with gardaí, following the murder. Two possibilities were that Doyle had been killed by the Russians over the reported fight in a nightclub, or that a Turkish criminal syndicate had decided to make an example of him after he and Mr A had failed to pay for a consignment of heroin seized in Dublin, in August 2007. However, after analysing the intelligence gathered by their European counterparts, the Spanish police eventually came to the conclusion that Christy Kinahan had ordered Doyle's death because of missing money.

The previous November 2007, an English drug dealer, 43-year-old Simon Cowmeadow, had been found dead with a single bullet wound through the eye on a deserted Amsterdam street. Cowmeadow was on the run from the British authorities after being caught with 100,000 Ecstasy tablets in Essex. He had been sentenced to eighteen years in absentia.

The Spanish police had received information from their Dutch counterparts that Doyle had hooked up with Cowmeadow, known as 'Slapper', during one of his visits to Holland and had agreed to act as his enforcer.

When up to half a million euros of Christy Kinahan's drug money later went missing, both men got the blame. The Spanish file stated:

> The violent character of the organization is evident. Up to six murders are now linked to this organization. In November 2007, the killing in Holland of Simon John Cowmeadow coincided with the disappearance of €400,000 or €500,000. It appears Patrick Doyle and Cowmeadow were responsible for the disappearance of this money which belonged to the Kinahan organization.

Gardaí suspect the Kinahans may have contracted the job out to Eric 'Lucky' Wilson, one of the most unhinged killers the force has ever come across. Wilson was an assassin for hire who had been on the run from gardaí since they found two sawn-off shotguns hidden under the sofa of his rented home in County Carlow.

Wilson is the chief suspect for up to eight gangland murders in Ireland and is currently serving a twenty-three-year term, after drunkenly shooting dead an Englishman who had stepped in to stop him harassing a woman in a bar.

After the Englishman's assassination, Spanish cops raided the run-down farmhouse in Coín, near Mijas, where 'Lucky' Wilson was staying. They were stunned when they found plastic explosives, an anti-tank grenade and military-issue heavy machine-gun ammunition. Gardaí also suspect Gary Hutch knew Doyle was about to die and had been complicit in setting him up. They believe he tipped off Wilson, telling him exactly where the black SUV in which he, Mr A and Doyle were travelling would be at a particular time on the day of the murder.

Paddy Doyle's murder came two days before gardaí

arrested Eddie Van Boxtel and seized €3.5m worth of cannabis in Newbridge, County Kildare. It also preceded the seizure of a cache of weapons sent by Daniel Kinahan, in London, a month later.

There was also Cowmeadow's murder to consider and the fact Europol believed Christy Kinahan to have been the source of two shipments of drugs sent from Holland and Spain to the northern English city of Newcastle and seized there.

The cartel was at the heart of all these incidents and it was clear to the authorities across Europe that they would have to co-operate more intensively if they were to get a handle on what was happening.

On 7 July 2008, senior officers from An Garda Síochána, Belgian Police Fédérale, Spain's Policía Nacional and the Dutch Korps Landelijke Politiediensten (KLPD) held a top-level meeting in The Hague. It was jointly agreed that the Kinahan cartel had become far too powerful. It was time to take them down.

But the authorities knew that cracking down on their drug- and arms-running activities would only deal with part of the problem. The cartel had developed a wide-ranging and refined money-laundering wing which helped both shield illicit profits and provide further financing to buy more narcotics and weaponry. Unless this was unravelled, any operation against the Kinahans was doomed.

8. Filthy Lucre

'The hidden wealth of the Organization both in
Spain and in other countries is incalculable,
given that the majority of their assets are in the
names of third parties.'

The Anti-Money Laundering
Brigade of Spain's National Police

The billionaire financier George Soros – 'the man who broke the Bank of England' – espouses the traditional investment strategy of diversification to lessen risk, while also emphasizing the importance of betting big, based on research and instinct. It was a policy Christy Kinahan, an avowed admirer of the Hungarian-born tycoon and who recommended his books to others, would follow closely when deciding how to launder the massive amounts of money he was reaping from his drugs and arms wholesale business.

By the late 2000s, Kinahan was making so much cash, he literally did not know what to do with it. The gang had taken over a local Irish bar called the Auld Dubliner in their Estepona base on Spain's Costa del Sol. Spanish authorities had long noted the use of the pub as a spot for Christy to meet underlings on a daily basis, and where Daniel, Gary Hutch and other gang members would party late into the night.

It was difficult to infiltrate, as the predominantly Irish and

British clientele made it almost impossible for anyone who was clearly local to pass unnoticed inside. In addition to extensive CCTV coverage, both inside and out, the windows had been plastered with four rolls of wrapping paper to make sure prying eyes were kept out.

With some investments, the gang were prepared to take a financial hit to have a secure place to do business. This was the case with the gym they ran just outside Marbella. It had just 58 members, but cost them €4,500 a month to run. In one call, Daniel's secretary burst into laughter as she told another cartel launderer it was making no money and she would have to invent income for tax reasons. It was purchased by the gang and acted as Kinahan's bank. Cash was left there in envelopes and stuffed into jars or hidden in safes.

The Auld Dubliner was also a loss-making enterprise for the Kinahans, who regularly complained about how much both it and the gym were costing them. Nonetheless, the value of the two locations – as dropping-off points, as storerooms for cash and mobile phones, and as business meeting venues – meant they both stayed open.

While Kinahan did not quite resort to Colombian drug lord and drug trafficker Pablo Escobar's tactics of burying his money in isolated areas, Spanish phone taps revealed he was running out of places to stash it.

For the cartel's empire to work, huge amounts of dirty money needed to be regularly laundered and the family patriarch took a hands-on approach to how it was done. Kinahan was already quite experienced in this area from his efforts in Belgium.

While living there, he had carefully reinvested his drug profits in properties both locally and in Cyprus, but he had learned a valuable lesson when Operation Excalibur, the

Belgian probe into his money-laundering activities, seized his assets. The problem was, the fixed location of these property assets within the EU made them much easier to impound. Christy was not going to make the same mistake twice.

According to Spanish investigators, Kinahan's new financial model for laundering the cartel's drug money worked in four distinct phases. In the first phase, illicit cash would be introduced into the banking system by lower-ranking cartel figures, such as Daniel's Spanish secretary. She would make small lodgements, via Kinahan-controlled companies, to set up accounts.

In the second phase, once the accounts were up and running, goods, shares or other assets would be purchased. They would then be sold, and the funds would be transferred to tax havens, such as Gibraltar or the Cayman Islands, and back, creating a credible money trail which would be difficult for the police to unravel.

Phase three would see money 'cleaned' through the sale of previously purchased assets. Property purchases were an old favourite, as constantly shifting values could be used to justify large profits. The sale of the property would often be made to fictitious companies based in tax havens. The activities, or even the very existence of these companies, were impossible for the authorities in Ireland or Spain to track.

In the fourth phase, fake invoices were issued by non-existent companies for work done by Kinahan-owned firms, usually involving amounts of at least €40,000.

Once laundered, the cash was sent to tax havens or countries with iron-clad banking secrecy regulations, such as Cyprus, Gibraltar, Liechtenstein, Switzerland, Panama and the tiny Pacific island of Vanuatu, which lies off Australia's eastern coast.

*

Having had his fingers burnt in Cyprus and Belgium, Kinahan fixed his gaze on Brazil. With a massive tourism industry, historical connections to Europe and a notorious corruption problem, Latin America's largest nation was ideal for the cartel's needs.

Perhaps heeding his hero George Soros, Kinahan bet big. The cartel created a Spanish-based firm, Greenland Securities SL, with Daniel set up as one of its directors.

Greenland Securities SL invested heavily in Brazil's northeast region, the country's poorest area. It was known for its year-round sunshine and popular with European tourists, particularly Italians.

The Kinahans soon built up a sizeable property portfolio there. Spanish police who trawled through Greenland's holdings found the cartel had five separate property portfolios, with each comprising over 300 dwellings, in and around the city of Fortaleza.

The estimated value of the Brazilian properties, numbered at over 1,500, was €500 million, on top of the €150 million property portfolio the cartel was believed to be sitting on in Spain.

While the location had changed to South America, the way the money laundering was carried out remained the same. Spanish police tracked one transaction in Greenland Securities which exemplified the gang's strategy. An associate in Greenland Securities sold half his shares in the company to Daniel for €1,500. Months later, Daniel sold the shares onward to another member of the firm for €50,000, though only €5,000 in cash was handed over by the buyer, with the remaining €45,000 to follow. A clause was inserted in the sale contract that unless the €45,000 balance was paid by the gang member within one year, the apartment would be transferred to Daniel's name as compensation. Unsurprisingly, the money was never handed over and the end result was that Daniel Kinahan became the legal owner of a high-value, luxury apartment in the Oasis do Mar resort in the city of Joao Pessoa, Brazil.

It was a process that worked quite smoothly for Christy's heir. Within two years of the creation of Greenland Securities, Daniel was recorded on Spanish surveillance taps telling his secretary that he owned more than €4m worth of property in Brazil's north-east region.

With its lax oversight on money laundering, transferring his funds to Brazil was starting to work out very well for Christy Kinahan. Soon he was taking calls from criminal associates in Cyprus who wanted to invest in forty-two of his property units there. Christy, of course, creamed off a fee for his 'management' activities.

The Brazilian scheme was so popular with other criminals the gang could not get their hands on enough real estate. By November 2009, they were buying land in Brazil's Amazon region, far from the usual tourist spots. The strategy behind these unusual purchases soon became clear.

Daniel's secretary was recorded telling her boyfriend, 'The Irish are going to ask for a loan in Brazil, offering some lands as a guarantee. They won't pay it back and the bank keeps the land.' A figure of €2 million was mentioned for the planned swindle.

But property was not the cartel's only interest in Brazil. Christy was also investing in energy firms, and was recorded telling one associate how his involvement in a firm called 'BMCC Energia do Brasil' would earn them 'two million a week'.

Money was funnelled through Panama, known as the 'Switzerland of the Americas' due to the discretion of its banks. In Panama, foreigners could open an account just by showing two forms of ID – a tax return and proof of banking elsewhere for at least three years – all documentation which could be easily faked.

The Kinahans were quick to take advantage and laundered money by creating Panamanian firms which subsequently bought shares in their Spanish-based companies or transferred funds into them for bogus purchases. One Kinahan-controlled Spanish outfit, Local Blue SL, was bought entirely by the Panamanian Trio Investments Ltd Inc., before receiving a cash injection of €466,400. Spanish investigators believe both were controlled by the cartel, via a frontman.

Large amounts of cartel wealth were also kept in cash, in safety deposit boxes and safes. The money was distributed by hand in envelopes, with the Auld Dubliner functioning as a drop-off and collection point. Daniel, for example, preferred to deal in cash and once gave his secretary enough money to cover three months of his mortgage payments.

Though Christy was heavily involved in deciding how to launder his money, he was happy to delegate the day-to-day administration to Christopher Jr. While Daniel was in charge of the actual business of drugs and arms dealing, Junior was, to quote Spanish police, 'in charge of money-laundering activities'. He is the money man who looks after the details of the gang's finances, including keeping an eye on the gang's lucrative Brazilian ventures.

Christopher Jr became quite adept at moving cartel assets around and investing in ventures such as waste recycling and carbon credits. As part of his role as cartel treasurer, Junior had ready access to cash and kept large amounts in the safe at his home outside Marbella.

Ahead of one of their father's frequent trips abroad,

Daniel rang his brother looking for €9,000 in cash for Christy's spending money. This was not a problem for Junior, who was able to supply €11,000 there and then.

Christopher Jr travelled regularly with his father on their trips to Barcelona and Brazil and liaised with those running Greenland Securities SL. He also got on well with John Cunningham, with whom he regularly golfed.

In February 2010, Christy took a call from a man asking if he was 'still doing that stuff in Brazil' because he had 'friends interested in doing things there'. Christy immediately passed the phone to his younger son, who took over the conversation, albeit speaking in typically vague language in case anyone was listening.

Christopher Jr was also involved in attempts by the gang to re-structure their property portfolio in Cyprus, and he knew intimate details of some mortgage amounts there. He consulted frequently on the phone with his father and brother about how much money was in different accounts. Christopher Jr was also recorded telling an unidentified third party that a lawyer was to be paid €50,000 to take care of the purchase of a Spanish bar.

Police were sure that he had been made responsible for paying all the cartel's bills and signing off on the purchase and sale of land for money-laundering purposes. They noted:

> It is telling that in these operations, Christopher (Jr) shows little interest either in the characteristics (quality of construction, location) or price of these assets. He shows great interest in carrying them out as quickly as possible.

Some of the deals the gang became involved in not only laundered their dirty money but also returned a sizeable profit on their initial investment. The cartel expanded into diverse areas, including cement, gold, precious stones, sugar, cereals, cucumbers and bio-combustibles, with Christy buying and selling huge amounts of these commodities using the Chinese website alibaba.com.

Investing in the cement industry proved a particularly huge earner for Kinahan. He would buy it at $55 per tonne and sell it on for $97 per tonne to builders in construction-booming Dubai. In one transaction, he discussed placing an order of 15 million tonnes, but later revised this down to a more conservative 1.5 million tonnes – still enough to earn him a cool $63 million.

Sugar appeared to be a fixation of Kinahan's, so much so that police initially suspected it was a code word for something else. Christy would not buy just any old sugar, it had to be a special variety known as ICUMSA 45. It was only when he told an associate he had learned from the *Financial Times* that sugar prices were at a twenty-nine-year high that cops understood what was going on.

Buying merchandise at high prices meant it was easier to justify the drug profits being laundered through legitimate transactions, especially when buying from Latin America, where false invoices and a fictitious paper trail were easy to create. The transport of such merchandise provided a double opportunity for the gang. With commodities, such as rice or sugar, coming from Latin America, they could stash drugs and arms amongst them. Apart from Christy's sugar fixation, cartel members' conversations about transporting the merchandise usually displayed far more interest in the type and frequency of boats available than the quality of the goods they would be carrying.

The 'testing' of routes with legitimate merchandise also

ensured the cartel had the greatest chance of landing illicit goods unchallenged. The gang could check which ports were most heavily policed, and which had the weak points essential for their smuggling operation.

Christy Snr was always looking for a new angle. In one phone chat with an Israeli-Arab subordinate based in Belgium, it emerged he was musing over buying his own marina, the location of which he was too cautious to mention. Apparently, his idea was to provide a more secure facility into which he could import drugs. In another call, he discussed getting a €10 million loan from a bank to buy two ships, ostensibly for the transport of gold from Colombia, Bolivia and Brazil, though cops were sure of the real purpose of the purchases. Neither plan ever came to fruition.

Police believed the Kinahans were storing tonnes of drugs and arms in and around their Costa del Sol base at any one time, ready to be shipped onwards to Ireland and the UK. Spanish detectives were not surprised to overhear one of his secretaries make inquiries about renting two warehouses measuring 1,615 square feet, in neighbouring Nueva Andalucía.

When the owner of the properties innocently inquired what the warehouses would be used for, she was told *el señor* wished to keep the goods for a second-hand store there.

The Dapper Don's eye for a deal was endless. Before Christmas 2009, he got on the phone to an unidentified Spanish associate following his return from a trip to Hong Kong. Kinahan wanted to set up a deal where he would buy discarded chicken feet, duck necks, poultry innards and pigs' ears from a slaughterhouse somewhere in the UK. He also wanted donkey, goat and bull penises. According to Christy, chicken guts commanded a higher price than beef in the Far East, where 'they eat all that stuff'. The Spaniard suggested just buying a farm in China to sell it all locally, but Kinahan felt the potential for profit was higher if the offal was sent from Europe, where it was generally just dumped after slaughter. The scheme also seems to have come to naught in the end.

Chats with a Spanish lawyer the cartel was using indicated the Far East was an area of considerable investment for Christy. He told his legal adviser he was setting up a deal with the state-owned oil firm PetroChina, but that the transaction was being held up by official red tape and even the service of a public notary wasn't helping. 'I have experience with notaries in China and they pay a lot of attention to detail, so I'm surprised at what's happening,' he admitted.

Other opportunities for money laundering and investments came in the form of construction projects, particularly in countries not overly worried about where the money came from. Christy travelled on more than one occasion to Slovenia, where money-laundering rules were somewhat laxer than in western Europe

In one incident, a Slovenian firm was poised to take up a €9 million motorway contract in Libya. Christy wanted to invest in the enterprise, as it would go a long way towards justifying several million euros of questionable provenance.

The gang were also keen to legitimize their operations by linking themselves with charities. They even discussed setting up their own non-governmental organization (NGO) to act as a front. Christy commented:

We need projects which will create jobs that are humanitarian, directly humanitarian. Remember, we need a project which will absorb some of this. What I said is, if we do this together, we can absorb it and what the real price is, we'll split the difference.

On a separate occasion, Kinahan also discussed setting up a foundation to do 'humanitarian work'. It could then purchase other institutions and use them as a 'guarantee fund' in which to shield assets and capital.

At the other end of the scale, Daniel was making inquiries, on behalf of his father, about opening a high-class brothel on the Costa del Sol. Prostitution operates in a legal grey area within Spain. It is technically outlawed, but most brothels get around this by branding themselves as something else. This accounts for the proliferation of garish neon-signed 'singles clubs' on the outskirts of virtually every Spanish town and city. The combination of the law's blind eye and the massive Spanish tourist trade make them a huge earner for pimps. All of which made the 'singles clubs' a very attractive proposition for the cartel.

The Kinahans had commissioned one of their UK-based contacts to review the possibility of opening a 16,000-square-foot brothel, which they felt would earn them up to €100,000 a week. Despite Daniel's enthusiasm, the Briton was not overly impressed and made plans to fly to Málaga to outline his reservations to them in person. Like many other projects discussed by the gang, this one never got off the ground.

As the 2010 World Cup in South Africa approached, the gang were keen to get in on the action. Ticket touting, with its mark-ups of up to 500 per cent on the set ticket price, represented a serious earner to the cartel and, while abhorrent to fans, it is not illegal in most countries. In fact, touting is so profitable that well-known sports figures, including Steffi Graf and Andre Agassi, act as directors of one of Europe's biggest firms, Viagogo.

Christy Senior took an unusual level of interest in the

administration of the touting business and flew into a rage when he was told the name of the company he wanted to register, Global Sporting Events, had already been registered by another firm in Spain. Afterwards, he calmed down and accepted the more pretentious-sounding Corporate Sporting Events, though he still insisted Daniel's secretary let him see the logo that was being designed for the new outfit.

Once again, Christopher Jr was appointed to oversee daily operations. He was recorded expressing a desire to 'dominate' the touting market for the tournament. While Spanish cops were not able to confirm details of the scam, they believed the gang had set up a network of firms in South Africa to resell tickets to desperate fans.

Daniel made plans to travel to South Africa in November and December 2009, ordering his secretary to reserve him a first-class ticket via Dubai, costing €3,000. Having grown used to the good life, Daniel was not about to slum it in economy.

The gang had hooked up with the brother of a well-known Irish football international. The footballer's brother had a serious gambling addiction and was up to his neck in touting. He ran a number of Irish and UK-based firms involved in the lucrative trade.

Not surprisingly, the Kinahans accepted the gambler with reservations, as he was not averse to betting with other people's money. In one conversation between Daniel and Matthew 'Mr Bean' Dunne he was described as 'one of the biggest bettors in Ireland' and Dunne said the wayward tout owed so much money 'Mr Bean' was on sleeping tablets because of the stress. On another occasion, Daniel heard that the footballer's brother had gone into hiding in London because of his massive gambling debts. The gambler was apparently pinning his hopes on a loan from his well-paid sibling to bail him out of trouble.

On 22 November 2009, Christopher Jr flew to Ireland to discuss their proposed South African operation, before Daniel headed down there. Christopher met with the tout to discuss the logistics. The gambler was to become one of the firm's directors, but he was basically touting for the Kinahans and taking a slice for himself. Daniel subsequently told his brother he had warned Matthew Dunne that the man 'better help us and not try and rob us, 'cos he owes me big time'.

By December 2009 Junior was deeply involved in the business, regularly placing orders for tickets for games, such as Man United vs Arsenal and the Carling Cup final, and musicians like Black Eyed Peas, Lady Gaga and Michael Bublé – many of which appeared to be for him and his friends. He took advantage of his position in charge of ticket touting operations to order multiple freebies for himself and his pals. He enjoyed flying in and out of the UK for Premier League matches, Six Nations rugby games and concerts.

Nothing but the best would do on these occasions. On one weekend away to see Ireland take on England at Twickenham, Christopher Jr told Daniel's secretary not to book him into the Hilton hotel, as he didn't like the luxury chain's beds. He also ordered her to find him tickets for a West End show.

Like his younger brother, Daniel was fond of the good life. He lived in the same luxury apartment block as Christy in Estepona, in Spain, and on long-distance flights abroad he would insist on business class, despite his secretary nagging him about the cost. On his visits to Dublin, Daniel would stay at upmarket hotels like the Westbury, off Grafton Street, in central Dublin.

The touting business seemed to be turning a tidy profit, despite the ever-increasing attentions of law enforcement. Detectives from London's Metropolitan Police raided one of the cartel's outlets there and questioned the footballer's brother over money laundering. He rang Christy and told him he had eventually been released at 1 a.m. that morning, and only after police had confiscated twenty-one tickets. He also confirmed that police had begun going through the company's emails.

The Dapper Don soothed the man's ruffled feathers and told him to call another associate. 'The business is going well,' he told him. That, it seemed, was all that mattered.

Other operations were not so successful. An attempt to invest in a wind farm in Cyprus came to naught, while the Kinahans were 'fucked over' on a separate deal involving a landfill site. This prompted Christy to whinge, apparently without irony, 'They are not people of their word. This is the problem with all these business people; there's no real honour.'

Another scheme of his which the authorities had uncovered involved a professional futsal team called FORCOM in Belgium, which Kinahan was supposedly sponsoring. In reality, he was handing over cash to corrupt individuals connected to the club, who would then give him a sizeable portion of his money back.

As the end of 2009 approached, Kinahan was irritated at the prospect of having to go to jail again. His laundering activities in Cyprus had been seriously hampered by Operation Excalibur in 2008 and the Belgian court orders had also frozen his €380,000 Cypriot stash. In September 2009, Kinahan had been convicted on ten counts of money laundering and ordered to serve four years. However, the sentence was suspended while he appealed. He did have some holiday villas which he had managed to keep out of the reach of the Belgians, but as his appeal hearing approached, the Dapper Don was aware he was on borrowed time. He needed to offload them before their seizure could be ordered – even if it was at a loss.

The life of a drug trafficker is not an easy one and Christy on occasion admitted to his associates that the pressure got to him. With Europe in the midst of recession, the price of holiday villas had plunged. Worse still, the vacant properties had suffered a bird infestation and would require extensive cleaning.

'Everyone is going through a bad time,' remarked the Cypriot man who was looking after his investments.

Christy replied:

It's happening everywhere, and Spain is worse than Cyprus. Sell them off cheap because I want to pay off the debt. Get rid of them all. You know my money's frozen in Cyprus, I can't do anything there. I'm a bit pissed off with how things have turned out. I've been going round in circles, travelling to this place, that place. People understood that what happened was out of my control. It pisses me off, though. The prosecutor is claiming that AB Eureka is a dodgy firm, a front, even though they've been there and seen it. They said that clearly before the judge and he accepted it. It's difficult for me to go against the prosecutor when he's lying.

Kinahan was referring to AB Eureka Developments Ltd, a company he had set up in March 2005 and which was dissolved in December the following year, without filing any accounts. The gangster's outrage against the Antwerp court dealing with his case seemed genuine.

Days before his appeal against his conviction was due to begin, in January 2010, he again rang his man in Cyprus and ordered him to flog off his three villas in Paralimni, for €300,000 each. Even if he made no profit, it was important to offload them, he said.

Kinahan told his contact that the court was continually accusing him of building properties in Cyprus. This was a lie, as the place was only a means of money laundering and that kind of thing, he insisted, admitting his crimes in a rare lapse. His associate replied, 'They won't find anything here, pal; they're angry because they didn't find anything.'

In another call to John Cunningham, on 10 March 2010, Kinahan complained bitterly that the judge and the prosecutor had been 'mocking' him throughout the court proceedings until his lawyer intervened and told them to have more respect.

Christy's sense of injustice cut little ice with the court, however, and the Dapper Don's four-year sentence, on ten counts of money laundering, was finally confirmed in December 2010, after repeated adjournments. The delay was in large part due to Christy's attempts to frustrate the process at every turn, by raising vexatious legal arguments, each of which would eventually be thrown out by judges. Reporters who were present at the December 2010 hearing revealed how Kinahan once more reacted with indignation when he felt his lawyer was not given enough time to sum up, comparing it to 'speed dating'.

Kinahan's talent for networking and his fluency in foreign languages meant that, by the end of 2009, he had built up contacts in Latin America for his cocaine, Afghanistan for heroin and eastern Europe for weapons.

Christy was dealing directly with suppliers, and the cartel would come to be responsible for 90 per cent of the cocaine imported into Ireland. But it was not only Ireland it was supplying. It also had a sizeable chunk of the UK's much more lucrative drugs market and was amongst the top five suppliers of cocaine, heroin, Ecstasy and hash to Britain.

Daniel was a heavily experienced drug trafficker by this stage, trusted by Christy, who was delegating more and more to his heir apparent. And Daniel, now firmly on the radar of several European police forces, had plans aplenty on how to add to their filthy lucre.

Law enforcement agencies had known for years that impoverished countries in West Africa were a major part of the drug export route to Europe. The attractions for narco-traffickers were obvious: these were poor countries with corrupt authorities, where drugs could be repackaged and sent onwards to Europe with little fear of interference. Few countries presented more opportunities than Sierra Leone, a country still recovering from a horrific decade-long civil war, and Daniel was anxious for a slice of the pie.

The extent to which the region had become a trafficking hub was highlighted when a Boeing 727-200 belonging to the Colombian mob crashed ten miles from a makeshift airstrip in the desert of northern Mali. Back in the eighties Pablo Escobar used to send small planes, heavily laden with cocaine, to fly below the radar into the southern United States. His successors had upped the ante to an industrial level.

Britain's Serious Organized Crime Agency (SOCA) believed Daniel had tasked a Birmingham-based businessman, who had mining interests in Sierra Leone, with contacting locals who used to work for a jailed group of Latin American drug lords called the Perezes. It is not clear if the plan ever came to fruition, as Spanish wire taps subsequently revealed Christy's dislike of operating in West Africa. The patriarch always preferred going straight to the source in South America, and he could 'clean' his money there as well.

Ireland too featured on the money-laundering trail, with Matthew Dunne acting as the Kinahans' main man in Dublin. Dunne ran a dry-cleaning business, appropriately enough, to launder drug money.

Dunne listed his Irish occupation as a taxi man. Daniel's Spanish secretary was put under surveillance by gardaí after she was collected by Dunne in his 'mega taxi' on her arrival at Dublin Airport. She was there to discuss the proposed purchase of a Costa del Sol hotel by the gang in February 2010.

Kinahan's secretary was regarded as someone 'actively participating in money-laundering activity', who had, on one occasion, 'left cash' in envelopes at the Auld Dubliner pub. The police file concluded:

> She is one of the fundamental parts of the money-laundering set-up. She's in charge of managing a corporate and financial system in Spain, through which the organization introduces illicit cash into the monetary circuit. She has accounts in Gibraltar, Zurich and Cyprus.

In one recorded conversation, the secretary and her English criminal boyfriend, who had been linked to the 2008 London arms seizure, spoke about investing money in Dubai. He explained:

> I have one million euros stashed in Dubai. But the money is only about twenty per cent of the work I've done. I'm terrified of being arrested in the UK and that's why I get my father to take out the money and reinvest it. I've also some money tied up in the Cayman Islands.

In another call between Daniel's PA and a female friend, she outlined how her boyfriend from London was paranoid. 'He's freaking out,' she said. 'He says he has private detectives following him, and he has no money.'

Despite her mistrust of her gangster boyfriend, she remained in close contact with him as he moved around the UK, regaling her constantly with tales of woe to persuade her to wire him money. It was obvious to investigators the Englishman was lying, and it soon became apparent why.

In a separate recorded telephone conversation, the man outlined how he was coming under pressure from the cartel because of his gambling habits. 'Daniel has taken over my company and I was punched in the face in Puerto Banús,' he explained.

Matthew Dunne was still involved in the ticket touting business, but he was not involved in the debt collection side of the cartel. His focus was on hiding its money once gang members had collected it.

Dunne lived within sight of businessman Ben Dunne – no relation – in upmarket Castleknock, in west Dublin, in an 'enormous' house. Daniel's secretary also talked about watching in bemusement as the former supermarket tycoon was collected regularly by helicopter.

Matthew Dunne was the sole administrator behind Matdunne SL, and was also involved in Sun Dream Homes SL, Warm Beach SL and Sea Dream Homes SL, all of which were Kinahan-controlled firms.

The declared activities of these firms ranged from shoe sales to property development, but investigations by Spanish police found they were primarily used to receive funds and then transfer the money onwards in another money-laundering scam. For example, Matdunne SL received a capital injection of €500,000 in 2007. Sun Dream Homes SL had also received separate capital injections of €1.4 million and €651,000 in 2006 and 2009, neither of which had any evident explanations, and investigators found that there was no apparent justification for the transfers.

A Spanish arrest warrant was eventually issued for Matthew Dunne, on 18 May 2010. His Dublin home, another apartment in Castleknock, north Dublin, and his luxury chalet in Estepona were raided and documents were seized and taken away for examination.

The warrant read: 'According to investigations into his finances, he owns a large number of assets in Spain, which does not correspond to his stated profession.' For a taxi driver, Dunne had a lot of spare cash. He planned big, but appeared to be somewhat out of his depth.

In one venture, the Dubliner wanted to carry out a €1.5 million upgrade of a downmarket one-star hotel near Marbella. However, a lawyer for the gang crunched the numbers on the project and informed Dunne that the project was 'not viable'. He advised Dunne to pay off the builder for the work he had already done, advice Dunne appeared reluctant to accept.

Dunne was later arrested at Schiphol Airport, in Amsterdam, in October 2010, on foot of a European Arrest Warrant. He was extradited to Spain, where he was placed under formal investigation for money laundering and criminal association alongside his boss. He remains on bail while his case is considered.

In any case, Matthew Dunne and his outlandish ambitions for money-laundering schemes were a minor problem compared to the crisis his first cousin was causing in Dublin.

9. Don vs Don

'You need to get out of there for a while, because it's better to be on the outside looking in than on the inside looking out. If I were you, I'd leave the country tomorrow morning.'

Daniel Kinahan, 24 April 2010

Three weeks before Christmas 2009, a group of about twenty men had gathered in the National Stadium on Dublin's South Circular Road. Amongst them were some of the cartel's biggest figures, including brothers Liam and David Byrne, Mr A and Greg Lynch. Also present were representatives of the INLA in the North and members of the McCarthy-Dundon gang from Limerick.

Gardaí watched as the men laughed and joked in their ringside seats and watched boxer Matthew Macklin defend his European middleweight title against Rafa Sosa Pintos. Ostensibly they were there to cheer on Macklin, a Birmingham fighter with Irish roots who has no involvement in crime but is a personal friend of Daniel Kinahan.

But the real reason for the gangland night out was because one of their associates, Eamon Dunne, known as 'the Don' even by his fellow criminals, had murdered eleven of their contemporaries and nobody was sure who was going to be next.

Then just thirty-five years old, Dunne was viewed by gardaí as one of the most unstable individuals ever to emerge on the Irish gangland scene. A highly intelligent man who came from a middle-class family, he had taken a conscious decision to make his living from crime.

Dunne was born in February 1974 and grew up in Cabra, on the northside of Dublin. Unlike many other teenagers who later became immersed in crime, Dunne sat his Leaving Certificate and ran a motor business after he left school.

The business, however, turned out to be a front for his criminal activities and Dunne was soon involving himself with local shady characters, including major drug dealer Martin 'Marlo' Hyland.

Dunne first came to Garda attention in 2002 when he was caught with a large amount of cocaine and Ecstasy during a raid on a house in Finglas. He was charged with possession and was released on bail.

Five months afterwards, he was stopped by gardaí in a car carrying a bound and gagged man in the boot. The man was a pusher who owed Hyland money and Dunne had been sent to sort him out. The man was freed, but was too terrified to make a complaint, so no charges were brought against Eamon Dunne.

Over the next few years, he continued to progress in the criminal world and quickly learned the tricks of the trade. Just like Christy Kinahan, Dunne would use every means possible to try to intimidate gardaí investigating his activities. When stopped, searched and questioned, he would take out a Dictaphone and begin recording the gardaí concerned. He also took pictures on a small digital camera he kept in his car. He took down officers' identification numbers and made complaints to the Garda Ombudsman, claiming gardaí were colluding with the media to have him killed. After these allegations were thrown out, Dunne took an unprecedented case to the High Court, alleging the same conspiracy. That too was rejected by a judge. Nothing was off limits or too underhand for the stocky, bald man from Cabra.

Dunne's first murder victim was Andrew 'Chicore' Dillon, a former member of the Westies gang who had been accused of stealing drugs belonging to another dealer. The Don killed Dillon in August 2005, at the behest of his then boss, Martin 'Marlo' Hyland, who had lured Dillon back from England to make an example of him. Gardaí believe Dunne also participated in the cold-blooded murder of Latvian mother-of-two Baiba Saulite in November 2006, which had been requested by her estranged husband, Hassan Hassan.

The Lebanese criminal was serving time for abducting the couple's two young boys, along with a four-year sentence for involvement in a stolen car ring. He asked his cellmate in Portlaoise Prison, notorious Limerick criminal Wayne Dundon, to arrange her death. Dundon in turn passed the request on to Marlo Hyland, who subcontracted the job further to Dunne.

Hyland, however, would soon learn that Dunne could just as easily bite the hand that fed him. Though Eamon Dunne had worked for veteran narco-trafficker Marlo for over a decade, Dunne had decided it was time for him to die. Hyland, who was feeling the pressure over both being suspected of organizing Baiba Saulite's killing and of losing a substantial amount of drugs after a number of recent Garda seizures, was taking large amounts of cocaine.

Dunne viewed his master as a spent force and saw an opportunity to eliminate him and fill the void. Increasingly aware of his weakened grip on those under him, Hyland was moving around constantly. He kept a samurai sword near him at all times and had been given a formal Garda Information Message (GIM) that his life was under threat.

A month after the shooting of Baiba Saulite, Hyland was staying at the house of his niece Elaine, in Finglas. Eamon Dunne decided this was the perfect moment to strike. Two hitmen were watching the house and entered after they saw Elaine and a plumber, who was repairing radiators at the property, leave. What they hadn't reckoned on was the presence of Anthony Campbell, the plumber's twenty-year-old apprentice, who had been left behind while his boss went to collect some parts. The innocent youngster was held at gunpoint, as one of the pair went up to where Hyland was sleeping and shot him in the back of the head as he lay face down on the bed.

Returning downstairs, the hitmen took a decision not to leave any witnesses. As the stunned youngster instinctively put his hands up to protect himself, the main hitman fired a single shot, which passed through Anthony's left arm and hit him in the side of the head, killing him instantly.

The public was disgusted and outraged at the slaughter of the innocent young man, but Eamon Dunne was only just beginning.

The Don's next victim was Finglas armed robber John Daly, who had shot to public attention for ringing RTÉ's *Liveline* programme on an illegal mobile phone. Daly was serving time in the supposedly maximum security Portlaoise Prison when he made the call.

John Daly was a violent criminal suspected of involvement in a number of shootings. He had once threatened to shoot a garda and rape his wife after being arrested for an assault on St Patrick's Day, in 2003.

There was personal animosity between Daly and Dunne, and the armed robber had plans to set up his own gang following his release from prison, in August 2007. Spotting a potential challenge to his new domain, Dunne acted quickly. Daly was shot five times as he was getting out of a taxi on the night of 23 October 2007.

More killings followed, with all the victims viewed by the Don, correctly or not, as a threat to his authority. Next to die was Paul 'Farmer' Martin, a convicted armed robber who was a friend of John Daly and who was known to be fond of throwing his weight around. Martin was shot dead trying to flee gunmen who entered the Jolly Toper pub, in Finglas, where he was drinking after a funeral, in August 2008.

Meanwhile, the Don had also been feuding with another northside heroin dealer, Michael 'Roly' Cronin. Cronin, who had once suffered a hiding at Paddy Doyle's hands in Amsterdam, was an experienced criminal. He had been jailed for thirteen years after he was caught with IR£16,000 worth of heroin at his north inner-city council flat, in 1996, following a dedicated Garda operation aimed at taking him out.

Cronin was no shrinking violet and was also actively trying to eliminate Dunne as they vied for control of Marlo's former turf. But, yet again, Dunne's deviousness won the day. Aware that Cronin was selling directly to an addict named Christy Gilroy, he hired him to murder 'Roly'.

On 7 January 2009, Cronin and his pal James Moloney drove into town from Finglas, where they had been topping up their colour at a tanning salon. 'Roly' had arranged to meet Gilroy to sell him drugs, and would not have been suspicious of a man he considered no threat to him.

But minutes after getting into the back seat of Cronin's car in Summerhill, in the north inner city, Gilroy shot both men in the back of the head. The car then rolled down a side street and out into the middle of the thoroughfare, where it crashed into the railings which divide both carriageways.

Gilroy, far from an experienced assassin, panicked. He opened the rear driver's side door, got out and ran off, leaving behind the gun, a mobile phone and his jacket, all replete with his fingerprints and DNA. The hit was so botched, gardaí who arrived on the scene first thought they were dealing with a traffic accident. It was only when a witness told them they had seen a man carrying a gun get out of the car, and officers saw the smoke still rising from the hole in Moloney's neck, that it became clear it was something far more serious.

Detectives believe Gilroy went to the Don and confessed he had screwed up. Dunne spirited him out of the country to Spain and promised help for his drug addiction. Gary Hutch was instrumental in organizing the favour, with the sanction of the cartel.

Gilroy was booked into a rehab clinic in Marbella under a false name, but left within a few weeks when he was picked up by two men. Gardaí understand one of the men was contract killer 'Lucky' Wilson, who promptly shot Gilroy and buried him in an unmarked grave. The other man was Gary Hutch.

Gilroy's remains have never been found, despite repeated pleas for information from his family so they can give him a proper funeral. Once more, Eamon Dunne was tying up loose ends.

Then came a murder which illustrated the depths to which Dunne's paranoia had descended. Graham McNally, a veteran associate of Marlo Hyland was a long-time friend of the Don and thought he had no reason to fear his pal. They had arranged to meet within hours of McNally's return to Ireland from Amsterdam, on 20 January 2009.

Gardaí, seeking to stop Dunne's reign of terror, had swamped the area with checkpoints. They halted and searched McNally's jeep as he drove through Finglas at 5.15 p.m. that evening. The gangster, who had once been jailed for biting three cops attempting to detain his mentally ill brother, appeared relaxed and was not wearing his usual bulletproof vest.

Within half an hour of being stopped, McNally went to a cul-de-sac off the old Ashbourne Road, where Dunne shot him three times in the head and face and dumped his body on the side of the road. It is believed Dunne feared McNally was conspiring with associates of 'Farmer' Martin to strike back against him, but there is no evidence any such plot was ever in motion.

The blood continued to flow. Drug dealer Michael Murray, who had been the subject of two previous murder bids by Dunne, was gunned down on his orders, in Finglas, in March 2009.

At the time of his death, Murray was facing charges over the possession of a handgun found under the saddle of his motorbike. He had also been named in court as the killer of another man, Ian Tobin, shot through the letter box of his home, in May 2007. Murray had actually been after Tobin's brother Blake, following a fist fight between Blake and Murray's daughter's boyfriend.

The following June, Paul Smyth, 'Farmer' Martin's brother-in-law, was found with a bullet wound to the head in a ditch in Balbriggan, north County Dublin.

By this stage, Dunne's paranoia was causing deep alarm within Dublin criminal circles. While safe from any major collateral damage in their fortress in southern Spain, the Kinahans were looking on with concern at the divisions which were opening up in one of their key markets.

Gardaí had launched an operation specifically to target Dunne, and the Criminal Assets Bureau (CAB) had also begun examining his finances. But they could not watch him 24/7. On 9 October, David Thomas, who was not involved in organized crime, was shot dead as he smoked outside the Drake Inn, in Finglas.

That night, Liam Byrne rang Daniel to inform him of the shooting, tell him the victim's name and that 'the Don was probably the gunman'. Gardaí believe Dunne shot Thomas as a favour for a pal whose associate had been beaten to death by Thomas, in a bar fight back in 1998.

Christy decided it was time to try to bring an end to the spiral of killings. He organized a gangsters' peace summit at Macklin's fight at the National Stadium, in Dublin, on 5 December 2009. Dunne, flanked by his goons, was there, as were other senior gangland figures. The Kinahans themselves did not attend.

When the media got wind of the event, Daniel was furious. He rang his brother and read out an article, complaining that there was a photo of Christy and him in the papers. Daniel fumed as he told how the report said 'Dad' controlled all Dublin's criminal gangs and the proof of this was the 'fifty tickets he had given to the "top gangsters" and "mafia elite" for the Macklin fight'. Referring to the seats that had been kept for those invited, he told Christopher Jr:

> Someone is talking and has squealed that 'Kinahan has sold the tickets'. That 'Kinahan' is you. Think about it. I'm thinking of those around me. It has to be something like that, or someone is talking on the phone, you know.

The efforts of the summit came to naught, largely because the other criminals felt they simply could not trust Eamon

Dunne. Even Daniel Kinahan was wary over the poisonous atmosphere across the city. He told a pal in advance of the fight that he was not sure if he would attend because he was 'a little paranoid about how things are in Dublin'.

The cartel found itself increasingly sucked into rows created by Dunne's determination to wipe out anyone who showed the slightest resistance to his reign. One of those figures was a criminal in his early twenties who had been released from prison that December, and who had been an associate of John Daly. Despite his relative youth, the gutsy young thug, nicknamed 'Shooter', was not prepared to have Dunne tell him what to do.

The next person on Dunne's hit list was a drug-dealing Traveller named John Paul Joyce. Dunne wanted Shooter to help set Joyce up, to prove his loyalty. The young criminal was reluctant to get involved.

Days after getting out, Shooter had received a call from one of Dunne's henchmen, Alan 'Fatpuss' Bradley. A masked man had been spotted outside Bradley's Finglas home on his CCTV and Bradley claimed it was one of Shooter's friends. It was a sighting that, days later, would have extremely serious consequences.

Shooter swore his friend was not involved and the conversation moved on, Bradley reassuring him that Dunne, who he referred to as 'Ace', had no issue with him. But at the end of the conversation, Bradley suddenly switched tack. He told Shooter, 'Look, I'm just putting you wide, be careful because there's a group out looking for you.'

Shooter then met with Dunne and his loyal sidekick, Brian O'Reilly, in a shopping centre and told the Don to his face he was not afraid of him. Shooter was smart enough to know how much trouble he was in after the confrontation and he reached out to the Kinahans, via Gary Hutch, for help.

One of Shooter's friends rang Hutch, telling him of a conversation Dunne ('the baldy man') and Shooter had:

> He was chatting to the baldy man with no arguments, no shouting, saying, 'What's the problem, pal?' The baldy man said, 'Look, I'm hearing stories that when you get out, you're going to sort everything out. The Dalys are saying you're the man, that you'll sort everything out.' He's telling him, 'You have to understand that I'm going to respond to these threats.'

Hutch received the OK from Daniel for Shooter to move to the Costa del Sol, which took him out of danger.

It was more than could be said for John Paul Joyce. Joyce had also been freed from jail just before Christmas, after serving a sentence for beating a man so severely, he had left him with brain damage. Before being put away, Joyce had also already survived two attempts on his life.

Dunne was determined there would be no escape this time. After being summoned to a meeting early in the New Year, Joyce was abducted, shot in the head and his body was dumped in a ditch down a remote laneway at the back of Dublin Airport.

In the meantime, an increasingly paranoid Dunne was still looking for whoever had been outside 'Fatpuss' Bradley's home. It was a situation one wannabe mobster felt he could exploit.

Gary Howard, who lived around the corner from Dunne, in Finglas, already had over forty convictions for assault, hijacking and arson, and was desperate to ingratiate himself with the Don. Howard claimed the masked man on the

CCTV was Brendan Molyneux, from the north inner city. The same weekend the Don murdered John Paul Joyce, he sent Howard around to Molyneux's flat on Pearse Street.

Howard's uncle, Thomas Nalty, was drinking there with Molyneux's friend Paddy Mooney, and Howard pretended he was there to deliver drugs to his relative. But once inside, he pulled out a gun and shot both Molyneux and Mooney, as his stunned uncle looked on.

Nalty later gave a statement to investigating detectives, but Gary Howard's trial heard that, following his arrest, he had asked his mother, Celine, during a supervised visit, whether he should say anything to gardaí. Her response was, 'All I want to say is I'd rather have a son that's murdered than a rat.'

Howard was not murdered, but he was convicted of the double killing and given two life sentences. His reputation as a patsy preceded him into jail and while on remand awaiting trial, Limerick gangster John Dundon attempted to get him to admit to the shooting of innocent rugby player Shane Geoghegan. The popular Garryowen prop was murdered in a housing estate in Dooradoyle, in November 2008, as he walked home after a night out. He had been mistaken for drug dealer John McNamara, who lived nearby and was of a similar build. Paddy Doyle's brother Barry, who had moved to Limerick to work as a hitman for the McCarthy-Dundons and screwed up his first assignment, is currently serving life for the killing.

Meanwhile, Eamon Dunne had by now adopted Marlo Hyland's extensive cocaine habit, which only worsened his psychosis. He regularly boasted about having flings with several other gangsters' partners. One of them was a former girlfriend of convicted hitman Craig White, Paddy Doyle's getaway driver during the murder of Noel Roche, in 2005. White, serving a life sentence, was furious and began demanding his pals on the outside take action. But other events meant Dunne's fate was already sealed.

As the recession bit, he had turned his attention to extorting other criminals and had hooked up with the INLA to threaten those who failed to cough up. One of those targeted was cigarette smuggler Noel 'Kingsize' Duggan, who received a demand for €150,000.

Duggan had extensive paramilitary connections, as illicit tobacco was a major earner for republicans. He met with the INLA leadership in Belfast, who confirmed they were backing Dunne. Duggan returned south and held talks with his criminal associates in Dublin, who feared they were next on the Don's extortion list.

Duggan's associates agreed the Don had become too much of a loose cannon and would have to be dealt with. Nothing could happen without the assent of Christy Kinahan, however, but he shared their concern and a decision was made to take Dunne out.

Dunne was 'a good earner' and had tightened up operations compared to the mistakes made in the sloppy last days of Marlo Hyland. But aside from the consternation his killing spree was causing, and the extra Garda attention it brought, there were other factors.

The Don was facing a trial for trying to carry out a €900,000 armed robbery at Tesco in Celbridge, County Kildare, in 2007. Dunne, along with Alan 'Fatpuss' Bradley, Bradley's brother Wayne and three others, had been caught in the act after months of Garda surveillance. The Don, who was clearly in charge of the raid, was likely to be sent away for a long time.

Weighing up their options, the Kinahans decided removing him from the scenario altogether was the simplest choice.

Making the decision was the easy part, but carrying out the killing was another matter. Dunne did not want to end up like his old boss Marlo Hyland, and he was moving about constantly. He had been responsible for up to seventeen murders himself by this stage, so he knew how such things worked. However, the cartel leaders soon settled on one event they were sure he would attend.

The birthday party for taxi driver John Fairbrother was in full swing in the Faussagh House pub in Cabra, north Dublin, on 23 April 2010, when the gunman walked in. One witness later said he seemed quite sure of his surroundings, and strode over to the corner 'very deliberately, as if he knew where he was going'.

His target also knew instantly what was coming. Eamon Dunne grabbed the Chinese lounge boy as a shield, holding him close in a desperate bid to hide himself from the masked assassin who was there to kill him.

The teenager had just served Dunne a 7Up and was waiting for payment. 'I thought it was a joke,' Geng Zian later admitted.

It was to no avail. The hitman opened fire on Dunne from around four feet away, as his horrified seventeen-year-old daughter looked on. Geng was shoved aside and a further eleven shots were fired at the man widely known as the 'Don', even within the criminal fraternity.

The inquest into Dunne's murder heard that those who carried it out were well informed. John Fairbrother's birthday party had been due to take place at another pub, but the venue had been cancelled at short notice two days beforehand. Fairbrother himself said he believed someone in the pub had texted exactly where Dunne was sitting to the gunmen waiting outside.

Another witness gave gruesome evidence of watching Dunne die right in front of him. 'I saw Eamon's head splatter on the back, top right of his head,' Graham Farrell told the coroner's court. 'I knew he was bollixed.'

Dunne's grief-stricken father, Eamon Snr, would later tell how he had asked his son if he would abandon crime if he won €20 million on the Lotto. 'He said no,' he admitted, sadly. 'I think he loved the buzz of it all too much.'

In the aftermath of the murder that night, gardaí swarmed the area, establishing checkpoints aimed at catching any of the hit team foolish enough to linger on afterwards and in the hope of finding potential witnesses.

One of those stopped, albeit on another part of the northside, was a key Kinahan associate, who gardaí would later learn had been one of the hit team. The man had been a member of the nascent cartel since his late teens and was close to both Daniel Kinahan and Gary Hutch. Daniel trusted the man as his eyes and ears on the ground in Dublin and was in regular contact with him over both business and personal matters. The morning after the shooting, Daniel rang his man, seeking an update on the latest murder.

'Last night on the way home, they were there and went through the phonebook of my mobile and all, they took out all the numbers and rang them,' the gunman told Daniel.

'Who was it?' Daniel asked.

'Two big SWAT guys,' answered the hitman, in a reference to the Garda's Emergency Response Unit (ERU), the force's main tactical armed response body. 'They were talking about some car on a hill, I've no idea what they were on about. I told them it wasn't me, but I'm telling you because they had the phone in their possession for a long time, you know?'

'Where did they stop you?' Daniel demanded.

'They stopped me around Portland [Row]. I wasn't even near that area, but they said they saw a car driving strangely,' replied the hood.

'They're going to pick up and question loads of people, and you too,' said Daniel. 'Why don't you come over here for a few days? You don't want to be there right now, and we can talk.'

The flustered gangster said he was not quite sure what to do. 'They're going to get me at some stage anyway,' he answered. 'They've already rung Gary's buddy too, and they went to his door.'

'They'll be going to everyone's house,' said Daniel. 'Those who don't get on with each other are going to finger the others to fuck them over. You need to get out of there for a while, because it's better to be on the outside looking in than on the inside looking out. If I were you, I'd leave the country tomorrow morning. Things are going to get very messy there.'

Daniel was fixated on what was appearing in the media following Dunne's murder and rang another unidentified associate on Sunday, two days after the shooting. The man read a newspaper report verbatim down the phone, which quoted 'a Spanish source' linking Daniel's father to the crime.

'There's another bit about the baldy fella and it has to do with a load of shit that happened years ago and mentions that thing in New Street too,' said the man, in an obvious reference to the murder of Raymond Salinger in Farrells pub, in the south inner city. 'It's saying the "old man" ordered that other shit.'

'What does it say about the sources? Tell me about the sources,' Daniel insisted with some urgency. 'Do they say a Spanish source said that, a criminal said that or someone else said it?'

'Just a Spanish source, that's all they say.'

Daniel, apparently reassured, thanked the man and hung up.

Gardaí are certain the murder of Eamon Dunne was organized by Christy Kinahan. For one thing, Dunne was too important to be taken out without assent from the top. As a criminal named Michael 'Mickey' Devoy would learn some years down the line, anyone who tried to eliminate a rival connected to the cartel without permission would pay the ultimate price.

True to form, however, Daniel was keen to muddy the waters and began one of his periodic disinformation campaigns. Having mentioned the day after the shooting that phone taps would likely be put in place, he began acting as if they were, unaware that he had already been under surveillance for months.

A staged phone call to the gunman who had been stopped on the evening of the murder saw the pair act as if the killing had nothing to do with either of them. They discussed how gardaí had called to the home of a now deceased cartel member named Gavin Abbott as part of their investigation, but the gangster was on holiday at the time and not there.

'This is strange,' declared the hitman, playing his part to perfection.

'It's very strange,' replied Daniel. 'It smells like someone's trying to cause problems and has a campaign against us.'

The farce continued even with his own mother, who

Daniel seemed keenest of all to convince. 'I heard "the man" has been killed,' he said to Jean in a phone chat the Monday after the murder. 'I can tell you we've tried, but it's impossible that it was us who did it.'

Jean said that Christy would not be happy, 'because people are talking', but Daniel was quick to blame a media conspiracy, ironically a key legal gambit used by the man whose death his father had just ordered.

'It's that fucking Paul Williams [the crime journalist] talking. He has sworn against my da, you know?'

'That's clear,' answered Jean. 'That stupid newspaper.'

The brothers were very close to their mother. They regularly rang home and sent large sums of cash to make sure she was comfortable and brought her to Las Vegas to celebrate her birthday.

At one stage Daniel was recorded inquiring whether €6,000 had reached her, telling her €1,000 of it was for her and to distribute the rest to various others. He had appointed a heavy, a former boxer, to look out for her and was incandescent with rage when he learned his mother's flat had been burgled by a local junkie that same April 2010.

He rang the heavy, demanding to know what had happened and why he had not been contacted straight away. He warned him:

> Never do this again. My family is the most important [thing] and you have to look after them because I've always given you money. Tell me what happened to my family or you're finished. I need to trust you one hundred per cent, so go find out who it was and promise me you won't tell any of them except me.

Gardaí were aware of the ex-boxer's role, and that he was ferrying cash between Daniel and contacts in Dublin. A year beforehand, the heavy had been stopped at Dublin Airport and €28,450 was seized from him as he attempted to board a flight to Málaga. The man claimed he was bringing it to Málaga to invest in property, but the Circuit Criminal Court ruled it was most probably the proceeds of crime and ordered it forfeited to the State. The application was not contested.

Daniel also called the ex-boxer, anxious to know what had been in the papers about Dunne's killing. He told the man:

This is going to change a lot of things anyway, so don't talk much on the phone because now they'll be tapping and listening in on everyone, because anything anyone says, they [gardaí] will say it was the motive.

Needless to say, Daniel's charade about the Don's murder was not enough to pull the wool over the eyes of anyone involved in Dublin's gangland scene, least of all Eamon Dunne's associates. Brian O'Reilly even approached the Kinahan gang seeking money to pay for Dunne's funeral.

A Dublin-based cartel underling told Daniel that O'Reilly had 'just come up to me saying that they want the money for the funeral, to pay the family'.

'Who does he want the money off? There's more to it than that,' answered a suspicious Daniel.

'I know Brian. But if we do that, the papers will blame us for carrying it out, you know?' Referring to Dunne's pals, the cartel member continued, 'I haven't called them yet for the moment, because I haven't had to, because if they start mouthing off, I'll ring them and tell them to shut their faces. They all know me, but I don't want to call over something as stupid as that.'

In the weeks that followed, Daniel continued to take a

1. Christy Kinahan as a young father. Already he had embarked on a career in crime.

2. *Above* A 1980s mugshot of John Cunningham.

3. *Right* A 1980s mugshot of a young Gerry Hutch.

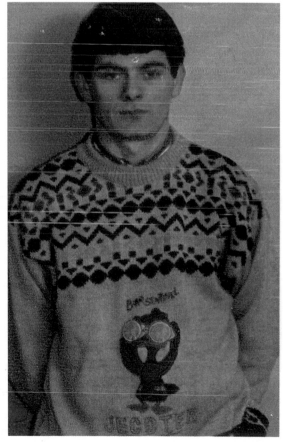

60. *Above* Detective Superintendent Anthony
Howard from the Drugs and Organised
Crime Bureau.

61. *Above right* Chief Superintendent Pat
Leahy from Store Street station. Four of the
killings have happened in the north inner city.

62. *Right* Former Assistant Commissioner
Michael O'Sullivan, who retired in
February, 2017.

63. *Below* Detective Inspector Paul Cleary from
Kevin Street station. He runs 'Operation
Thistle' with Detective Superintendent Peter
O'Boyle. The operation targets mid-level
members of the cartel.

keen interest in what was reported on Dunne's shooting. He received regular verbatim updates down the phone from gang members in Dublin, swearing extensively when something which displeased him was published.

Daniel told associates, 'Keep your ears open and tell me what people are saying,' leading one to respond, apparently without irony, 'Sure you know more than me.'

Police surveillance files showed that – just as with Christy – the crown sometimes lay heavy on Daniel's head. He was recorded on several occasions complaining about how he was working hard, but business was not going well and he was worried.

The gangster was acutely aware of the realities of his chosen profession. During a chat, earlier in 2010, with the gunman later involved in Eamonn Dunne's death, who had wanted to discuss the problems caused by Dunne, Daniel had replied that he had concerns of his own.

'Things are very bad and worse than you can imagine here,' he confided. 'Someone said to me literally, "Can you be happy here because someone will go for you?"'

The clearly shocked man replied, 'For you?'

'Yeah, but I don't want to talk about it here,' answered Daniel.

A couple of months earlier, Daniel had also told an unidentified pal in Ireland that he was nervous about travelling home for a cousin's wedding, in Cavan. A friend of his had been arrested upon arrival at Dublin Airport and was told to present himself to gardaí several days later. Daniel said he could not go through Northern Ireland, as he had 'something outstanding in England'. When his pal suggested travelling through Shannon, Daniel told him to spread gossip that he was not going to attend the nuptials at all.

Feeling the pressure was a familiar refrain that surfaced time and again on the surveillance recordings. Christy Kinahan confessed in one call that he had not had a personal phone for some time.

'This is a family number,' he told an associate. 'But you get paranoid about everything and everyone when something happens here.'

It was something which his long-time accomplice John Cunningham had picked up on. After one apparent row between Christy and a senior cartel member over the latter's use of cocaine, Cunningham rang him the next morning to ask if he was still angry.

'I'm all over the place the way things are now,' Christy replied.

Christy was extremely wary about speaking on the phone except when it came to legitimate business deals to wash the gang's dirty cash. Possibly the only time when Christy dropped his guard was when he spoke to his third wife, Nessy. It was clear the pair had a great relationship, with Christy sending her texts telling her how much he loved her.

But there was no 'love' shown for Eamon Dunne. As with other former associates who the cartel turned upon, there was no appearance by any of the Kinahans at the funeral, on 4 May 2010, eleven days after Dunne was hit by eight of the twelve rounds fired at him at close range.

The Don had made detailed preparations for his demise. He had organized his own funeral the year before, selecting his grave in Dardistown cemetery, in north Dublin, in a plot beside fellow gangland killer Paddy Doyle.

The bling funeral service had a dress code for those attending – black suits, white shirts and black ties. Mobile phones were banned and some of the mourners held vicious-looking Rottweilers on chains.

The murder of Eamon Dunne had the desired effect. The unpredictable cycle of violence he had perpetrated came to a close, and the tension which had permeated Ireland's gangland eased. Meanwhile, the cartel was aware it was facing increasing pressure from the Spanish authorities and had decided it would respond in kind.

10. Watching the Watchers

'This is going to take us to a different level.'

Christy Kinahan

Across the sun-scorched southern Spanish coast lie a series of towers known as the SIVE. The Sistema Integrado de Vigilancia Exterior towers are designed to be the country's eyes and ears over the narrow Strait of Gibraltar, long a favoured channel from North Africa for smugglers of drugs and humans alike.

The towers, which look like very sophisticated CCTV poles, about the size of lighthouses, monitor the seas up to 10km offshore. They use a combination of radar and extremely high-definition FLIR (forward-looking infrared) cameras. Whilst most of Spain's cocaine is brought in through the jagged, inlet-strewn coastline of Galicia in the north-west, hash is ferried in by low-riding speedboats from North Africa. They aim to get in, dump their wares and take off again before the authorities can react.

The smugglers play a constant game of hide and seek with the overstretched Police and Customs services. At times the traffickers sail directly across the Strait, which is less than nine miles wide at the narrowest point, or they pick the narcotics up from a mother ship sailing backwards and forwards in international waters, until the moment is right to launch.

The odds are usually heavily on the smugglers' side, particularly when they travel at night. But the cover of darkness was not enough for the cartel, who wanted to tilt the balance even further in its favour.

The cartel planned to hack into the SIVE control centre in Mijas and put the whole network out of action. This would allow the gang's own suppliers to land their drugs from Morocco without the risk of being seized. As an added bonus, the service could possibly also be rented out to other trusted smugglers.

The Policía Nacional knew nothing about this plan until they came across surveillance-style photos on a pen drive seized at the home of the cartel's main counter-surveillance expert. He was an Englishman that Christy consulted on electronic and other anti-tracking strategies. The pair would chat regularly about technical matters, with the Englishman attending counter-terrorism fairs across Europe, to scout for the most up-to-date technology which could be used by the cartel.

Having listened in on conversations between the pair, cops anticipated finding security cameras and other assorted equipment in his house. Detectives were surprised, however, when they opened the drive and recognized the images of the SIVE towers in Estepona and of the system's control centre in the mountains outside Mijas. There were also pictures of what would become known as 'the man with the pliers'.

Further searches at the Englishman's home uncovered a radar signal interception device and technical details of the FLIR cameras and their thermal sensors. Other items discovered included photos of backup power generators at the Mijas control centre, images of a van with the livery used by the company outsourced to maintain the SIVE towers, and shots of their operatives at work, all taken with a long-distance lens.

The discovery came as a considerable shock to police, who had no idea of the scope of the cartel's plans. They noted:

> It's probable that along with already recognized services offered by the Kinahans, such as drugs and arms trafficking and money laundering, they were preparing to offer a service to other crime groups to 'blind' temporarily the SIVE and/or police channels, thus allowing these groups to bring in drug or arms shipments on the coast.

It was not the first time the SIVE towers had become a target. Two towers in Vélez-Málaga and Almuñécar-La Herradura had been the subject of crude attacks, as criminals tried to put them out of business – in the first case through attempted arson and in the second through vandalism. In a third incident, a shot was fired at the FLIR camera at the tower in Estepona, which temporarily put it out of action too.

The cartel's plan was more sophisticated and was thought to have involved either hacking into the system or putting it out of action by cutting its power. By accessing the system's operational centre in the hills outside Mijas, the gang could have paralysed the whole network.

Detectives investigating the photos of 'the man with the pliers' discovered that they had been taken near a similar maritime traffic control centre in Gibraltar. Police assumed the operation was part of a sabotage attempt on the Rock itself, but as it was not under their jurisdiction, they could not do anything.

Spanish police also found emails between Christy and the Englishman about a police scanner which had been input with frequencies used by police in the Caribbean island of Puerto

Rico. In one message, the Englishman told his boss that he had 'confirmation on the Dominican', but added he wanted to discuss the matter face-to-face. The Spanish investigators concluded that the radio frequencies used by Puerto Rican authorities could be scanned from the neighbouring Dominican Republic, a known stop-off point on the drug-smuggling route to Europe. However, there was nothing they could do and they decided to concentrate on issues closer to home.

The police report explained:

> The Kinahan family and their electronic IT equipment could 'blind' or inhibit the nodules of the SIVE of the Telecommunications Nucleus in Mijas-Benalmádena. Even if for a few moments, it would be attributed to a full systems crash without suspecting the real cause. This electronic IT attack would allow them to operate entirely on their own, without the need to run the risk of bribing police.

The understated acknowledgement in the report of potential police corruption played down an issue which has plagued Spain for decades. The country has three separate police forces: the Guardia Civil and Policía Nacional, both of whom handle serious crime (with separate territories), and the Policía Local, which generally handles public order incidents and other minor issues.

Cops in all three forces are relatively well paid by Spanish living standards, but a member of the Guardia Civil with ten years' service will earn less than €25,000 per annum, while an inspector in the Policía Nacional gets just over €27,000. This makes police prime targets for bribery, particularly on the south coast, where many police resources are concentrated to combat the twin problems of drug trafficking and illegal immigration.

Dozens of cops have been arrested down the years after succumbing to the temptation. The gangs usually target police officers with financial problems, such as gamblers. There could be an element of carrot and stick, once they've got their claws into them – the criminals will keep paying them, but the cops know they can't walk away. In March 2016, three Guardia Civil agents were arrested in an operation which seized five tonnes of cannabis. Officers have also been caught trying to let mules through Madrid Airport, helping drug gangs steal €500m worth of cocaine from their drug gang rivals in Barcelona, and setting up their own trafficking ring in the northern region of Navarra. In one infamous episode in Alicante, a Policía Local chief was caught red-handed as he supervised the unloading of a boat filled with hash.

The Kinahan phone taps also showed they had at least some of the local officers who were meant to be watching them on their payroll. In one instance, Gary Hutch was stopped driving without a licence, but he told the gang's mechanic, 'They know one of the cops, so it'll be sorted out.' One senior Garda officer who put a halt to Kinahan's first major drug operation, way back in 1986, said gardaí were aware not all European colleagues could be trusted implicitly. He commented:

> There's no doubt his organization has been assisted by rogue police officers in Europe. You have police in Europe who live in squalor, and often in the same areas as the criminals, so it's easy for them to get sucked into assisting criminal gangs because that's what they do – they prey on vulnerable people.

Another senior Garda source who worked closely with his Spanish counterparts while monitoring Kinahan's activities in Estepona had high praise for the officers. He said the problem can often lie with the involvement of civil servants in the investigation:

> The Spanish police are doing a great job but they are often restricted by the judicial process. For example, when investigators apply for a warrant it can take a few days and by that time news can filter out. A court official also has to accompany the police on any raids so the question of keeping details of the arrest operation under wraps can prove a difficult task.

The SIVE plan had indicated the lengths the Kinahans were willing to go to in order to protect their territory. While the cartel members were planning their own counter-strike against the forces of law and order, they continued to hone their skills in the areas of both counter-surveillance and surveillance itself.

The Spanish investigators were used to dealing with criminal gangs who took precautions. It was precisely because they had always been careful about talking on the phone and watching for tails that the biggest mobs became important enough to show up on the police's radar. But even seasoned officers of the Policía Nacional were surprised by the lengths to which members of the cartel went.

As well as constantly drilling into their subordinates that no business was to be discussed on their phones, Christy and John Cunningham set up a complex communications system. It was to ensure any attempts to listen in on their operations would be frustrated as much as possible. For lesser members of the gang, pay-as-you-go (or 'burner') mobile SIM cards would be stored in several spots around

Marbella, such as at the Auld Dubliner pub and in lockers at the gang's gym.

When contacted by their bosses, the foot soldiers would be instructed to go to one of these locations and use a burner to call another predesignated number, belonging to a 'clean' SIM card, which would later be disposed of. If that was not convenient, they would be sent to find a phone box, though told to avoid using the same one regularly – another lesson Cunningham had learned painfully in Holland.

The investigators noted:

> Throughout the telephone surveillance, it was clear the legally intercepted phones were receiving frequent calls from telephone boxes located both in the UK and Ireland, thus obscuring the identity of the caller. Checks with police in both countries showed these boxes obeyed a logical sequence and are located near the front companies used by the organization.

Lower-ranking members also hid clean burners in safe locations which could be easily accessed in case of emergency. Ironically, the gang would regularly joke about their phones being tapped, unaware of just how right they were.

'They're all over me, it's not that I'm paranoid, everyone's watching me,' Kevin Lynch quipped once to a pal when complaining that his mobile would not send messages properly.

Lynch was a former international boxer turned armed robber who was used by the cartel as an enforcer, but he also took a hand in the money-laundering end of things. He had been sent several times to Brazil and regularly spoke directly to Christy, his two sons and John Cunningham.

Gary Hutch also told James Quinn, a cartel member

employed for his kickboxing skills, that his phone was not ringing properly. Quinn and Hutch were close and even shared prostitutes, but like many friendships within the cartel, it would end badly between them.

'That didn't ring there, you know that?' Liam Byrne informed Hutch on another phone call from Dublin to Hutch's Spanish number.

'Did it not, no? Don't mind them anyway,' Hutch answered.

But all these counter-surveillance measures were still not secure enough for Christy and the 'Colonel'. Towards the end of 2009, Kinahan began to make inquiries about getting his hands on encrypted phones known as PGPs – Pretty Good Privacy – which are virtually impossible to tap. Along with their anti-eavesdropping capabilities, PGP email and text communications are routed through secure servers in Holland, using software which also makes them extremely difficult to intercept.

Normal emails use the same key to scramble text before it is sent and then unscramble it at the other end so it can be read by the recipient. This means all email service providers, such as Gmail, can access individual account holders' messages if required to do so by court order. The PGPs, however, apply another level of security, using different keys for both the scrambling and unscrambling of the message, ensuring only the holder of the handset can read what is sent.

Christy was determined to have the secure phones but, ever concerned about appearances, he wanted to know how the PGPs would look. He told an English fixer he was using to source the devices that he wanted the ones used by the British royal family.

'Check what make they are,' he said. 'Because if they're Ching Chong Changs, it's no good. They have to be Nokia or Samsung or LG. A recognized name; if not, people are going to say "this is a bit strange".'

The fixer assured Christy that he had one of the phones available for him to take a look at, but it would cost him STG£2,000.

Kinahan, who seemed to take a Ryanair-style attitude to costs incurred by cartel places like the Auld Dubliner and the gang's gym, expressed dissatisfaction and said he thought the devices would have been cheaper.

'My number one priority is to take the SIM from the others, so I can get rid of them, you know?' he said. He went on to explain how he had bought SIMs from a local computer store, but now wanted as many as he could get his hands on. Christy continued, 'I did it for myself and my friend, but now I'd like the SIMs too, because if they're cheap enough, I'll get someone to put credit on them and I can share them out.'

While Kinahan awaited the arrival of his new toys, the gang continued to use code words to describe the merchandise they were flogging. 'Computers' stood for handguns, 'waiters' for more serious weaponry and 'cars' signified drugs. Christy occasionally referred to 'fridges', and once received a call from someone in England seeking permission to set up a 'jeans business'. However, more often he and his cohorts simply talked about 'that', 'the thing' or 'the stuff', making sure to never once mention a giveaway location.

At times the conversations could appear almost farcical, such was the heavy use of code. On one occasion, a Dublin associate rang Gary Hutch to tell him he had left 'a pair of new shoes' in the Golf.

Gary replied, 'I saw the girls who have husbands; he's the one who has connections and you're the one who has to make the calls.'

The other man answered, 'Everyone is waiting for the shoes on the coast.'

And Gary responded, 'They have to go towards where you are there.'

Confusingly, however, on other occasions when the gang members referred to cars, they actually were talking about cars. Particularly when they discussed what the Spanish believed were the stolen vehicles ring, which was one of the cartel's stock-in-trades.

Gary Hutch was heavily involved in this racket and frequently spoke with associates back in Dublin about the prices which could be fetched for cars or car parts. At one stage, he discussed a deal in which seventy Land Rovers, presumably stolen, would be shipped to Iran.

Christy wanted gang members to be proficient at surveillance themselves, in case the need ever arose. But the cartel's plan went beyond just technological measures. Police watched and listened as Daniel Kinahan, Gary Hutch and other gang members trained in what was an extremely lifelike series of surveillance and counter-surveillance war games, which went on for up to six hours at a time.

Daniel was gung-ho for the whole thing, and was recorded ringing around several subordinates the night before one outing was due to take place looking for a beige sports bag which contained bullets for his gun.

The elder Kinahan son threw himself wholeheartedly into the SWAT-style training and expected his subordinates to do likewise. He was regularly heard telling them excitedly how good the course was and how much he was learning.

The instruction consisted of shooting practice, martial arts and street exercises, all perfect for a man like Daniel, who viewed himself as an alpha male. English-speaking Spanish police – clearly unused to strong Dublin accents – logged one call as Daniel telling one of his cronies, the killer of Eamon Dunne, that they had been studying 'forced aid'.

'What?' the man replied.

'For when they shoot or stab someone and all that shit, you know?' answered Daniel. 'It's a brilliant course, I'm enjoying it, you know?'

The first-aid study was due to continue for two weeks before they would move on to something more serious – a hostage rescue situation.

'We want it for two weeks in the summer and they have a group there and a house, and we have to go in and take some-one out of the house, get past security and take over the house,' Daniel explained. 'Later there's another group who take us out into the country and they give us a fifty-mile radio and a two-hour head start. If they catch you, you'll end up in hospital.'

'Serious?' answered the clearly disbelieving hitman.

'Yeah, serious, but on the other hand, we can also send them to the hospital,' Daniel laughed.

Just like their Dutch colleagues, who had catalogued Cunningham's calls, the Spanish struggled with the inner-city Dublin slang they occasionally faced. A remark by Mr A that he had 'just seen the Old Bill there' was recorded as 'I've just seen the old builder'. They also had to seek clarification on what 'coked up' and 'telling porkies' meant and what a 'Nordie' signified.

The heir to the Kinahan crime empire did not joke about, however, when it came to the war games. When an unidenti-fied minion rang to tell him he could not make it to one such exercise because his car had broken down, Daniel did not take it well. 'This is fucking ridiculous,' he raged down the line. 'When I ask you to do something, I want you to do it.'

The operation was due to take place in the Costa del Sol town of Manilva, a short drive from the gang's Estepona base. Daniel, Mr A and two gang members, Ross Browning and Davin Flynn, drove there and entered an apartment complex. What happened next was initially unclear to watching police, who were unable to follow communications between the gang members as they used walkie-talkies. However, it soon became apparent some sort of surveillance exercise was under way.

It then became obvious that it was not all going smoothly when Daniel rang Browning and told him a cop had arrived: 'Get out of there.'

Daniel added that he had told another subordinate, Davin Flynn, to stay seated and keep his eyes open because there was another cop at the end of the street. Browning said he had hidden himself in some shrubs, and Daniel told him to warn Mr A not to come near the place.

A further series of calls between Daniel and Browning took place, and it appeared they had been following a man who had just walked out of a building. But within minutes, the amateur sleuths had lost their target and the war game finished up shortly afterwards.

The objective of these exercises became clearer to the police the following day in a phone call one of the instructors made to Gary Hutch. The gangster listened as the man explained that any person they came across within the complex – apparently of apartments – was to be watched and followed.

The equipment the gang members were using for such drills underlined how seriously they were taking the course.

Ahead of a second war game, days later, Daniel rang Gary Hutch and asked him, 'Do us a favour when you come: the telescope, the camera, the camera charger, under the bed, the pistol, the rifle for the telecom thing, they're all in the bed in the back room on the lower floor.'

It was almost hard not to feel for Daniel at times, given the intelligence of those he had to deal with. Having dispatched gang members to buy wigs for camouflage, he received a call back from one of the men asking if a black hairpiece with green stripes would suffice.

That day's operation too was eventually scuppered, with Hutch first reporting someone was tailing them in a van, before Mr A excitedly came on the phone saying he had 'security all over him'. It appeared the gang had blundered into some unconnected police operation.

Daniel, who was following proceedings by phone, was becoming more and more frustrated. He finally put an end to the outing when he received a call from Ross Browning, who was cracking up laughing.

Browning had dressed in drag but the disguise was not foolproof, as a small child who he passed in the street had shouted, 'That woman is a man!'

Daniel quickly rang Hutch and told him, 'The operation is over.'

Farcical elements aside, the training was successful. It made it more and more difficult for the Policía Nacional to keep their eyes on the cartel's movements. The gang switched cars regularly and continually checked to see if they were being followed. The cops noted:

They drive at high speed, carrying out evasive manoeuvres, circling several times around roundabouts, stopping abruptly, and carry out counter-surveillance when they are on their way to important meetings.

Cartel members became expert at spotting a tail. In September 2009, trained surveillance officers had to abandon an attempt to follow Daniel, a Scottish convicted drug dealer named Kevin Kelly and two others in Kelly's Volkswagen Golf, because the car continually pulled in at roundabouts to let traffic go past, or parked suddenly on the street.

Kelly would later fall foul of the Kinahans in a row over a drugs debt. He was rescued in September 2012 by the Policía Nacional when they stormed a flat in Manilva. Cops found Kelly inside, handcuffed on a bed. He had been abducted four days beforehand and badly beaten.

Christy continued to look for new ways to deal with any attempts to keep tabs on him. Analysis of the English technical expert's emails showed the patriarch had inquired about ANPR (automatic number plate recognition) technology, which cops believed would have been used to check if any vehicles in the vicinity belonged to the State, or if potential clients they were meeting were undercover officers.

The technical expert had also discussed buying STG£5,000 worth of pinhole cameras and audio devices with Christy, who again hesitated on the grounds of cost. Meanwhile, the Englishman was making plans to attend a counter-terrorism expo in London, where he could further beef up on potentially useful equipment.

The Englishman's van was of particular interest to police who raided his home, as it had been turned into a sort of counter-surveillance vehicle. The van, which had blacked-out windows, contained a device for following GPS trackers which could be attached to the underside of cars. It was also fitted with directional microphones, cameras, police-style lights and a siren.

Elsewhere in the house, police found five paramilitary-style uniforms similar to those worn by Policía Nacional agents, bulletproof vests and a Glock pistol. The police believed the uniforms may have been intended for use in robbing other drugs gangs, while they regarded the van as clear evidence the gang wanted to watch anyone who was watching them, possibly with a view to intimidation. The hunted, police realized, had become the hunters.

Christy also regularly rang the tactics expert the cartel had contracted for the SWAT-style training. He wanted progress updates and urged the instructor to be stricter with 'pupils' like Hutch who were not pulling their weight. Christy was clearly frustrated with Gary Hutch due to his half-hearted participation.

The trainer told him that Kevin Lynch 'gets it', but that Hutch was 'not taking it seriously'.

This was clearly not news to Christy. 'Gary has a good heart, but he lacks attention,' he replied.

Neither Christy nor his younger son, Christopher Jr, took part in the SWAT-style training, but it was evident Daniel was keeping them well briefed on what he had learned.

In April 2010, the patriarch flew to Brazil, along with Junior and another Dubliner who was part of their money-laundering set-up. The trio were dropped to Málaga train station by Daniel's Spanish secretary, who received a lecture from Christopher Jr en route about how his dad was going to travel by himself because he could not go under his own name, and how they planned to pretend they did not know each other at all.

The startled woman protested that she had only been making conversation and insisted she 'didn't want to know'. She clamoured, 'Don't tell me; it doesn't matter. I only asked if he was going with you!'

All three men took the train from Málaga to Madrid's Atocha Station, from where – after ducking in and out of several buildings in an attempt to shake any tails – Christopher Jr and his companion disappeared in a taxi. Two trained surveillance cops stuck with Christy, who loitered around Atocha for around half an hour, frequently doubling back sharply in the direction from which he had just come.

The Dapper Don then spent half an hour sitting on the terrace of a bar, scrutinizing everyone within view, before suddenly getting to his feet and walking off quickly in the direction of the nearby Reina Sofía square.

There, Christy, who had paid cash for his €3,706 business-class flight to Rio, booked himself into a grotty two-star hostel, using a false British passport in the name of Michael Leslie Swift. Subsequent investigations discovered Kinahan held an account with Banco Sabadell in the same name. A Spanish social security number for his fake ID had been registered to the Costa del Sol home of his British-Indian money man.

Attempts to have the Kinahans followed by their Brazilian counterparts upon landing did not work out, which must have annoyed the Spanish greatly. Evidence of Christy and his son meeting with the people taking care of the cartel's property empire on the ground would have greatly aided the money-laundering case against them. However, the success of such requests often comes down to the strength of personal relationships between officers from different countries, and it was clear the Spanish did not have enough clout with their Brazilian counterparts to pull off a surveillance operation there.

Despite all this training, some of the less clued-in gang members still rather enjoyed press attention and even courted it. It was clear this was not the case with Daniel. He regularly rang pals back in Dublin, looking to see what was in the papers about the gang, and would curse and swear if something he obviously did not want out had been published. Daniel would also often ring his mother, Jean, to tell her there was something about him and his father in the papers, and to reassure her that it was 'shit'.

In the end, most of Christy's more ambitious schemes, such as the plan to paralyse the SIVE tower network, never happened. But it was his move towards the use of PGP phones which would have more lasting consequences for police forces across Europe, including the gardaí.

In time, the expensive phones became de rigueur for any self-respecting gangster wanting to do business at the highest level. True to his service-provider ethic, the Kinahans soon began wholesaling the devices to other criminals, ensuring yet another revenue stream was flowing into cartel coffers.

PGPs, which are not illegal, are now in widespread use amongst drug dealers in Ireland and regularly pop up for sale on websites such as DoneDeal or Gumtree, costing between €1,000 and €2,000. Several PGPs were seized in Dublin and Estepona during joint raids between gardaí and the Guardia Civil, in September 2016.

Combatting such technology will prove difficult. In July 2016, the Government updated laws regarding covert surveillance to allow gardaí to access encrypted messaging services such as WhatsApp, Viber and Facebook. This is unlikely to help in cracking the use of PGP handsets, widely viewed as the most secure phones on the market. In April 2016, Dutch police shut down a company called Ennetcom, which it claimed was 'the largest encrypted network used by organized crime in the Netherlands'.

It is known that some Irish crime figures, including the Kinahans, were using encryption firms based in Holland, but it is not clear if Ennetcom was one of them. Ennetcom's servers were based in Toronto, Canada, and the encrypted data on them was copied with the co-operation of the Canadian authorities. However, it is far from clear how long it will take the Dutch to crack the codes in question. Also, it is likely servers will be stored in less co-operative and more technologically backward nations in future.

How gardaí and other police forces deal with this obstacle will likely decide the outcome of countless gangland investigations over the years to come. Ironically, with all their surveillance training, Daniel and the rest of the Kinahan gang were unaware that they were under constant scrutiny — and that the Spanish investigators were now ready to strike.

11. Tumbling Down

'I don't speak Spanish!'

Christy Kinahan at 5 a.m.
on 25 May 2010

In February 2010, Christy rang his elder son to ask him if he wanted to collect the 'bits and bolts' he had for him. Daniel, who seemed drunk, did not understand. 'The laptop I have for you,' an exasperated Christy explained, in what police believe was code for a gun.

At that stage, the cartel members were aware that they were being watched and occasionally followed by Spanish police. Officers regularly stopped gang members at check-points and asked them pointedly if they were Irish, while they searched their cars.

But it was clear Christy Kinahan regarded this as run-of-the-mill harassment and nothing to get overly worked up about. 'It's not as if they're on top of us, but I don't want to be bringing it again and again to the house, so I left it in the car glove box,' he continued to Daniel.

By 2010, Kinahan was well aware of his own notoriety. He was on Europol's list of the 'Top 10' drugs and arms suppliers in Europe, putting him alongside the likes of Italy's Cosa Nostra and the 'Ndrangheta (the Italian mafia based in Calabria, with close links to Colombia's narco-gangs and Mexico's ruthless drugs gangs), the French Unione Corse (one of the biggest suppliers of cocaine in western Europe) and various other British and eastern European gangsters.

Christy and the rest of the gang appeared to have grown used to overt police attention, so when agents from the Policía Nacional's Drugs and Organized Crime Unit (UDYCO) burst into the homes of the Dapper Don and twenty-one of his subordinates at 4 a.m. on 25 May 2010, it caused predictable panic throughout the gang.

Veteran criminals like Kinahan and Cunningham had been through all this before. But when Spanish police broke down the door of Cunningham's 3,500-square-foot villa in Estepona, in May 2010, they were particularly careful. The 'Old Man', as the Kinahans respectfully referred to him, had protected his home with armoured glass and extensive CCTV camera coverage. Cops were also aware from sur-veillance that he had two large dogs – one a husky – and they considered him a 'weapons expert'.

His arrest and incarceration in Holland had left Cunningham with a marked reluctance to discuss anything business-related on the phone. Nor was he inclined to repeat the costly mistake of keeping contraband in his own home.

A thorough search of his villa during the raid found very little incriminating evidence. The only real item he could be charged over was a fake British passport in the name of Hugo Young which featured a photo of the 'Colonel'. Cun-ningham put up a fight as he was cuffed anyway, and he received a shiner for his trouble. After his home was searched, he was led away into the early morning darkness.

Meanwhile, multilingual Kinahan had the chutzpah to claim he didn't understand Spanish while he lay handcuffed in his underpants on the floor as a police officer read out the warrant to him.

Daniel and Christopher Jr were also detained at their homes and taken into custody while a thorough search of the properties was carried out. Others, despite their 'hard man' reputations, were thrown into full-blown consternation.

Both Gary Hutch and Mr A escaped arrest because they were in Holland that day, a coincidence which would raise suspicions with Christy and John Cunningham about their loyalties. After the raids, a flurry of calls took place between the absent pair and other Kinahan gang members, as they tried to find out exactly what was going on and who had been arrested.

It took several hours, and keeping abreast of media reports, before the cartel members who had not been picked up understood the size of the unprecedented operation against them. The confusion was furthered by the multiple calls they were receiving from Dublin, where gardaí had carried out forty-five searches that same morning. This was 'Operation Shovel' – a co-ordinated move by the Spanish, Irish and British authorities to take the cartel by surprise in a number of raids on gang members, their properties and other cartel premises. The gardaí would perform another nine raids the following day.

Only one person was arrested in Ireland, a man in his twenties who was an associate of Gary Hutch. The disgruntled criminal later rang Hutch and told him how his attempts to resist arrest had not ended well. 'They got me at the door, half on the ground,' he moaned. 'I tried to hide under the sheets, but the guy caught me by the feet and pulled me out of the bed. I tried to fight back, but they put a cushion on my face and the other guy was screaming, "Turn around so we can see your face." Then they were insulting me and they put something around my neck, the bastards.'

'Why did they lift you?' a clearly perplexed Hutch asked.

'Two and a half years ago, they found a little coke in one of my bags with an automatic pistol. They found a print on the bag the sniff was in,' replied the man in Dublin. 'I think that's why they came. It's all over drugs, that's what's coming out on the telly. They took money, my laptop, paperwork, they said, "We know there are drugs in your house," and all that.'

Hutch quickly sent two minions round to check his own house on the Costa del Sol. They reported that the doors and windows had been bashed in by police. One of the men rang him to tell him the cops had dismantled the air condition-ing, 'destroyed' the sofa and the DVD player.

Hutch was most concerned about the safe in his bedroom. His contact had bad news for him – the safe was empty.

'There's nothing in it?' asked a clearly disbelieving Hutch.

As news kept filtering through, it quickly became appar-ent how much trouble the cartel was in.

'They're all over us, buddy,' a panicked Mr A told an unidentified colleague back home in Dublin. 'Keep your head well down because there are at least twenty-nine people arrested in Spain, England, Ireland and Seville.'

'They got my boss and four others too,' added Hutch. 'I've no idea what's going on; I'm dizzy.'

Hutch dealt with the stress of the situation in his usual manner – by 'going to buy a bag of weed'. But there would be no respite for those of the gang who were still in Spain. The raids were filmed by Spanish police and footage of Christy Kinahan in his underwear was the lead story on the evening news, both in Spain and Ireland.

The country's interior minister, Alfredo Pérez Rubalcaba,

did not hesitate to crow over the high-profile spectacle from an EU borders conference in Warsaw. The minister described the Kinahans as 'a fairly well-known mafia family in the UK and Ireland', before going on to accuse them of being involved in human trafficking, which was news to the gardaí and the Spanish investigators.

Anyone connected to the cartel was fair game. In October 2009, Christy had hooked up with 'Mad' Mickey McAvoy, the notorious London gangster who masterminded the STG£27 million Brink's-Mat gold bullion robbery at Heathrow Airport, in November 1983. Spanish police had watched as Kinahan, McAvoy, a Spanish fraudster and an Indian criminal met at the Holiday Inn in Valencia. The police were unable to get close enough to hear what the quartet were discussing, as they gathered around the Spaniard's laptop, but they knew McAvoy had moved into drug trafficking after his release, in 2008, from a twenty-five-year sentence over the Brink's-Mat heist. Intelligence had suggested the Kinahan cartel was his supplier.

Later phone taps between the Kinahan gang and McAvoy's associates referring to 'containers', 'the stuff', 'the black something' and 'the itchy stuff' seemed to confirm the Spanish police's suspicions, and McAvoy was also arrested in May 2010.

Along with the Spanish and Irish arrests, British police also pulled in eleven people for questioning about drug trafficking, though all were subsequently released without charge. That brought the number of detentions under Operation Shovel to thirty-four people – twelve of whom were Irish. Over 750 police officers had been involved in the co-ordinated operation.

*

Christy, his two sons and Cunningham were all photo-graphed, looking bedraggled, being led into court. In a closed session they were questioned by the investigating judge appointed to oversee the probe, María Carmen Gutiérrez Henares. Spanish police put on a massive show of security around the small courthouse in Estepona. Heavily armed, balaclava-wearing officers kept watch as the trio and other cartel members were led inside.

Spain's criminal law is based on the Roman inquisitorial system rather than Ireland's British-style legislation. This means an investigating judge must review all the evidence collected by police and question the suspects before he or she decides what charges will be brought.

Anyone under investigation will not actually be charged until the opening day of their trial, meaning an *investigado*, who is merely suspected of wrongdoing, can be locked up on remand for years despite not having been accused of any-thing. This was the case with Christy, Daniel and Christopher Jr who – following a lengthy interrogation by Judge Gutiér-rez Henares – were packed off to a remand prison near Málaga. They were under formal investigation for drugs and weapons trafficking, money laundering and membership of a criminal organization.

Despite police protestations, the judge remarkably accepted Cunningham's flimsy excuses that he was merely a tourist on holiday in the area. While Christy and his two sons were sent to prison, the 'Old Man' was freed on bail after three days of questioning, as were several other key figures.

Given the evidence that the Spanish had gathered on the Ballyfermot native, it was hardly a surprise. Most of the phone taps Cunningham featured in were anodyne discus-sions about the weather, walking the dog or chats with his golf coach. Any conversations Cunningham had concerning business were suitably short and vague, with nothing that could really be used to incriminate him. His frequent calls usually ended on instructions to talk face-to-face or to meet by some other method.

Cunningham on one occasion referred to himself as 'John the Mailman', on another he promised to 'think on it' when asked by an unidentified caller to 'sort' a problem the man had. At times, the indignation of the man who once considered ending it all with a grenade during the Jennifer Guinness kidnapping siege came to the fore. Ringing home for a chat with his brother Mick, he discussed how someone they knew had been caught downloading something illegal in Limerick Prison and how some prison officers there had also been nabbed trying to sneak prostitutes into the jail. 'And then they criticize us?' Cunningham ranted.

Cunningham had once been a close associate of, and even subordinate to, John Gilligan. But by now, their roles had been firmly reversed and Gilligan was still serving his twenty-year term for drug-trafficking offences. In one episode, he was desperately trying to contact Cunningham from behind bars. A Dublin-based associate rang the 'Colonel' to tell him he had received five calls from 'the man with the little legs', Cunningham's disparaging nickname for his one-time friend. The 'Colonel' laughed as the associate told him Gilligan had a problem he really needed help in resolving. The pair joked as the man told Cunningham he had informed Gilligan the communication would only go in one direction, and he would see what he could do. Cunningham said he would sleep on it and clearly dismissed the matter from his mind.

However, when the 'Colonel' did occasionally let his guard slip, the results could be unexpected. The month before the

Operation Shovel raids, he rang Daniel, somewhat panicked, and was a little more forthcoming on the phone than usual.

Cunningham told the elder Kinahan boy something 'very strange' was going on and asked if Daniel could come round to his place straight away. 'I'm OK, but I'm taking photos here in the house and the entity keeps appearing in the photographs,' he said.

'That's not possible,' Daniel responded.

'Get in the car and come round,' insisted Cunningham.

Twenty minutes later, Daniel rang his aunt, Christy's sister Denise Kinahan. 'John's taking photos inside the house and in all of them a woman appears in the background,' he told her.

Denise was a businesswoman who had been joint director of three import-export, dry cleaning and interior design firms with Daniel, in Dublin. She had also been a prominent taxi driver, heading up the Taxi Company Owners Association and sitting on the National Taxi Council, with former Garda Commissioner Pat Byrne as chairperson. She subsequently moved to join her brother in Spain.

When Daniel called her in a panic, Denise asked him to email on the snaps.

'The woman is in all the photos,' her nephew wailed. 'On the stairs, in all the corners. There's something scary about this.'

There would be a lot worse than ghostly apparitions for Cunningham and Daniel to worry about in the months to come. The cartel was in complete disarray. Supplies of heroin in Dublin dried up within weeks. Robberies from pharmacies for prescription drugs were at an all-time high as desperate junkies sought ways of getting their fix. It was a solid indicator that the Kinahan empire, which now completely controlled the city's market, was in a tailspin.

*

Back in Ireland, the Criminal Assets Bureau (CAB) had identified twenty bank accounts which it believed the Kinahans were using to launder their profits. Betting was still a favoured strategy for Irish criminals to wash their dirty cash. The investigation team found it continued to be used by the cartel, 'cleaning' an estimated €2.5 million of dirty money, with only €200,000 lost in the process.

Business had clearly been booming for the cartel. In one conversation in December 2009, John Cunningham had been recorded discussing selling a property in Marbella for at least €590,000 and buying a different one for €1.6 million. He was also contacted by agents of the Spanish bank, CatalunyaCaixa, who politely informed him he would have to submit documentation to justify why he was regularly receiving transfers from Ireland of more than €35,000 into his account. His wife, Mary Cunningham, ran a clothing store named Cose Belle – Italian for 'Beautiful Things' – which police suspected, but could not prove, was selling counterfeit designer wear. As a laundering front, the store was perfect and Daniel Kinahan had been recorded by the Operation Shovel team ringing his secretary to tell her to find out about renting two units in the four-star Andalucía Plaza Hotel complex, as Cunningham wanted to open a further store there. Just like the businessmen they were, they viewed the monthly €600 rent as too high, and ordered her to negotiate something lower.

Hairdressers, dry cleaners, solicitors and accountants were among the businesses searched in the joint Spanish-Irish operation. In Ireland, CAB officers took away large amounts of documentation, computers and bank records for examination, while Spanish police confiscated dozens of forged blank Irish and British passports.

Each member of the gang had their own aliases for their illegal passports. Along with Michael Leslie Swift, Christy was known as Thomas Richard Hassett, born in London. The first passport had knocked two years off his age; the second five years. Daniel had a British passport in the name of Zachary Brian Goodman and an Irish one for an Alan Ennis. Cunningham's alias was Briton Hugo Young, while Bernard Clancy, a long-time cartel member with convictions for drug dealing in Ireland, was Irishman Gareth William O'Connor.

Ross Browning, a driver for the Kinahans who carried out his first armed raid in Dublin aged just eighteen, was Michael Chaney, while Mr A had two passports – an Irish one for John Fox and the second a Slovenian passport in the name of Slobodan Babic.

In further raids, Spanish police found €100,000 in cash and fifty-one mobile phones. More than two dozen top-of-the-range cars were taken to a compound at Málaga port after being seized. They included Christy's €180,000 Bentley, Cunningham's Corvette and BMW and a yellow Lamborghini, also worth €181,000, which consumed petrol at a wallet-draining 14 miles to the gallon.

But far more important for the cartel – and the various police forces who had spent years investigating them – was the seizure of their money-laundering apparatus. Judge Gutiérrez Henares froze the assets of thirty-one companies linked to the Kinahans. This list included Greenland Securities SL, which was controlling the Kinahans' Brazilian property empire.

The gang members were not the only losers here. Dozens of innocent investors had ploughed their money into the Brazilian property deals promoted by Greenland Securities SL. The company had been plugging its Palma do Mar resort in Brazil as a chance for people to get in on an expanding market before it took off.

Unfortunately, the only thing that took off was investors' money. A class action was started to retrieve the investments but with Greenland Securities' assets frozen, and allowing for the notoriously slow Brazilian legal system, the innocent investors have little chance of getting their money back any time soon.

After seven months in jail, all three Kinahans were released on bail in November 2010. The gang threw a lavish fancy-dress party to celebrate their freedom. Christy had to hand over €60,000 in bail and his passport was confiscated, though this was unlikely to bother a man with such easy access to fake IDs.

The cartel leaders were quick to apply to get their cars back, with John Cunningham asking for his Corvette C6 and BMW X5 and Christy requesting that a seized Volkswagen Golf R32 and a Toyota Land Cruiser be returned. Daniel also wanted a different Golf R32, while his brother queried the status of a BMW 1 Series taken away from him.

Operation Shovel rolled on; Mr A was detained in Dublin on a European Arrest Warrant. Never short of neck, he applied for free legal aid, despite having been observed frequently flying to Spain, Holland and Morocco, while having no apparent legitimate income.

The High Court gave short shrift to his claims that his elderly mother was funding his wanderlust, and turned down his request. Aware he would most likely be released on bail by the Spanish court, Mr A consented to his extradition and impatiently requested he be sent to Spain 'straight away'.

Mr A was proved to be correct. He was extradited to Spain at the cost of thousands to the Irish taxpayer on a Friday and was granted bail the following Monday. Another celebratory gangland knees-up was held the following night in a cartel-controlled pub.

Shortly afterwards, Christy was packed off to Belgium to serve the remainder of his four-year sentence for money laundering when the Antwerp court finally rejected his appeal, in December 2010. He would serve just a couple of months of the four years before being allowed out pending the result of his challenge.

Predictably, the gang were using every method at their disposal to fight against Shovel. Daniel Kinahan's lawyers moaned about leaks to the press and insisted their client had never been questioned properly by the authorities about any of the crimes of which he was suspected.

Daniel's legal team wrote to the court complaining that the confidentiality applying to Spanish proceedings was being ignored abroad:

> What is more surprising is that, given that arrests and searches took place in Ireland and England, apparently the secrecy order has not been extended to these countries, as the Irish press published information, including names of the people involved, the companies under investigation, phone taps carried out, etc.
>
> We attach documents 1 to 16 featuring different publications from the day of the arrests and the subsequent days, which had much more information in the press than to which we lawyers had 'access', and probably the court too.

However, the reality was that press reports were the least of the cartel's worries on the home front.

12. Goldeneye

'If you didn't do what you were told, then you would
be killed. It was as simple as that.'

Former Detective Superintendent Gabriel O'Gara

On the surface, things looked bright for Michael Fitzgerald
as June 2010 entered its third full week. A few days earlier,
the 29-year-old builder had married his sweetheart, Aisling
Gallagher, in a civil ceremony in the capital. He was looking
forward to life with her at the house they shared in Cush-
lawn Park, in Tallaght, south Dublin.

The couple had booked a wedding reception in a hotel on
the sun-soaked island of Tenerife for the following month.
They were set to celebrate their nuptials in style, with 200
of their nearest and dearest. Unfortunately for the new bride,
it would never come to pass.

On 24 June, several uniformed and plain-clothes gardaí
swooped on the newly-weds' home, along with other properties in the Walkinstown and Crumlin areas. At the Tallaght
house, officers discovered €2m worth of cocaine and mixing
agents for the substance in the family home's kitchen, main
bedroom, attic and small front bedroom.

In what was described by gardaí at the time as an 'advanced
drug-mixing operation' officers also recovered a compressor, digital scales, mixing equipment, duct tape, plastic

wrapping, metal moulds for packaging cocaine and €60,000 in cash. Brought in for questioning, Fitzgerald would be held in custody for the next seven days.

Bad as things were for him, they were about to get even worse. Four days into the suspect's detention, detectives received an unexpected call from Fitzgerald's father to say that he had recovered a 'large holdall' bag that was 'suspicious' at his home in Corrib Road, Terenure, south Dublin.

Obtaining a warrant from Peace Commissioner Patrick Morton, officers combed the Fitzgerald family home. Searching a bedroom at the property, officers discovered a 'large quantity of white powder'. The powder, later identified as cocaine, was valued at €8.5 million. As the search continued, investigators also discovered a Colt semi-automatic pistol, a 9mm handgun and five .45 calibre rounds of ammunition hidden in DVD boxes.

Questioned over a period of twenty interviews, Fitzgerald admitted possessing the huge drugs and weapons haul at his own home and at his father's. He was jailed for eight years at Dublin Circuit Court, on 24 November 2011. At a previous bail hearing, gardaí had made it clear they considered him to be a 'flight risk' because of the serious nature of the charges but they did admit that he had 'never previously been before the courts' and was 'not known to be a drug user'. Bail was refused.

During Fitzgerald's sentence hearing, the court was told gardaí were satisfied he didn't own the drugs and was struggling to pay his mortgage. In return for agreeing to store the drugs and firearms for the cartel he would earn a 'modest profit'.

Jailing him for the eight-year period, Judge Martin Nolan commented that he had been caught with a 'huge amount' of drugs but maintained he was a 'good candidate' for rehabilitation following his release from prison. During his time in jail, Fitzgerald has distanced himself from the gang members and is regarded as a model prisoner.

One senior prison source explained:

> He has kept his head down and has undergone a few courses. He found it hard adjusting to prison life when he first came in and he was the last person you would expect to see in the system. He just wants to do his time and then get back to some sort of normality when he's freed. He's hasn't aligned himself with anyone and is doing his best.

The seizure was the first major success for 'Operation Goldeneye', a Garda initiative set up to run in tandem with the wider-reaching Shovel. Just twenty-four hours before the offensive began in Spain, in May 2010, a specialist Organized Crime Unit was established in the gardaí's South Central Division.

Following several high-level meetings with Garda management, Goldeneye was born and placed under the command of senior investigators Detective Superintendent Gabriel O'Gara, now retired, Superintendent Thady Muldoon, also now retired, and Superintendent Joseph Gannon. The objective of the new unit, which included some of the most experienced gangland detectives in the country, was to 'specifically target' senior cartel figures.

The unit was made up of a Detective Sergeant, a Sergeant and eight other officers, ranging from the ranks of detectives to uniformed gardaí. They used the Emergency Response Unit when dealing with the movement of weapons and were all based in the A District, which was home to many of the major gangland criminals. They already had extensive knowledge of their targets.

Former Detective Superintendent O'Gara considers the huge drugs seizure a 'spectacular success' for his team of investigators. 'We were targeting the Kinahan gang and its associates and there's no doubt the Fitzgerald seizure was one of the highlights of this operation,' he says.

Fitzgerald was just one of many young men in the south inner-city area who were under the spell of the cartel. It had made a speciality of seeking out people they viewed as being 'under the radar', who they could exploit for their own ends. People who were vulnerable, experiencing cash problems, those who owed debts because of their addictions, and others with no previous convictions, or who were not regarded as gang members by detectives, were deliberately identified by the cartel. O'Gara explains:

> Once these guys got their claws into you there was no way out. They used the classic examples of intimidation and fear to make people who had otherwise no convictions store drugs and weapons. If you didn't do what you were told, then you would be killed. It was as simple as that. There were families all over the south inner city who were living in terror. Many parents were forced to remortgage their homes to pay for drug debts because they didn't want their children being shot.

The cartel also conscripted children. Use of kids by drug dealers was not invented by the cartel, but it is one of their specialities. The youngsters are recruited early, aged ten or more, and are told to transport drugs and money around on their bikes or to act as 'spotters', keeping an eye out for gardaí or rival gangsters.

If they are stopped and searched by gardaí, little or no action can be taken against them. There are only around forty detention places for children in the State and these are reserved for those who display the worst behaviour. Any youngster caught by the authorities will most likely be placed under the supervision of an already overworked probation officer, or ordered to take part in a 'youth diversion scheme'.

However, those who lose drugs in a search may be beaten or stabbed as a warning to others in the gang. On one occasion, an investigator recalled how a young man was attacked in the street and his father's car was damaged after a small batch of heroin was seized by gardaí in the New Street area. Gardaí also uncovered examples of parents taking out loans against their homes because their children had become hooked on drugs, mainly heroin.

Operation Goldeneye aimed to prosecute those gang members who were preying on vulnerable children and their families. In O'Gara's words:

> Goldeneye was an initiative designed to infiltrate and disrupt the activities of organized criminals who were aligned to the Kinahan faction. The Kinahan cartel had a major network of criminals within the south inner city who they used as a distribution chain in the sale and supply of drugs. This network had its leading lights in the form of . . . Liam and David Byrne, Greg Lynch and other associates.

In a file later submitted to the Director of Public Prosecutions, detectives maintained they were targeting a gang:

> . . . whose sole area of expertise was the importation, sale, supply and distribution of controlled drugs within the greater Dublin area. The unit was deployed with a specific remit of targeting organized crime and all persons associated with this prominent criminal gang who live and operate

this illegal enterprise within the Dublin Metropolitan Region, South Central Division.

The senior cartel figures who would come under the spotlight of the new unit included Mr A, who Garda intelligence classed as having associations with ninety-one of the country's most serious criminals. Another target was 31-year-old criminal Greg Lynch.

Lynch, a convicted heroin dealer, was relatively unknown to the general public. He rarely left his heavily fortified home in the south inner city over concerns that, if he did, he would feature in many of the national media outlets. On the rare occasions he was seen in public, it was to attend illegal horse races on beaches in remote parts of Ireland, events where huge bets were placed.

Banned from driving for life, because of amassing a series of traffic offences, Lynch cemented his position within the cartel after he was jailed for eight years, in 2004, for possessing €400,000 worth of heroin. During one hearing at the Appeal Court over the young criminal's driving ban, Garda Diarmuid O'Donovan told the court how Lynch had fifty-seven previous convictions and had been banned from driving for 'lengthy periods' from a young age. Lynch's solicitor also told the same court how his client had an 'appalling record' and was battling a 'drugs addiction'.

Lynch was quickly elevated to a position of trust within the criminal organization because his father, Ger 'Bra' Brady, from the Oliver Bond Estate, was a childhood friend of Christy Kinahan. In the summer of 2010, Lynch, who was also a close associate of enforcers Gerard 'Hatchet' Kavanagh and Paul Rice, was suspected by Garda intelligence of controlling sixty dealers in the south inner city, making him one of the most senior members of the cartel on Irish soil. O'Gara says:

> Without question, Greg Lynch is one of the main men for the Kinahan organization in Ireland. He has his own personal driver and is always driven around in top-of-the-range jeeps. When it came to targeting senior members of the Kinahan gang in 2010, he was at the top of the list.

Another officer adds:

> He's somewhat of a recluse and has a team of young dealers around him to sell his drugs. He got involved in serious crime from a young age and it was no surprise he was caught with such a huge amount of heroin in 2004.

The Operation Goldeneye investigations meant that Lynch and his associates were under the Garda spotlight. He was often stopped and searched as he was being driven around the inner city. However, despite these measures, and the arrest of the cartel senior members in Spain in the summer of 2010, it was business as usual for the gang.

The cartel carried on recruiting individuals without previous convictions. One of those men was 'Tommy' (not his real name)*.

Born in the mid-1980s, and growing up in Dublin's Oliver Bond Estate, the childhood home of Daniel and Christopher Kinahan, Tommy was the perfect candidate for the gang. Unlike many of his childhood friends from the area, the father-of-one had never been before a court. His only interaction with the gardaí had been when he was stopped in

---

* At the time of writing 'Tommy' is facing fresh drugs charges so for legal reasons identifying details have been removed here.

Oliver Bond on two occasions and found in possession of cannabis for his own use.

In mid-summer 2010, Tommy was in full-time employment, earning a yearly salary of just over €32,000. Despite being in work, he continued to associate with his old friends in the pubs around the south inner city at weekends. Many of them were working directly for Greg Lynch. And it was during a social outing that gardaí believe he was offered the chance to earn an extra €1,000. Regarded as someone they could trust, because of his long-term associations and close links to Oliver Bond, Tommy became a paid-up member of the cartel.

His first job for the gang was to find a property, away from Oliver Bond because of the Garda activity in the area, to be used for the weighing and 'bagging' of a heroin shipment. It had been smuggled into Ireland by the cartel's associates, just after Operation Shovel.

Tommy contacted a younger cousin, 'Mary' (not her real name), who had been renting a one-bedroom apartment on the fourth floor of the Smithfield apartment complex. It was used by professionals and young families living in the city centre. Mary was someone who had never come to the attention of the authorities and had no previous convictions. A single mother-of-one, she had previously been employed as a cleaner. Mary was unemployed and in receipt of social welfare payments. Like her cousin, she was the perfect candidate for the gang.

On a morning in late July, the single mother received a telephone call from her cousin asking if he could use her apartment to 'bag some stuff' for a payment of €150. She agreed and they made arrangements for him to use the apartment two days later, to cut and bag the drugs.

At 4 p.m. on the agreed day, Tommy received a key and made his way to the apartment. Once there, he was in the process of cutting and weighing the drugs when he was disrupted. His cousin's ex-partner had unexpectedly called to the apartment. Terrified of being caught, Tommy left the building before returning at 5.16 p.m. to meet his cousin.

Handing back the keys, he explained he was 'unable to bag the stuff' and would come back to complete the task a few days later.

Four days later, Mary received a text in the morning: 'Cuz, can I do that message again today.' She agreed and they arranged for Tommy to return to the apartment that afternoon. Arriving shortly before 3.30 p.m. the new cartel employee was invited into the apartment and directed towards the living room, while Mary went to her bedroom.

At the same time as Tommy was preparing the drugs for distribution, the Goldeneye investigators received intelligence the property was being used to store heroin. Less than an hour after he had arrived at Mary's apartment, gardaí arrived at the apartment complex armed with a warrant. However, just as the search team reached Smithfield, Tommy received a telephone call from a mystery individual who has never been identified. The caller informed him that officers were at the complex.

Telling his cousin of the impending bust, the pair left the apartment in different directions. Mary was arrested in a stairwell, while her cousin was stopped at 4.30 p.m. in the atrium of the building by Garda Sean O'Neill. Searching Tommy, investigators recovered €475,000 worth of heroin from his rucksack.

Tommy was taken to Kevin Street Garda Station where officers also recovered another small package of drugs that he had concealed in his rear passage. Questioned during nine interviews over a two-day period, he admitted bringing the drugs to Smithfield to cut them before returning them to an individual he 'refused to name'.

He insisted it was his idea to use his cousin's apartment for the illegal enterprise, and that he had been ordered to cut the drugs into 125g bags. During his fifth interview, he also outlined how he knew he was involved in heroin because of his experience growing up in Oliver Bond.

During her cousin's nine interviews, Mary admitted she knew that 'bag up' referred to the packaging of drugs. As gardaí were preparing their file for the Director of Public Prosecutions, they concluded that Tommy had been 'clearly motivated by the financial gains to be made from being a vital cog in the wheel of the illicit drug trade within the greater Dublin area'.

In another submission, investigators rejected Tommy's assertions that he was a 'quiet and unassuming guy'. While gardaí did not regard him as a key player within the organization he was a key player in terms of this particular enterprise. He refused to name those involved in the operation because they had been childhood friends and because he knew what the consequences would be. They said:

> The idea that [Tommy] wished to portray himself during interviews as someone who was asked whilst out socializing to bag is entirely absurd. His reluctance to fully account for his involvement within the organized criminal gang reflects this.
>
> [Tommy] goes on further to state that he was in fear to refuse this request because of the persons concerned, and this was the reason why he found himself to be in

possession of this large quantity of illicit drugs. [Tommy] was the chief perpetrator in this case and it was through his criminal associates and position of trust within the hierarchy of a south inner-city crime gang that he was entrusted with his task.

[Mary's] involvement in the case stems from knowingly allowing her apartment to be used on at least two occasions to facilitate the cutting, weighing and bagging of these controlled drugs for sale and supply.

Throughout the course of the investigation, officers also recovered a 'vital piece of evidence' that linked Tommy to 'drugs distribution'. The evidence was a text message on his mobile phone outlining a coded 'tick list' of people who owed money to the gang. The biggest amount owed was €2,300 for 'go' and the least amount €150 for 'col'.

Two days after the raid, Tommy was charged at Dublin District Court with possession of heroin with intent to supply. Mary was charged with allowing her home to be used for the preparation of drugs.

At his trial, a year later, Tommy received a five-year prison term after he pleaded guilty to possessing the drugs with intent to supply, while his cousin was placed under a probation bond for a year for allowing her home to be used as part of the drug-smuggling operation.

Just two months after the establishment of the specialist unit, Goldeneye had secured another major success against the cartel. It would not be their last victory in 2010.

Meanwhile, Lynch's foot soldiers were forcing people from their homes in the south inner city over unpaid drug debts. And one of his associates in west Dublin, vicious gangster

Mark 'The Guinea Pig' Desmond was linked to the murder of 28-year-old James Kenny McDonagh, on 27 October 2010.

The father-of-two, from Islandbridge in Kilmainham, was last seen in the Ballyfermot area before he was abducted, shot in the head and dumped in a shallow grave. His remains were found on 8 January 2012.

The murder victim's mother, Jackie, who vowed to confront the gang she blamed for her only son's killing, passed away in June 2016. Although several people were questioned about the murder, no one has ever been charged. The main theory being investigated by gardaí is that he was targeted by Desmond, a mob boss who was responsible for up to four murders and would sexually assault drug addicts who owed him money, after they had a falling out. Another theory is Kenny McDonagh may have been killed by mistake. Desmond himself would get his comeuppance in December 2016, when he was shot dead in a gangland assassination gardaí said could have been carried out by any one of his numerous enemies. He had gained his unusual nickname as a consequence of taking part in pharmaceutical drug trials in return for payment earlier in life.

In a previous interview with the authors, James's mother summed up how gangland violence had destroyed her life:

> I've no life if I haven't got James. I know he's gone but I still keep waiting by the phone for him to ring me. I don't know why anyone would want to harm him because the only thing he lived for was his beautiful daughter and his horses. I haven't slept or eaten properly and I just want this nightmare to end. I'm on all sorts of medication but I don't know how I'm going to get through this. I'm not going to let this go for the rest of my life. He was my only child and I love him with every bone in my body.

The killing of James Kenny McDonagh would not be the only murder linked to Lynch's mob. His associates also remain the chief suspects for the killing of career criminal Mickey Devoy, who was found shot dead at Foxhill, Bohernabreena, at the foot of the Dublin Mountains, on 18 January 2014.

Detectives believe Christy Kinahan sanctioned the murder, after Devoy was linked to an attempt to kill Lynch outside Hanlon's pub on Dublin's North Circular Road, on 13 October 2013. Lynch, who was hit in the face and left with a permanent scar, had a lucky escape after using three innocent women as human shields. The three women were also extremely fortunate not to be killed that night.

As the authorities in Spain continued to examine thousands of documents and computer hard drives in 2010, in their quest to follow the cartel's trail of laundered cash across the globe, the focus for Operation Goldeneye remained the identification of those who were moving drugs and weapons for the cartel on the ground in Ireland.

In another file to the DPP outlining the work of the unit, gardaí maintained the 'remit' of the investigators was to:

> . . . specifically target an organized crime gang who are also involved in the importation of firearms which are used as the 'tools of the trade' to enforce and copper-fasten their criminal enterprise within the area of this illegal drugs trade operating within the South Central Division.

As the unit maintained its work on the streets of the Irish capital, detectives received intelligence that the cartel was still actively involved in importing arms into Ireland.

On 22 September 2010, the unit was tipped off that a Paul

O'Neill, who was unknown to gardaí, was involved in storing weapons for the cartel at his place of work. Born on 7 September 1972, O'Neill lived with his mother and brother at Smithfield Terrace, in Dublin city centre.

A father of a teenage boy and girl, for twenty years O'Neill had been employed at a recycling company in west Dublin. Working as a forklift operator and earning €430 per week, his only contact with gardaí was in July 2010 when he was cautioned for refusing to pay his motor tax. Like many others, O'Neill, who was battling a cocaine addiction, was viewed as easy prey by the cartel. He was offered the chance to earn some cash by holding drugs and firearms, and he succumbed to temptation.

Moving swiftly to obtain a warrant, the specialist unit sent experienced Detective Garda Richard Kelly, also now retired, to undertake surveillance at O'Neill's workplace. O'Neill left the facility in a silver Peugeot 207 at 4.15 p.m., driving the short distance to the Lidl supermarket car park in Clonee village, County Meath.

Leaving his car unlocked, O'Neill spent fifteen minutes placing bets at a local bookmaker's before returning to his vehicle and driving back to work. Once there, he was observed leaving a black laptop bag in the boot of his car before bringing another one into a small blue Portakabin.

The forklift driver left his employers at 5.05 p.m. and drove along the N3 towards Mulhuddart, in west Dublin. Closely followed by gardaí, his car was intercepted at 5.10 p.m. when officers from the Garda's heavily armed Emergency Response Unit (ERU) surrounded the vehicle. Once secured, the Goldeneye investigators recovered the black laptop bag. Inside they discovered two Ingram sub-machine guns, two silencers, four loaded magazines and 9mm ammunition.

O'Neill was immediately arrested by Detective Garda Linda Williams for the unlawful possession of firearms and brought to Kevin Street Garda Station in the south inner city for questioning.

The following morning, Detective Sergeant Adrian White-law, one of the capital's most experienced gangland investigators, returned to the recycling facility to search the Portakabin. He discovered another two Ingram weapons, two silencers, four loaded magazines and a quantity of loose 9mm ammunition. During the search, Detective Garda Richard Kelly recovered €31,500 worth of cocaine hidden in a metal cabinet used to store maintenance tools.

During his interrogation, O'Neill admitted that he had received a telephone call on 21 September to his mobile from an 'unknown' male instructing him to transport the cocaine to a location that would be disclosed to him in another call the following morning. When the call duly arrived, he was told where to park his car and to leave it 'unlocked' and 'take a walk for fifteen minutes' before he would receive another call informing him the item was in the boot.

Held over the next two days, O'Neill would also admit in his interviews to hiding bags of cocaine in a filing cabinet at work and using the facility to cut and bag cocaine on six previous occasions. He disclosed that he earned €200 for each successful drop.

In a prosecution file sent to the Director of Public Pros-ecutions, gardaí maintained O'Neill had made:

> ... full and frank admissions, however the specifics con-cerning the identity of the persons involved in this organized crime gang were not elaborated on by Paul O'Neill and it is the belief of investigating gardaí that Paul O'Neill holds a

genuine fear of the repercussions he would face if he were to disclose the identity of these persons.

As part of their probe, officers also outlined O'Neill's position within the gang:

It is obvious that Paul O'Neill plays an active part in the mechanism of this organized criminal enterprise [. . .] He can be considered a vital cog in the wheel of this criminal gang as he knowingly facilitates the transportation, storage and preparation of firearms and controlled drugs for these persons.

He is clearly motivated by financial gains to be made carrying out the orders which emanate from the top echelons of this crime gang. It is through his own admissions that this assertion is without doubt, as he has transported either drugs or firearms for this organized crime gang on at least three occasions prior to this incident coming to light.

O'Neill was not at the higher echelons of the criminal organization but through his willingness to accept responsibility for the transportation of weapons and drugs, this made him a valuable asset to the criminal gang. He continued to feature in this criminal organization as he would not only have been considered below the Garda radar but was also in a position of trust at [his workplace], which provided him with the opportunity of using this facility as a base to store illegally held drugs and firearms.

The discovery of the Ingram sub-machine guns, the first time they had featured in Dublin's gangland scene, was a major breakthrough for investigators. The weapons, often used by Mexican drug cartels for attacks on rivals in drive-by shootings, were considered as 'particularly lethal' because of their ability to fire 1,200 rounds per minute. 'Their potential use by criminals involved in the illegal drugs trade was most definitely a very worrying development,' according to investigating officers in their file to the DPP. The file explained:

> The Ingram firearm is an extremely deadly weapon and it was the firm belief of investigating gardaí that should these firearms have been deployed on public streets, the consequences of discharging such a weapon in a public place would have been devastating to not only the intended target but also innocent bystanders alike. It is clear that these firearms were destined to be part of the gang's arsenal and were to be used to intimidate, control and enforce the workings of their illicit drugs trade.

Former Detective Superintendent O'Gara also describes the seizure as a 'great success':

> These firearms were destined for criminals working on behalf of the Kinahan cartel. The damage and fatalities these weapons could have caused is unimaginable. Can you imagine if these weapons had been available to the cartel in 2016 as part of their feud with the Hutch gang? There would have been further bloodshed.

During O'Neill's trial, on 28 November 2011, Detective Garda Linda Williams told Dublin Circuit Court it was her belief the weapons were to be used by a major organized crime gang in the south inner-city area of Dublin.

In sentencing O'Neill to a five-year jail term, Judge Martin Nolan claimed O'Neill had been 'sucked into' a criminal enterprise. 'This was an incredibly serious offence and the accused has paid a heavy price for his involvement,' explained the Judge. 'He was used by a criminal gang because of his addictions.'

Anyone charged with possessing firearms can normally expect a sentence ranging from five to ten years. The DPP's file in this case outlined the serious nature of the offence because the weapons were destined for a major organized crime gang, but there have also been cases in the past where a judge has shown leniency to those with addictions and from vulnerable backgrounds.

Operation Goldeneye had successfully caused serious disruption to the activities of the cartel. The initiative ended in the summer of 2011, however, due to lack of funding and resources from the Government.

'It was unfortunate that the subsequent embargo on public service spending impacted on available resources,' explained O'Gara. 'The unit that was drawn together was reassigned to their districts and other duties.'

Although the specialist team's work had concluded, investigations into ways of breaking the cartel continued.

13. Streamlining

'After a few months, they got out on bail and they regrouped.'

Senior Garda investigator

In one sense, the cartel was almost better off when Operations Shovel and Goldeneye were over. The expensive round-the-clock surveillance could no longer be maintained in Spain or Ireland once the raids had taken place, and both campaigns had to be stopped. But gang members had learned from their mistakes and were highly unlikely to say anything of note on the phone, now they knew they had been under such scrutiny.

While Christy remained behind bars in Belgium, Daniel and John Cunningham took up the reins of the business in his absence. According to one senior garda, who has investigated the cartel's activities in Spain, once the fuss of Operation Shovel had died down, the gang members were soon back in business. He commented:

> They went to ground, as they were waiting to see what was going to happen with the investigation. But after a few months, they got out on bail and they regrouped. They knew they might be under surveillance this time, and they were a lot more careful, particularly on the phone.

The cartel could not allow the grass to grow under their

feet either. Any prolonged absence from such a cut-throat industry would soon see a competitor emerge to fill the void. But while they busied themselves building back up their drugs and arms network, Daniel was also devoting more time to extra-curricular activities.

When Birmingham-born professional boxer 'Tipperary Tornado' Matthew Macklin set up the MGM (Macklin's Gym Marbella) in 2012, following two narrow defeats in title fights for the WBA (World Boxing Association) and WBC (World Boxing Council) middleweight belts, the elder Kinahan lad saw an opportunity to climb the social ladder.

Daniel set up as manager of his own stable of fighters, operating out of the MGM. They quickly became recognized as a force to be reckoned with by the boxing fraternity. The uncomfortable truth about who was acting as manager, however, was rarely mentioned in coverage by boxing publications. When asked about Kinahan's involvement by the authors, Macklin, who has no involvement in criminality, insisted he knew nothing about his associate's widely reported activities.

Former Irish Olympian Paddy Barnes would also land himself in hot water when he declared Daniel could sit in his corner for his next fight after he signed for MGM Promotions, following a disappointing Olympic tournament in Rio de Janeiro, in 2016.

The remarks were enough to earn Barnes a rare rebuke from his old Beijing boxing teammate, Kenneth Egan. Egan, who won a silver medal at the 2008 Olympics in Beijing, is one of Ireland's best-known amateur boxers and is a regular TV panellist during the Olympics.

Egan, now a Fine Gael councillor in his native Clondalkin, west Dublin, described the comments as 'naive' and 'ignorant', adding that Barnes possibly was not fully aware of the cartel's activities, as he was from Belfast.

In an interview with the *Sunday Business Post*, Barnes said he had doubts over the extent of the gym's association with Daniel Kinahan. He said:

> MGM is Matthew Macklin. He is the founder of the gym; he is my manager and he'll be looking after me. I have nothing to do with any criminality. Matthew Macklin is not a criminal. I am not a criminal. So, if anyone wants to talk about criminality and about Daniel Kinahan and Christy Kinahan, they should go ask them themselves. I don't know anything about the Kinahans, I only know Matthew Macklin. But what has Daniel Kinahan been convicted of?

Barnes later accepted he was unaware of media reports about Daniel's gangland activity, but true to his mischievous manner, he posted a photo on Twitter of himself with Daniel at an MGM event in Portugal, adding: 'Didn't even know we had a picture together! Sure to cause a shit storm.'

Meanwhile, Daniel Kinahan had brazenly presented his credentials as a legitimate sporting figure in an interview with *Boxing Monthly*. Describing himself as a security firm owner who supplied staff to Marbella's bars, clubs and restaurants, Daniel boasted he was the real power behind MGM's rise to prominence. He was regularly described as a 'manager' for various fighters, despite not holding the required licence for such a position.

In the same interview, he outlined how he had come to know Macklin in the first place:

> I had never met Macklin, although I knew of him. I only met him after the Jamie Moore fight, in September 2006. He came

over a week after the fight. I met him at the airport and from there we became friends. Matthew is probably my best friend.

In another attention-seeking move Daniel also created his own Twitter account where he held forth on boxing, the movie *The Godfather* and the other daily inanities which typically appear on social media. It was a far cry from the actions of his publicity-shy, 'old school' father. In marked contrast, Christy once rang his Dutch partner to get her to take down all the photos her son had posted of Christy, Daniel and Chris Jr on Facebook. The patriarch is rarely seen in public. The only times he has been seen in recent years are when he is appearing in court.

In some ways, Daniel had faithfully adopted the evasive tactics of his criminal father, both on the phone and in public. When venturing outside, he often wore a baseball cap or some other type of headgear, to lessen the chance of being recognized. But while few photos of his father exist, the man known as 'Rasher' to close pals happily poses for any image that links him to the macho world of boxing or martial arts. A keen amateur fighter himself, Daniel loves the glamour that comes from mixing with professionals of the sport.

Criminal gangs tend to favour cash-based businesses, such as pubs and taxi companies, to launder money, as incomes can be greatly exaggerated. However, Daniel's lust for attention saw the gang set up its own publishing wing. In a sardonic nod to the press which had given the Kinahans so much unwanted publicity after Operation Shovel, one of their firms was called Toxic Publications SL. Daniel also styled himself the publisher of an English-language sports monthly, *Score Magazine*, which was distributed free across the Costa del Sol and in London.

Toxic Publications SL is on the list of the companies investigated by police and was referred to in the Shovel files as a firm which police believe may have functioned as another front company for the cartel. One of its administrators was the English boyfriend of Daniel's Spanish secretary.

It is unclear what financial benefits the publishing or boxing ventures actually offered the cartel. They may well have just been another means by which Daniel could raise his social profile.

The following year Christopher Jr and Daniel posed in a typical fighter's stance in promotional shots for the programme of a white-collar boxing event being held at the four-star H10 Andalucía Plaza Hotel. The proceeds of the evening, which was organized under the patronage of the MGM gym, were to go to Aspandem, a local special needs charity.

It is doubtful the organization was aware of the true nature of some of those who had attached themselves to its cause. The printed programme included a small pen picture of the pair, with Daniel grandly describing himself as 'MGM general manager'.

The programme also stated that the two brothers would fight on the night. The boxing matches were part of the event and both Kinahans won their fights.

'I've been involved since the start so it was about time I got in the ring,' Daniel declared. When asked to say something interesting about himself, he replied, 'I used to be a Liverpool supporter.'

Christopher Junior was less forthcoming. Giving his profession as 'researcher', he explained he had decided to fight because he 'wanted to test myself in a different environment'. Urged to give readers an indication of his character, Junior was self-deprecating. 'Everyone finds me uninteresting, even me,' he answered.

As well as being the quieter of the two siblings, Junior also lacked his older brother's need for attention. Like his father, not many pictures of him exist. Apart from his one-off appearance at the white-collar event, Junior shied away from publicity and concentrated on getting the cartel's money-laundering wing back on track.

According to a senior garda, with many years' experience of investigating the cartel, 'they were looking at other ways to launder their cash. They were really concerned about their money; that CAB might go after it, or the Spanish.'

While operations and shipments continued to run through-out 2012, it was clear the cartel was not as successful as before. Intelligence indicated that the gang was feeling the pinch in a recession-hit continent.

Immediately after his release from prison in Belgium, in 2013, Christy Kinahan had a meeting with his two main debt collectors, Paul Rice and Gerard 'Hatchet' Kavanagh. The word went out: all debts were being called in. Over the next few months, Rice and Kavanagh travelled over and back between Spain and Dublin, visiting anyone who owed money to the cartel and putting the squeeze on them to pay up.

Both thugs were well suited to the task. Gerard Kavanagh had been a drug dealer since his early twenties and was just twenty-five years old when he landed himself a four-year jail sentence, in March 1994. He had been caught red-handed in a park in Harold's Cross, south Dublin, with IR£3,500 worth of heroin and cannabis and IR£1,300 in cash stuffed into his pockets.

Cops estimated at the time that Kavanagh was making up

to IR£50,000 a week from his operation and had paid IR£65,000 cash for a house in Mayberry Park, in Tallaght. 'Hatchet' had up to ten dealers working for him. He kept in touch with them via mobile phone, with calls costing up to 50p a minute in those technologically backward days.

Few would dare cross him. Kavanagh was a keen boxer, and was not above using his fists outside the ring if it came down to it.

Rice had a similar pedigree. On 6 December 1993, he held up a publican at gunpoint, but escaped with just IR£460. Eleven days later, he stuck a sawn-off shotgun in a Securicor worker's face. His victim had collected cash from a Supervalu supermarket and Rice made off with IR£14,360.

In January 1994, however, Rice slipped up big time. He had been promised IR£15,000 to act as getaway driver for the hold-up at the Bank of Ireland in Kill o' the Grange, south Dublin. He did his job and the gang made off with an undisclosed amount, after shots were fired and a security guard was hit with a lump hammer.

Rice dumped the vehicle a few miles away at the Pineview Riding School, in Rathfarnham. He and a fellow raider put on helmets and rode off into a forest on two horses, past gardaí searching for the gang. He was arrested a few days later because a garda recalled seeing him on horseback.

Rice was sentenced to ten years for the bank robbery, with seven-year terms following for the Supervalu and publican stick-ups. In another example of the sentencing which infuriates gardaí, these seven-year terms were to run concurrently with the ten-year tariff, which itself had the last three years suspended. With remission for good behaviour normally reducing a sentence by one quarter, this meant Rice would serve just five years and three months for all three armed robberies.

Since then, Kavanagh and Rice had become the men the cartel sent to put the frighteners on those they felt owed them money. Most of the debtors Rice and Kavanagh were chasing in Ireland for the cartel were small-time dealers or junkies who would either cough up out of fear, or go into hiding if they had no money.

There was one dealer, however, who owed a significant amount but he could not or would not pay. Christopher 'Git' Russell was a Dublin criminal who owed Christy Kinahan €2 million. The Dapper Don wanted his money but Russell insisted the cash was tied up in a separate second-hand car business he was using to launder it.

On top of that, Russell, who a High Court judge described as having 'extensive links' to 'the upper levels of crime', was being actively pursued by the Criminal Assets Bureau. He pleaded for more time to settle. The cartel's response was to send Rice and Kavanagh to threaten him with a bullet.

Rice had bought Kavanagh's old home in Mayberry Park, in Tallaght, after his colleague moved to Spain in 2001, and was largely tasked with pursuing Irish-based debts. Kavanagh would assist him, but also had responsibility for collecting cash on the Costa del Sol.

In July 2014, Kavanagh travelled from Spain to Crumlin to demand payment of what sources described as a 'relatively small' debt from a drug addict. When it was not forthcoming, 'Hatchet' gave the man a severe beating. Unable to pay and fearful of what was coming next, the junkie fled the city. Kavanagh returned to Spain and the enforcement business there, and began visiting English, Turkish and Russian criminals who owed the cartel money. At some point, however, the Drimnagh 'hard man' went too far.

At 4.30 p.m. on 6 September 2014, he arrived at Harmon's

Irish pub in Elviria, a short drive from Marbella, in the company of a young man. Kavanagh went inside and ordered two blackcurrant cordials. He returned to the terrace outside where the pair continued to chat at their table.

What happened next was caught by the pub's extensive CCTV system. A black BMW X5 pulled into the kerb outside the pub. Two black-clad men, wearing balaclavas and carrying handguns, jumped out, leaving the engine running.

They rushed towards the table where the two men were sitting. The video shows how Kavanagh, engrossed in conversation, did not notice them until the pair were a few feet away. He immediately leapt to his feet and ran the few yards to the pub's front door.

He was too late. One of the gunmen fired repeatedly after Kavanagh as he tried to push his way into the bar, hitting him several times in the back. He managed to stumble his way inside, where he collapsed on the floor and curled up in the foetal position.

The gunman stood over him and shot him several more times in the head and body. His body had so many entry and exit wounds – twenty-nine in total – even an autopsy was unable to tell how many bullets had hit him.

The shock in the pub was palpable. Two other customers in football shirts had been at the bar drinking and joking when Kavanagh burst in, with the gunman hot on his heels. The pair were so slow to react to what happened that the Guardia Civil initially suspected they might have been in on it. Neither of the men tried to check if Kavanagh was OK, simply picking up their drinks and edging away from his body. But though the duo were never traced after they fled the scene, cops don't believe they were involved, just simply too stunned to help.

Another suspect ruled out was the young man with whom Kavanagh had been chatting in the moments before his murder. In fact, only the young man's quick reflexes saved him from being killed. While the first gunman went after Kavanagh, the second turned his gun on his stunned companion, who leapt from his seat and ran in the other direction.

The trigger-happy assassin aimed a round after him which was later found buried in the fender of a nearby parked car. The two hitmen ripped off their masks as they fled, and witnesses told detectives one of the men was blond, with the other described as bald and chubby. Their BMW X5 was later found ablaze nearby.

Police briefly hoped the pair might be caught, as they had exposed their faces in their haste to get away. In the end, they were never found and the investigating judge put in charge of the case shelved it in June 2015, effectively meaning they probably never will be.

In any case, Kavanagh's murder was a professional hit. Of far more interest to gardaí probing the Kinahan gang was who had ordered it. Several initial theories arose, with a female associate of the terrified car dealer, 'Git' Russell, coming under the microscope. There were also rumours 'Hatchet' had been killed for skimming off some of the debts he was supposed to be collecting for the cartel.

The theory now given most credence by gardaí is that Kavanagh had stepped on too many toes during his debt chasing in Spain, and the blowback became too much to handle. It is believed a compromise deal was worked out with Christy, where 'Hatchet' would be sacrificed to settle a row with a group of Russian gangsters Kavanagh had insulted.

The Kinahans were noticeably absent from Kavanagh's funeral in Dublin, though leading Irish cartel figure Greg Lynch attended, as did Paul Rice, who carried Hatchet's coffin.

Just a few months earlier, Daniel and Christopher Jr had returned to Dublin for their mother's funeral. In her final years, Jean had moved to southern Spain to be with her sons and her grandchildren. She was said to have never approved of the lifestyle her two boys had chosen, but was powerless to prevent them following in the footsteps of the father they looked up to so much.

Jean Boylan was no fool and, at times, confronted her elder son about Christy's activities. In one incident, when Daniel called her the day after gardaí had seized €6.6m worth of cannabis from a van and a warehouse in Dunboyne, County Meath, he was met with a direct question.

'There's something in the paper about your father,' Jean said, without preamble.

'Again? What paper?' answered Daniel.

'In the *Sun*,' Jean said. 'All that hash that they seized was from the drugs godfather Christy Kinahan, who lived in Amsterdam. That was your father,' she added accusingly.

'It probably was him, Ma, you know what he's like,' Daniel laughed. 'Ah, I'm only messing with you. You know now they'll blame him for anything.'

He then asked his mother if there was a photograph of Christy accompanying the article, and was told there was not.

'OK, we'll talk later, alright?' said Daniel, hanging up.

The newspaper report was not inaccurate. Detectives believe the €6.6 million haul had been organized by Christy's associates in the south inner city.

When Jean died, in May 2014, her sons were to the fore, helping to carry her coffin into the well-attended ceremony, but Christy was notable by his absence. No reference was made to him, during the funeral or in the death notice.

Gardaí discreetly observed the service, as Daniel had ordered a squad of young local toughs to act as spotters around the church and the Oliver Bond complex. He was determined to keep the inquisitive away. When gardaí attempted to search several foreign-registered cars entering the complex, he emerged from his mother's flat with five well-built men, acting aggressively towards gardaí and calling them 'bullies'. He had to be persuaded to return inside by detectives, who warned him he would be arrested and taken away if he did not desist.

Investigating gardaí believe that Jean Boylan's death removed the last hope of any civilizing influence on her elder boy, as the Hutch family would discover to their cost in the years to come.

While the Kavanagh family and the Kinahan boys were in mourning, Christy had cause to celebrate. Spain is notorious for its bureaucracy and the natives have a rhyming proverb, *las cosas de palacio van despacio* (official wheels turn slowly), which they often quote to frustrated foreigners. The refrain is particularly true of the Spanish judicial system, where *investigados* can spend years waiting to find out if they will actually be charged with a crime.

Kinahan was finally called back before Judge Gutiérrez Henares in August 2014. She informed him he was no longer under investigation for arms or drugs trafficking. A thorough review of the evidence had convinced her that only the money-laundering charges would stick.

The dropping of the drug- and arms-trafficking probes came as no surprise to gardaí who were familiar with the Spanish end of Operation Shovel. The two-year surveillance campaign had been set up with the aim of catching the cartel red-handed running their drugs and arms business. It had failed.

Much of the drug-trafficking evidence presented by the police relied on linking a company, based in Murcia, south-eastern Spain, to the gang. The cartel used to transport their narcotics via companies based in Málaga which paid the Murcia firm's bills. But the cartel had been so successful in muddying the financial waters that Judge Gutiérrez Henares felt the accusation was shaky, and would not be enough to support a conviction.

The cartel's confidence that they would be let off the hook was illustrated by the way they had gone back to business – and agreed to the elimination of gang members such as 'Hatchet' Kavanagh who were no longer considered of use.

At his funeral, Kavanagh's coffin had been carried by several associates, including his brother Paul, who was almost twenty years his junior. Like his sibling, he was involved in drug dealing and debt collection and was quite close to Paul Rice.

He took over the job of receiving cash from 'Git' Russell following 'Hatchet' Kavanagh's demise. But just like his older brother, Paul Kavanagh was suspected by the cartel of keeping some of the money which had been given to him, in his case €100,000.

On 26 March 2015, 27-year-old Paul Kavanagh left the rented house he shared with his partner and two children on Church Avenue in Drumcondra, on Dublin's northside, at around 11.30 a.m. He had just got into the front seat of a

Volkswagen Passat when two men wearing balaclavas appeared and opened fire through the vehicle's windscreen.

The two assassins had clearly been waiting for their target to exit the property, but in their haste to flee the scene they crashed their stolen white Audi A1. The pair then set the car ablaze and ran off on foot down Gracepark Road. The Garda helicopter was deployed in a vain attempt to find them.

Hundreds attended Paul Kavanagh's funeral in Drimnagh, including UFC fighter Conor McGregor, a friend of boxer Jamie Kavanagh, Gerard 'Hatchet' Kavanagh's son. Again, however, the Kinahans were notable by their absence. The dead man's distraught partner, Gemma Roe, told mourners that 'the day his brother Gerard died, a part of Paul died too.'

This was merely the beginning of the bloodshed – a lot more deaths were coming.

14. Lighting the Fuse

'You cannot trust these people.'

Hutch family statement

Were it not for the locked gate, Gary Hutch might well have survived. The one-time cartel stalwart emerged from his apartment in the Angel de Miraflores complex, Estepona, wearing shorts and a bright orange T-shirt for a morning run at around 11.20 a.m. on 25 September 2015. He found a tall, masked man carrying a pistol awaiting him in the garage of the complex.

CCTV footage subsequently recovered by Spanish police showed the assassin had been hiding there since 8 a.m., patiently watching for his target. The killer approached Hutch and raised his gun to fire, only for it to jam.

Hutch fled. With a lead of several feet, the north inner-city criminal circled the adjoining pool with the hitman in hot pursuit, shooting continuously at him. Police would later extract several bullets from the walls nearby.

It was then Hutch made his fatal mistake. Panicking, he ran towards the back gate of the complex which led out on to waste ground, desperately seeking an escape route. The testimony of witnesses – who thought they were watching a terrorist atrocity – later revealed to police how close Hutch had come to getting away. But Hutch was out of luck, the large gate was firmly closed and locked. He turned back, frantically glancing around for another way out, but his tormentor was upon him. Hutch turned once again to flee and the gunman fired a shot into his back.

CCTV cameras, which had captured Hutch's sprint down the long driveway towards the locked gate, also caught the moment he was shot. He fell forward, as if he had tripped. The assassin fired the coup de grâce into Hutch's body from ten feet away.

The hitman was so exhausted after the chase that he was unable to run from the scene. Instead he was seen by neighbours trudging up the hill from the pool to the kerb where he had parked the silver BMW X3 in which he drove off.

The attempt to burn out the vehicle in Marbella, a ten-minute drive away, was partially foiled by an alert local, who saw the blazing car and ran out with a fire extinguisher. This allowed cops to retrieve a balaclava laden with the assassin's DNA, a mobile phone and two pistols from the car. The bullet ejected from the jammed gun in the garage was also recovered.

The murder of Gary Hutch took place in an area overseen by the Guardia Civil, but the BMW X3 used as the hitman's getaway car was dumped in an area controlled by the Policía Nacional. Even though the evidence garnered from the partially burnt-out car was a major breakthrough in the case, the Policía Nacional initially refused to hand it over in an episode which showed the levels of pettiness to which rivalries between the two forces could descend. In May 2014, two Policía Nacional agents had helped catch a gangland murderer who was also transporting cocaine in the area. The confrontation had taken place on Guardia Civil territory, so the investigation – and, it was felt, the glory from the arrest – was given to them, leaving Policía Nacional noses out of joint. Dragging their feet on handing over the BMW X3 seemed to be a passive-aggressive way for them to get revenge.

The evidence would prove crucial in securing a later arrest over the murder. But Hutch's criminal associates did not require any forensics to solve who was behind the crime. It was immediately clear to them who had ordered their friend's murder.

For Spanish police, Hutch's death was yet another in a grim series of such professional murders. It was the second gang-related assassination in the area in the space of twenty-four hours. The previous evening at 7 p.m., a Colombian criminal had been shot dead by a passing assassin on a motorbike. He was getting into his car on Aguila Street, near the centre of Mijas, when he was gunned down in what was quite evidently a planned hit.

As is so often the case, Hutch's neighbours had no idea who had been living amongst them, describing him as 'pleasant' but quiet. Gardaí who had investigated Gary Hutch's activities, both in Ireland and in Spain, for many years tell a different story.

Aged just eighteen, Gary Hutch acted as getaway driver for a gang which burst into the home of businessman Jeremy Byrne, in Malahide, in the early hours of 11 July 2000. Byrne and his wife woke up to find four masked men in the room, with one of them pointing a shotgun at the terrified couple.

Jeremy Byrne was handcuffed and dragged downstairs, where at gunpoint he was ordered to open his safe. The gang escaped with IR£32,000 worth of jewellery and IR£5,000 in cash. Hutch was given a six-year sentence for his role in the armed robbery when the case came to trial a year and a half later.

The term went on top of a four-year stretch he was already serving for stealing a motorbike. Hutch had been awaiting trial for that offence when he took part in the heist. His case featured in an article by the *Irish Independent*, highlighting the number of crimes being committed by suspected criminals who were out on bail.

Hutch had barely served the two sentences when he was before the courts on serious charges once more. In December 2006, he was arrested and charged with shooting a childhood acquaintance, Paul Reilly. He shot Reilly in the chest and back after a confrontation between the pair during one of Hutch's visits home from Spain.

Reilly gave a statement to gardaí saying Hutch had shot him after quizzing him over a missing gun. But when it came to trial, the victim changed his story completely. Reilly claimed he had told a 'pack of lies' to investigators because he had heard Hutch was sleeping with his girlfriend and wanted to get back at him.

'I thought I was going to die and I didn't want him to end up with my partner and my two kids,' Reilly said while being cross-examined during the trial. He then went on to insist he had taken crack cocaine shortly before he was shot and was hallucinating when he was talking to detectives. Asked why he had named Hutch to a detective while in hospital recovering from his wounds, he answered, 'I couldn't tell you. I could have said Mass and I wouldn't have known.'

Not surprisingly, Hutch was acquitted of the charge of possession of a firearm with intent to endanger life.

As Paddy Doyle would later learn, this would not be the only time Hutch would turn on a former friend.

Both Hutch and his younger brother Derek, aka 'Del Boy' Hutch, were suspects in the murder of drug dealer Derek

Duffy, in Finglas, in September 2007. Duffy, who was not aligned to any gang, was shot five times as he sat in his car, which his killers then tried to set alight.

'Del Boy' would subsequently be jailed for six years for stabbing another man to death at a house party. He then had another sixteen years added to that sentence for his role in a May 2009 robbery in Lucan, during which gardaí shot dead his accomplice, Gareth Molloy.

At that point, Gary Hutch was firmly embedded within the cartel, in which he was viewed as a trustworthy figure. He had been working with them since he was a teenager and was, of course, closely related to one of the city's most established criminals. Hutch was ambitious, however, and wanted to rise up the ranks. That would require money and Gary, who regularly bragged about his uncle Gerry 'the Monk' Hutch's armed robber past, knew exactly how to get it.

One night in February 2009, junior Bank of Ireland (BOI) employee Shane Travers was watching TV at the home of his girlfriend, Stephanie Smith, in Kilteel, in Kildare. Stephanie and her mother, Joan, were out shopping and Travers was babysitting his girlfriend's five-year-old nephew, who was asleep.

When Stephanie and her mother returned, a gang of six men were waiting for them just inside the gates. Dressed in black and wearing balaclavas, they ran at the two women, pointing their handguns at them. The terrified mother and daughter managed to get the front door open and tried to slam it in the gang's faces, but they were not strong enough to hold them back and the men forced their way in.

One of the men struck Joan in the face and threw her across the room. Her brave daughter tried to overpower one of the other thugs and was pistol-whipped. Shane Travers intervened to stop this happening and was also beaten.

The trio, who still had no idea what was happening, were tied up and had tape put over their eyes. The plan was then explained to them: Stephanie, her mother and the child would be held hostage the following morning while Shane would go to the College Green processing centre of the Bank of Ireland in Dublin city centre and take out as much money as he could carry.

To convince his colleagues to co-operate, Travers was given Polaroids of Stephanie with a pillow case over her head, plus one of another staff member's home. He was also handed a pay-as-you-go mobile phone on which the gang would call him and give him directions once he had the cash. Any deviation from the plan, the gang threatened, and they would 'blow her [Joan Smith's] head off' and Travers himself would be 'knee-capped'.

Left with no choice, Travers drove into the BOI processing centre adjoining the branch. He filled four laundry bags with €7.6 million in used notes and told one of his superiors what he was doing. Gardaí were not alerted, a major breach of agreed protocol which would cause serious issues in the days to come.

Travers drove his red Toyota Celica to Clontarf Dart Station, where he had been ordered to leave the car with the cash in the boot. He had been in constant phone contact with the raiders throughout, who ordered him to take a specific route.

The Smiths, who had been driven around in a van while the gang awaited the arrival of the cash, were dumped near Ashbourne, County Meath. They managed to free themselves, using a putty knife they found in the back of the van.

In the Dáil (Irish parliament) the following day, 28 February 2009, then Justice Minister Dermot Ahern severely criticized the Bank of Ireland for not following protocol and notifying gardaí when Shane arrived with the photos. The truth was the gang could have got away with a lot more money. Tens of millions of euros were stored at the processing centre, which is used to replenish bank branches and ATMs across the country.

During a Garda surveillance operation on a house at Great Western Villas in Phibsboro, north Dublin, €1.74 million of the cash was later recovered. A man called Mark Donoghue was spotted leaving the house carrying holdall bags, alongside another man. The pair got into separate cars before gardaí surrounded both vehicles. Donoghue fled, but at the junction of the N3 and the M50, he was blocked in by another patrol car and arrested. The €1.74 million was found in the boot of his Opel Astra.

Donoghue, a financially troubled construction boss from Longford, was given a five-year sentence for transporting the money. His trial heard he had been promised €5,000 for holding it and passing it onwards. Another man, 25-year-old Darren O'Brien from Gardiner Street, in Dublin city centre, was also charged with handling stolen cash. But he skipped bail, despite the lodgement of €150,000 with the courts.

Gary Hutch was one of seven men held and questioned in follow-up operations by gardaí after they received specific intelligence about his probable involvement. He kept his mouth shut while in custody and refused to co-operate with detectives. Upon his release, he wasted no time in investing most of his share of the €5.9 million which the gang had netted in the business he knew best – drug trafficking.

Proof of this came in September 2009, when gardaí raided a house in the middle-class Violet Hill Park estate, in Dublin's Glasnevin. A surveillance operation had watched as a taxi dropped off some bags there. Inside the suburban house they found 25kg of cocaine, mixing agents, a compressor and scales. The haul was conservatively worth €1.75 million.

Two men who had been hired to dilute the pure cocaine were subsequently jailed for their role. Garda intelligence later revealed that Gary Hutch was the wholesaler who had sold the cache to the man who had hired the pair.

Gardaí believed Gary Hutch was supplying a large amount of the drugs being sold in Dublin's north inner city. Despite his uncle's well-publicized anti-drugs stance, his nephew had gone into the trade in a big way. He was buying his merchandise wholesale from the Kinahans, before flooding the streets of his native area with heroin and cocaine. Some of his merchandise was also being sent onwards to Limerick City.

Drug seizures aside, these were good times for Hutch, who had become an established member of the cartel and was quite close to Daniel Kinahan. He had long hoped to rub shoulders with those at the top of the Irish gangland pile and he finally appeared to have achieved that ambition.

When Hutch interceded with Daniel to ensure 'Shooter' could escape the clutches of Eamon 'the Don' Dunne and move to the Costa del Sol, it was another example of his influence within the cartel. As he set up the arrangement Hutch had bragged that he'd had a previous run-in with Dunne himself and had 'put him in his place'. He insisted there was no way Dunne or his gang would now try anything against Shooter 'as they would know what they are getting into'.*

---

* In time, Shooter – by then one of the cartel's most effective hitmen – would reward Hutch's efforts on his behalf by shooting dead one of his uncles and a friend of another. But in 2009 this was all a long way off.

The Spanish investigators viewed this episode as proof of 'the great influence of the Kinahans' and it was clear that Hutch felt he himself had sizeable clout within the cartel. Despite this, Hutch was not above carrying out Dunne's dirty work when ordered to do so by Daniel.

When Christy Gilroy had been coaxed into moving to Spain in 2009, in the aftermath of the Michael 'Roly' Cronin and James Moloney murders, it was Hutch who had brought him to the expensive drug clinic and paid for his stay in cash. And when Gilroy checked out, never to be seen alive again, Gary Hutch was one of those who turned up to collect him.

One of Hutch's roles within the cartel saw both him and Mr A entrusted with important arms and drugs runs. These operations were under the direct supervision of Christy and John Cunningham, who they would meet for instructions beforehand.

On one such errand, in February 2010, the Spanish authorities listened in as the pair made their way to Portugal by car, Hutch following Mr A, never more than two or three miles close behind him.

The methodology was simple: both men would drive at speeds of over 120 miles per hour to flush out any possible tails, with Mr A acting as a decoy car who could warn Hutch of any impending problems; and the phone line between them would always be open.

On one operation, the Spanish police waited for the pair to pick up the drugs and weapons in Portugal, store them in the secret compartments of specially altered cars and return across the border. There police tried to intercept them, setting up roadblocks on the route they believed the two cartel members would use. The cops were out of luck, however, and both cars evaded capture. The haul Hutch and Mr A had collected was ultimately sent onwards to Britain and Ireland through France and Holland, using the same vehicles, driven by Irish gofers carrying fake documents.

Hutch was provided with a range of high-powered cars by the Kinahans, always registered in the name of Spanish civilians. These included a Bentley coupé, a Jaguar XK8, a BMW 3 Series, an Audi A3 and a VW Golf R32.

Hutch had been a car thief and joyrider in his youth, and high-speed jaunts remained a fixation. He would occasionally use the powerful cars to which he had access to drive at speeds of up to 125 miles per hour on the AP7 motorway between Estepona and Marbella, often while stoned.

The episodes both bemused and concerned watching Spanish cops, who began to wonder if Hutch had some sort of death wish. They also angered other gang members using the cars, who were concerned about the vehicles coming to police attention.

The gangster's familiarity with cars saw him handed the job of procuring vehicles which would then have the secret compartments added to them, to facilitate carrying hidden cash and drugs. Hutch oversaw several different gang-controlled workshops across Spain, particularly in Málaga, which worked full-time on such endeavours.

As would be expected from a criminal of his experience, Gary Hutch was circumspect about chatting on the phone. Workshops would be referred to as 'that tyre place', while other calls were replete with mentions of 'that thing', 'this area', 'that guy' and so on.

He was aware that chatter about his Spanish activities could get back to Garda ears and told one associate to warn people not to be gossiping about his 'lifestyle' on the Costa. This caution came shortly after he received a call from an unidentified pal back in Dublin. The friend joked that he was 'hearing things' about Gary out in Spain, how he was smoking a lot of cannabis and had 'gone crazy' since splitting from the mother of his children. It was a reputation guaranteed to raise the hackles of Christy Kinahan and John Cunningham, but Hutch did not seem bothered enough to change his lifestyle.

It was obvious he was enjoying himself on the Costa del Sol, having become accustomed to a different sort of existence to the life he had back in Dublin. Cops looked on as he visited the upmarket El Corte Inglés department store, akin to a Spanish Brown Thomas, purchasing cashmere sweaters to change his look.

He boasted in phone calls to his cousin that he was seeing the daughter of a senior officer in Spain's paramilitary Guardia Civil and that her father was not too happy about it. He even bragged the girl was trying to get him off a fine for not wearing a seat belt.

'Her auld fella is a copper . . . with like the army old bill over here,' he laughed down the phone to Ireland. 'I swear to God . . . thirty-two-year with like the greens over here. He's one of them he is. Her brother as well is a copper.'

As befitting his status, Hutch also had ready access to false documents. In April 2010, he approached the Irish embassy in Madrid to renew his passport. Embassy officials became suspicious about some of the details he had provided, however, and denied his request.

The gangster was subsequently recorded on the phone to a British man asking about getting 'the red things', a reference to acquiring fake passports. He discussed flying to Belgium to attend a boxing match, shortly afterwards, but the trip was ultimately cancelled by the volcanic ash cloud.

Towards the end of that same April, Hutch was hauled over by cops at a tollbooth. He was returning from dropping off Daniel at Málaga Airport and was charged with driving at 137 miles per hour. His licence was promptly confiscated, but the following day, he was again pulled over and produced a fake Italian driver's permit, which was detected and seized.

Worried, he rang a pal in Dublin and told him he was facing either six months in prison or a €1,800 fine. 'They also stopped me for speeding this week and when they put my name in the computer, something came up,' he whined. 'I've no passport and they've taken my licence for eight months.'

The Spanish Shovel team considered him a high-ranking figure within the cartel. The files declared:

> Gary Hutch is just under Daniel Kinahan in the organization's hierarchy. He is Daniel's right-hand man and transmits Daniel's orders to members of a lower rank.
>
> It can be inferred from telephone tapping and surveillance operations that as a result of Hutch's responsibilities within the organization, he is often in contact with other members of the organization. He carries out duties as a bodyguard, chauffeur and sometimes he is simply a messenger for the top members.
>
> He also monitors possible smuggling operations, transfers and stores narcotic drugs, etc. He always works under Daniel's orders. The analysis of phone conversations makes it clear we have before us a perfectly hierarchical and structured criminal organization in which each member, including Gary, has well-defined tasks.

Gary's relationship with Daniel had long transcended the professional to the personal. On one occasion, Hutch, along with Kevin Lynch, Bernard Clancy and their boss, were observed by police taking water-ski lessons on a yacht thought to be owned by Daniel, despite – typically – being registered in someone else's name. When Daniel spoke to his younger brother about his fears of leaks over press reports of the failed gangster summit at a boxing match, it was Gary he rang next. 'There's an article in the *Star* talking about you, me and the old man, saying we're meeting all the criminal gangs,' he told him.

Hutch was clearly anxious to please his boss. When Daniel's baby daughter was born, he rang the proud dad, asking if he should bring flowers to the hospital to give to the child's mother.

The gang were regular users of cocaine on nights out, but even they were not immune to receiving a bad batch of narcotics. In February 2010, Daniel was given some drugs by a McAvoy associate for his personal use, but they had the opposite of the desired effect. He confessed down the phone to the man that the substance had made him paranoid and he had had to go home.

When Hutch heard about this, he texted Daniel to tell him 'don't take that shit, man, it's not good.' When Daniel appeared unimpressed by his warning, Hutch's tone became almost pleading: 'Believe me, mate,' he said. 'That shit's no good, trust me.'

But while Gary Hutch was close with Daniel and Chris Jr, he could be treated with casual contempt by their father. In November 2009, Hutch was dispatched from Marbella to Madrid Airport to pick up Kinahan Senior from one of his frequent trips abroad. It was a six-and-a-half-hour drive and, upon arrival, a disoriented Hutch rang for further instructions. He received only vague directions to 'check the arrivals board for flights arriving from Shanghai or Hong Kong, or somewhere like that'.

Having cooled his heels around the terminal for a further five hours, Hutch then received a phone call at 2 a.m. to tell him Christy had decided to make his own way home, leaving him to do likewise.

Such behaviour was typical of Kinahan, who viewed all of those under his control as being at his beck and call. One senior garda familiar with Christy's attitude towards lesser-ranking gang members said the Kinahan patriarch probably just could not be bothered listening to Hutch, who would have viewed the journey as an opportunity to build rapport with his boss. The garda explained:

> He often looks down on members of his organization because they aren't on a par with him. He treated them with disdain and that was an example of this. Rather than wait for Hutch, Kinahan made his own way and the feeling among the investigators was because he probably didn't want to listen to Hutch rambling on because they were on totally different wavelengths.

Discussions taped between Christy and one of the English gang members revealed he considered Hutch to be 'hard work'. The Englishman believed this was because of Hutch's cannabis habit. 'Even Gary wants to quit because he needs to focus on something else,' he remarked.

This, however, appeared something of a stumbling block for Hutch, who was regularly recorded either talking about or ordering cannabis. A typical evening would see Gary smoking several joints, while texting pals back home about Jedward or Ronan Keating. He would then jump in the shower and head out to meet other members of the gang in the bars around Puerto Banús. Several lines of cocaine would ensure the party continued until well after dawn. In typical behaviour Hutch had passed the time on the long drive back from his fool's errand to Madrid smoking joint after joint, ringing Mr A to tell him he was driving at 135 miles per hour and was 'completely stoned'.

It was this kind of behaviour which made the gang, particularly Christy and John Cunningham, feel Hutch was not entirely trustworthy. He was a heavy user of steroids and would frequently boast about all the 'sters' he was taking while complaining they left his nipples feeling tender.

Career criminals are invariably caught in two ways: they become sloppy, or someone else rats them out. The Kinahans and John Cunningham have long been ultra-guarded against the first, and vigilant to the point of paranoia against the second. It was inevitable Hutch would come under suspicion in the wake of the Operation Shovel raids. The main strike against him was that he was in Holland at the time, even though Hutch had travelled there on 11 May on Daniel's orders. The fact that Hutch was later formally placed under investigation by a judge, along with the rest of the gang, did not dispel the uncertainty either.

Hutch continued to be a member of the cartel, but it was no longer the arrangement of old. Operation Shovel had ramped up the suspicion and paranoia that usually ran through the cartel, with the slightest incidents now being pored over for evidence of disloyalty. Senior figures would test the loyalties of underlings by feeding them tall tales to see if they resurfaced elsewhere.

Hutch had it worse than most, however. The 'rat' tag haunted him and he was eventually accused, most probably by Christy, Cunningham or Daniel, of being an informant because of a number of drugs seizures in Britain. He was fingered over the capture by police of a massive €10 million shipment of ketamine and cannabis, hidden in a van packed with frozen food, in Cheshire, in February 2014.

The successful operation had to have been the result of very specific intelligence, and it was obvious to the cartel someone was talking to police. Hutch, despite his protestations of innocence, became the chief suspect. He remained within the cartel, but more embarrassment followed.

When Daniel and Christopher Jr's mother, Jean Boylan, died in Dublin, in May 2014, a few months later, graffiti was scrawled outside a church near where her remains were due to be cremated at Mount Jerome cemetery. It labelled Gary Hutch a 'rat' and accused him of setting up a jailed former pal who was a relatively minor criminal. Gardaí believe this was an attempt by someone to paint Hutch in a bad light ahead of the funeral, and it did little to quell the rumours.

Hutch was also reportedly increasingly putting pressure on Daniel to see a return on the tiger raid money he had invested in drugs with the cartel and was said to be 'mouthing off' about his unhappiness to anyone who would listen. He was aware Daniel had double-crossed a Dutch gangster in a drug deal, and Kinahan was worried his loose tongue would cause the cartel serious problems. The tension between the two former pals was ratcheting up all the time.

Then came the incident which would cost him his life. In August 2014, former European light middleweight champion boxer Jamie Moore was leaving Daniel Kinahan's Estepona villa, in the early hours of the morning, when he was shot twice by a gunman wearing a Frankenstein mask.

Moore, who was shot in the hip and leg, initially thought it was a joke when confronted by the man in the mask. The former boxing champion almost bled to death. Only the fact that he had charged his phone, enabling him to call an ambulance, saved his life.

It was evident that Moore, who has no involvement in crime, was not the real target. Spanish police initially blamed 'Russian and Ukrainian' gangs, hinting that it was Daniel who was the real target. Gardaí agreed on this point, but differed on who had carried out the shooting. They believed it was a rash attempt by Gary Hutch to take out the man who was by now the de facto head of the cartel. Only the gunman blew it.

It was obvious to Daniel that the shooting was an attempt on his life, and he did not take long to figure out who was behind it.

In the meantime, he was quick to take advantage of the attempted murder of the innocent boxer. His Spanish lawyer, Javier Arias, publicly announced Kinahan would be seeking armed police protection as he was 'in fear for his life'.

Subsequent to the shooting of Gerard 'Hatchet' Kavanagh a month later, police explored the possibility that Moore had been shot by mistake when Kavanagh was the intended target. However, Arias insisted Kavanagh had 'no personal or working relationship' with Daniel Kinahan. 'The only link between Daniel and Gerard Kavanagh is that they're Irish,' he said.

Gardaí and Spanish police viewed the announcement about seeking police protection as a cynical ploy by Daniel to be able to claim victimhood in his upcoming trial. His request was denied.

Having once been a trusted member of the Kinahan mob, Hutch was under no illusions about what lay ahead. He fled

Spain for Holland and sought the protection of his uncle, the respected criminal figure Gerry 'the Monk' Hutch.

Normally in the criminal underworld, anyone suspected of having been 'turned' by the police would simply have been wiped out, never mind what would happen to a gang member who tried to kill his boss. But Hutch was from Irish criminal royalty. Killing him would have serious repercussions for the cartel's operations in Dublin. So it was that the 'Monk' and the Kinahans met in Amsterdam in 2015, for discussions on how the matter would be handled.

A deal was brokered, €200,000 'compensation' was handed over and Gary Hutch returned to Spain, sure the threat against him had been lifted. Hutch's misplaced confidence was in part due to his uncle's underworld clout. But, like many before him, on 25 September 2015 Gary learned that the cartel played by its own rules.*

In an unprecedented statement to the media after Gary Hutch's murder and the subsequent feud outbreak, the Hutches revealed their fury at the Kinahans' treachery. They told the *Sunday Times* newspaper:

> Gary had a falling out with the Kinahan organization. This matter was resolved and €200,000 in cash was paid over to the Kinahans. We shook hands and agreed to walk away.

* Hutch's friend and former associate, Martin Cervi, kept away from Gary's funeral. Once a key figure in both the Kinahan and Hutch gangs, nobody could have predicted what side Christy's 'third son' would have chosen when the two factions went to war. In the years after the Salinger killing, Cervi had distanced himself from both the Kinahan and Hutch gangs, often operating his own scams. He spent huge amounts of time along the eastern side of Spain and in Holland, and would only make rare visits to his hometown. Following his death from a suspected heart attack, in Holland, on 6 March 2016, the question of Martin's loyalty would go unanswered.

Gary was then murdered for no reason. You cannot trust these people.

Having taken care of Gary, the Kinahans then went after his brother, Derek 'Del Boy' Hutch. Gary had previously used his position within the cartel to make sure his brother was protected from the then all-powerful Real IRA, while he awaited sentence behind bars for his role in the cash van robbery. But after Gary's murder those who had watched his back were out to kill him.

Two weeks later, Derek Hutch was attacked in the exercise yard of Mountjoy Prison by two brothers. He received slash wounds to his arms from crude 'shiv' weapons, before three prison officers stepped in to rescue him. The incident was seen as a warning to 'Del Boy', rather than an attempt to kill him: he was to forget about any thoughts of avenging his brother's death. The cartel was confident they had made their point, but the message had not got through to some of Gary Hutch's old cronies.

On 7 November 2015, several members of the cartel, including Daniel, had gathered at the Red Cow Moran Hotel in Clondalkin, south Dublin. They had gathered ahead of a fight organized by MGM Promotions at the National Boxing Stadium the next day.

Cartel member Liam Roe was outside having a cigarette when a car pulled up and a handgun was aimed at him. Although connected to the cartel because of his ties to the Byrnes and Mr A, Roe is regarded by gardaí as a lower-level enforcer and driver. His only convictions are for minor offences. Detectives believe he is more concerned with his tan, white teeth and designer clothes than becoming directly involved in the cartel's operations. When they raided his home, in May 2016, due to his associations with his first cousins, Liam and David Byrne, they found dozens of pairs of expensive trainers, leading some cops to nickname him 'Imelda Marcos'.

Garda intelligence indicated Liam Byrne was the real target of the killers, who had only pointed their weapon at Roe because they recognized him. Fortunately for him, the gun jammed and Roe and the other cartel figures, including Daniel, scattered.

The incident was not reported to gardaí, who learned about it via informants. It was abundantly clear the Hutch gang was not going to take Gary's murder lying down.

In December, the cartel went after 'Del Boy' Hutch again. Hutch was in his cell in Mountjoy when two other inmates, armed with a shiv, came in and wrestled him on to his bunk. They were about to begin their attack when Hutch was saved by a familiar face.

Craig White, who was serving life for the 2005 murder of Noel Roche, which he had carried out with Paddy Doyle, waded into the cell with another prisoner and fought off the attackers. It was clear Hutch was not safe in Mountjoy and he was moved to Wheatfield Prison.

With Gary Hutch's brother out of reach, the cartel moved against his uncle. The 'Monk' had been spending much of his time living on the Canary Island of Lanzarote since his 'retirement' from crime. He had an apartment there and would fly out from chilly Dublin for months at a time during the winter.

On New Year's Eve, Gerry Hutch was in an Irish pub in Lanzarote. Shortly after he left the premises, two masked men entered the bar looking for him, but their target was already gone.

The Hutches claimed they had held more meetings with the Kinahans on the Continent following Gary Hutch's murder, in an effort to avoid further bloodshed, during which the cartel had demanded a further €200,000 in cash.

The statement to the *Sunday Times* newspaper continued:

> The Kinahan organization have attempted to kill Gerard on several occasions in recent months. We are being terrorized by the cartel. Kinahans' representatives said members of our family would be killed, or forced to leave their homes and Ireland if their demands for money were not met. Our extended family are under threat from these people.

As a PR stunt, it was not a bad move. There are no innocent parties in gangland, though the Hutch mob certainly seemed to be more sinned against than sinning in this feud. Certainly, the cartel seemed intent on pressing the matter as far as it could.

Gary Hutch's funeral had heard calls from his family for no retaliation. 'We don't wish our pain on any other family, let God be our judge,' a female relative said, in a prepared statement read from the altar.

But what was said in public did not necessarily correlate to what Hutch's aggrieved associates were planning in private, as everyone in Ireland was about to find out.

15. Clash of the Clans

'The ironic thing is that if Byrne hadn't stopped to
look for where his boss Daniel Kinahan was in the
hotel he might still be alive today.'

Security source on the Regency Hotel attack

It was not the type of interview boxer Vaidas Balciauskas
had imagined he'd be giving after a boxing weigh-in. The
fighter, from Lithuania, had been looking forward to the
'Clash of the Clans' event at Dublin's National Boxing Stadium, on 6 February 2016. All the participants had gathered
at the Regency Hotel, in north Dublin, for what was supposed to be the usual photographed weigh-in to publicize
the fight night a day later.

When the boxer spoke to the media twenty-four hours
before he was due to showcase his talents, however, there
was no mention of boxing. Instead, his interview focused on
the miraculous escape he, along with many others, had had
at the Regency Hotel only a few hours earlier. He explained:

I heard the shots . . . bang, bang, bang and then everybody
ran. Everyone was just worried about their lives. It was
shocking, very shocking. Everyone was trying to survive
and there was screaming everywhere. Of course I was
scared. I came here to fight – not for the shooting. I had to
run for my life and it was terrible.

The boxer's close friend David, also from Lithuania, was on his first trip to Ireland. He revealed his trauma, commenting:

> It was very shocking. I was there in the restaurant. The guy he came in and started shooting. In the air first and then at the people. It was just one guy with a gun I saw – an AK47. I don't know what he was shouting. I heard the shooting and we were running.

Another fighter, Jamie Kavanagh, due to be the main attraction at the following night's event, spoke of his relief. Kavanagh, whose uncle, Paul, and whose father, Gerard 'Hatchet' Kavanagh, had both been murdered by the cartel, took to Twitter: 'Anyone asking, I'm OK. Thank you for asking. I was lucky today is all I can say.'

He later explained:

> You had people there – everybody was running for their life. And nobody knew what to do, nobody knew which way to react. They were supposed to be police. These people were dressed in police uniforms. And from that point of view, you see the police and you think you're OK, that you're safe. But obviously, a few seconds later it was very different.

The boxers were just some of the hundred people who were at the hotel when all-out war exploded around them. As boxer Gary Sweeney took to the podium at the Regency Suite for the last of the weigh-ins, two men dressed in the Garda's Emergency Response Unit (ERU) uniforms entered the hotel. Then the shooting began.

Mel Christie, president of the Boxing Union of Ireland, was standing on a podium when the gunfire erupted and panic gripped the room. He said:

There was a horrific cracking noise in front of me. Boxers weren't being targeted. There was an incredible noise out there and that is where I saw a body, a corpse, lying literally at the edge of the reception desk. So, I'm sure he was trapped – he was riddled.

Another witness, who was staying at the hotel but chose to remain anonymous, also told how she initially believed the Islamic State terror group had launched their first attack on Irish soil. 'I ordered the children to get down and stay down on the floor of the bedroom,' explained the mother-of-two. 'We were staying directly above the room where the shooting was.'

Shocking footage of the gun attack was also posted online after the incident, in which a terrified child is heard to scream, while a man shouts, 'Get the f*** out of here!'

A team of photographers from the *Sunday World* newspaper had been hanging around outside the venue, in the hope of snapping some of the gangland figures expected to attend, particularly Daniel Kinahan. They were perfectly positioned when the drama began. Instead of Kinahan, they found themselves photographing a man dressed up as a woman and another man, who would subsequently become known as 'Flat Cap', fleeing the scene while carrying handguns.

When the dust settled, one cartel member, David Byrne, was dead and another, Sean McGovern, had been shot in the leg. A third, Aaron Bolger, had been hit in the arm.

Thirty-three-year-old David Byrne was a key cartel figure. He was a brother of fellow gangster Liam Byrne and a close associate of Mr A. David Byrne's death would hit the cartel hard.

Born in the Crumlin area of south Dublin, on 13 February

1982, he had been introduced to crime from a very young age. David Byrne, like many of those he hung around with, started his criminal career by selling small amounts of cannabis to fellow pupils in Ardscoil Éanna in Crumlin. One former classmate, who did not want to be named, explained:

> There was one person in the class who went on to become a guard but someone like Byrne was never going to end up in a normal nine-to-five job.
>
> He was always going on about how much he loved football but he never had the bottle to put his name forward. He would always go to the games and stand on the sidelines with Mr A. As he progressed through his teenage years he started throwing his weight around as a big-time criminal because of the family connections and friendships he had.
>
> A lot of his old school friends left him behind and everyone was saying how the only people that mattered to him were his family and the Kinahan brothers. They all knew each other, were related in some way and grew up in the same area, so it was no surprise they would all become heavily involved in drug dealing and crime.

Byrne's group of friends during his school years included his older brother Liam and Declan Gavin. His friend Gavin's murder would spark the Crumlin and Drimnagh feud and leave sixteen young men dead, over a fifteen-year period. Other close associates during David's teenage years included Shay O'Byrne, who was one of the sixteen who died during that gang war, in March 2009. His former classmate explained:

> David was always a bit of a poser when he was in school. 'He was expelled from school when he was caught with a block of cannabis on a school trip to the Delphi resort in

the west of Ireland. David was in and out of trouble but no one thought for a second he would have become a member of one of Ireland's most dangerous drugs gangs. He never showed any fear towards other pupils because he had his brother to look after him.

Elder sibling Liam was also a serious associate of the Kinahans and is seen as one of the cartel's most senior members, standing just behind Daniel and Christopher Jr in terms of rank. Liam Byrne is regarded as having a serious propensity for violence. In one case, he embarked on a three-year intimidation campaign against a couple who gave evidence against him in a serious assault trial, in March 2001. Just twenty-one years old at the time, Byrne was sentenced to four years after he left former League of Ireland footballer Trevor Donnelly with a fractured skull. He had battered him with a baseball bat outside a chipper, on 23 April 2000, after Donnelly had a row with Liam Byrne's girlfriend. At the time Byrne was on a four-year suspended sentence for burglary, dangerous driving and firearms charges.

Over fifty witnesses saw the incident, during which Byrne declared, 'If he wakes up, it's a bullet he's getting.' However, aware of Liam's reputation, most eyewitnesses declined to talk to investigating gardaí. After Donnelly's girlfriend decided to give evidence, Byrne sent an intermediary to offer the couple IR£50,000 to withdraw her testimony.

When they refused, and she testified anyway, he shot up Donnelly's house. He also took out a contract on the woman's life with the INLA, forcing the pair to leave their home and live in hotels.

During the court case, Liam Byrne was described as a member of a criminal gang. He had been involved in drug dealing since his late teens, in the company of his brother David and Mr A. As Mr A became more established within the cartel, from the middle of the decade onward, he took the Byrnes with him. When he was in Dublin, Liam Byrne's job within the cartel was to secure weapons.

He was known to have a fascination with fast cars and Liverpool FC, and bought a young relative a new Volkswagen during the summer of 2016. As joint owner of LS Active Car Sales, which was raided by the Criminal Assets Bureau (CAB) and was dissolved without ever filing any accounts, Liam's other role was to launder cash through the business.

By the mid-2000s, Liam Byrne was a major player in the cartel. Over the course of the next ten years, his brother David would also cement his position as a trusted lieutenant inside the Kinahan gang. His job within the gang was to distribute the drugs that were being sent to Ireland from associates in Spain and Holland.

Once the gang's product arrived in Ireland, David had a loyal team of 'runners' in place to transport it all over the capital. A big fan of fast cars, motorbikes, football and boxing, Byrne used the profits from the gang's drug-dealing activities to fund a lavish lifestyle.

As former Detective Superintendent Gabriel O'Gara explains:

> David Byrne was one of the main organizers for the Kinahan cartel in the south inner-city area of Dublin. He was up there with the main players and had been a target for gardaí for many years. He was an individual who had no problem in flaunting his wealth.

> As someone with no visible means of income, it was a common sight to see Byrne wearing designer clothes and

driving around south inner-city Dublin in high-end sports cars.

From 2006 onwards, David Byrne was a regular visitor to Spain's Costa del Sol and travelled to see boxing fights in Las Vegas. Byrne was also a massive fan of UFC cage fighter Conor McGregor and went on trips to the Crumlin man's fights in the United States.

Gardaí first became aware of David's interest in the fight game when he was spotted by detectives at the National Boxing Stadium Dublin, on 3 June 2006. At the time, intelligence indicated the Byrnes and their close criminal associate were working for the cartel on the ground in south Dublin, in close co-operation with the Hutch gang.

Just twenty-one days later, investigators also received further proof of the connections between the Kinahan and Hutch gangs when Byrne and his brother Liam were seen leaving a wedding in Francis Street, in the south inner city.

From there, they were all brought in a stretch Humvee to the reception in the Stillorgan Park Hotel, south Dublin. The luxury vehicle was owned by Gerry Hutch's company and provided an insight into the links between two of Ireland's most dangerous criminal gangs. Just under a decade later, however, the elite of Ireland's criminal underworld would be at war and David Byrne would be dead.

One security source says:

> The ironic thing is that if Byrne hadn't stopped to look for where his boss Daniel Kinahan was in the hotel he might still be alive today. The CCTV footage clearly shows him looking for Daniel but if he had run the other way, he would still be alive. When he was looking for Daniel, his boss was running out the back of the hotel to safety.

David Byrne's love for boxing was well known, as was his habit of always being present when the MGM was promoting a fight or staging a boxing match:

> The Hutch gang would have known this and after the murder of Gary Hutch he would have been a major target because of his senior role within the cartel. However, the main target for Gary Hutch's associates will always be Daniel Kinahan because they blame him for his death.

Alongside his work as a promoter for the MGM gym in Marbella, Christy Kinahan's elder son continued with his responsibilities in running his father's vast criminal empire. Although choosing to mainly stay in southern Spain after boxer Jamie Moore was shot by mistake outside his apartment, Daniel continued to make frequent trips to Ireland.

According to security sources, Daniel had visited Dublin at Christmas 2015. Gardaí received intelligence of a meeting between Daniel and 'Shooter', the young criminal who had defied Eamon Dunne and fled the country and subsequently become one of the cartel's main hitmen.

It was a tense time to visit, as Daniel's gang was being widely blamed, across many media outlets, for Hutch's killing a few months earlier, but the elder Kinahan son had shown no signs of fear.

'People have to remember that Daniel Kinahan is extremely arrogant, with no moral compass whatsoever,' explained one former investigator. When he returned to Dublin, in February 2016, the investigator noted:

> He was at the Regency without a care in the world, and if he had thought for one second he was under any type of threat, then he wouldn't have been anywhere near the venue. There

was also no specific intelligence to suggest any type of attack had been planned. If there had been, Daniel Kinahan would have been warned his life was in danger. As far as Daniel was concerned, the Kinahans were the only show in town and no one would have the nerve to take them on.

Unlike his close friend David Byrne, Daniel Kinahan had a lucky escape at the Regency Hotel because his bodyguard swung into action as soon as the shots rang out. From the moment he landed in Ireland, Daniel had made sure he was never left alone. He was not expecting an attempt on his life in public, but was taking no chances nonetheless. For the first time, his precautions seemed justified.

Pulling him through an emergency door, and up a flight of stairs, the pair escaped by clambering on to a small roof at the rear of the hotel, across which they fled. As his associate lay dead, Kinahan was being brought to a safe house in the capital, before flying to London and then on to the sanctuary of his base in Spain.

The audacious daylight attack made headlines around the globe, with the world's media descending on Dublin. Gardaí, including specialist teams such as the Emergency Response Unit, the Special Detective Unit, Regional Support Units and local detective units, were all placed on high alert in the traditional Dublin heartlands of the Kinahan and Hutch gangs.

David Byrne's killing also led to a political backlash, with Fianna Fáil opposition leader Micheál Martin calling on the Government to provide gardaí with more resources. He said:

Criminal gangs are now killing people without any fear of prosecution. We need more specialist resources to tackle organized crime. We need specialized approaches to this; we need specialized approaches in terms of gardaí. There is no question about that. In terms of specialized courts to deal with some of these criminals, who spread fear and intimidation across the land, and many people have been afraid to testify against them. Across the full panoply of mechanisms we need to double up in terms of our resources now.

It would not be the last time calls for more Garda resources would be heard over the months that followed.

Serious questions were also being asked about why gardaí had been so badly caught out by the Regency attack. The Garda Commissioner, Nóirín O'Sullivan, insisted there was 'no specific intelligence indicating any threat at the Regency Hotel'. She said:

> I think it's also important to say that gardaí are deployed on intelligence and risk assessment. We also have to be very careful how we divide hours of An Garda Síochána. The Regency was a sporting event and we cannot have members of An Garda Síochána going to every single event just because criminals may be there. If there was intelligence in place, there would have been a policing and strategy plan in place.

The Regency incident had not only stunned the public but it had also badly shaken the cartel's sense of invincibility. Furious, they sought not only to retaliate against those they believed to have carried it out, but also the media who had been reporting on their activities. After becoming aware that threats had been made against two journalists from the Independent News and Media group, the gardaí offered them armed protection.

Over the course of the weekend, Garda analysts also identified seventy-nine people, including mothers, wives and children, associated with the rival factions, who were possibly at risk. Detectives were not underestimating any potential response. Friends and former partners were all checked out and some were warned they might be in danger. One innocent relative of Gerry 'the Monk' Hutch was due to be married within weeks of the attack, but felt too fearful to go ahead with her reception in Ireland. She cancelled the ceremony altogether and decided to hold her wedding overseas later in the year instead.

Intelligence reports indicated that the cartel was busy plotting to avenge Byrne's killing. They had met in a Dublin pub just twenty-four hours after he was shot dead, planning their retaliation. It would come just two days later.

Taxi driver Eddie Hutch, the older brother of Gerry 'the Monk' Hutch, was well known to officers from Store Street and Mountjoy Garda Stations. Born on 12 April 1957, the father-of-five grew up in the north inner-city area of Dublin. He was involved in petty crime from a young age, before moving into small fraud scams in his adult years, earning a few convictions and suspended sentences along the way.

Eddie had also been used by his brother to launder the proceeds of his armed robberies. When the Criminal Assets Bureau (CAB) began operating in 1996, the Monk was one of its first targets. Three years later, its case against him reached the High Court, where the CAB told how it was probing the whereabouts of more than IR£4 million which Gerry Hutch had accumulated from bank raids and other criminal activity. Some of that money was passed to Eddie Hutch for safekeeping and, as part of the inquiry, the CAB seized a bank account in his name containing €160,000.

For his neighbours, however, the taxi man was just a regular fellow. One local recalled in an interview with the authors:

Eddie was a harmless character, absolutely no threat to anyone and certainly no 'Mr Big'. He was a gentleman who just did what he had to do to get a few quid for his family and a few drinks. He loved his younger brother Gerry, but that's as far as it went. He was no criminal mastermind and certainly wasn't involved in major organized crime. He was his own worst enemy, and when he was in his late forties and fifties the only thing that mattered to him was working as a taxi driver. He knew his younger brother was involved in serious crime but that world just wasn't for him.

However, Eddie had been sucked into the conflict engulfing his brother in early 2016, when he was approached by two senior associates of Daniel Kinahan. The pair warned Eddie that more members of his family would be killed if they refused to hand over a further €200,000. Security sources think the Kinahan threat was passed by Eddie Hutch to his younger brother just days before the attack in the Regency.

On 8 February 2016, as David Byrne's killing continued to dominate the news agenda around Ireland, the BBC reported a statement from the Continuity IRA claiming responsibility for the attack on the hotel. However, confusion soon reigned when another group, claiming to represent the dissident republican paramilitary faction, denied any involvement.

That same evening, Eddie Hutch returned to his home on Poplar Row, in Dublin's north inner city, after spending the day in his taxi. He parked his black Toyota Avensis and went off on a visit to the shops with his wife, Margaret. On his return at 7.45 p.m., the father-of-five decided to move his car, so it would be covered by the CCTV cameras at his property.

It was a decision that would cost him his life. Seconds after the car had been moved, the taxi driver noticed a silver BMW 3 Series speeding towards him. Hutch ran for the safety of his ground-floor apartment. He made it, but his desperate attempts to lock the door behind him failed and it was smashed in by three armed men.

Cornered in the living room of his home, Eddie was shot in the head four times as he lay on the ground. The gang escaped and abandoned their car in the nearby Whitworth Road area of Drumcondra. Their efforts to burn it out failed when a container filled with petrol did not ignite. DNA was recovered from a petrol canister and balaclavas in the vehicle, but has yet to lead to any arrests.

The following day, the victim's sister-in-law Ann Gavin described his killers as 'animals' in an interview with *Irish Sun* reporter Eavan Murray. She said:

> He got about three or four bullets, all into the head. It was the worst thing in the world. There was blood all over the walls.
>
> They had just been out shopping and they had brought the stuff inside and he was going back outside to move the taxi when they got him. They chased him in the door and got him just there in the living room. Eddie's wife, Margaret, is in an awful state. She heard the bang and she knew and started running out the back. She said to me, 'Ann, I couldn't get the door open.'
>
> Then when the gunfire stopped she ran out and she couldn't see him coming behind her. She looked back into the house and all she could see were his feet coming out of the sitting room. Margaret didn't see him like that, thank God, because when we went in I looked in and tried to

check for a pulse and there was nothing. We closed the door over to protect her. It was horrible to see something like that. I ran over to see was there a pulse or anything and the blood was like soup. Margaret's in bits. If it was one of the others you'd expect it, but Eddie was lovely and not involved in anything. It's going to kick it all off now.

Expecting further assaults, prison authorities moved quickly, isolating Derek Hutch inside Wheatfield Prison to prevent a third attack upon him. Meanwhile, the Garda Representative Association (GRA) called for detectives in Dublin to be given Heckler & Koch MP7 sub-machine guns so they could match gangs in a firefight if need be.

The Government responded by promising an extra €5 million in funding, along with a new armed support unit for the capital. In the meantime, the Emergency Response Unit (ERU) was being pulled back from the border to patrol the streets of Dublin.

Even the dead were not considered to be safe. On 12 February, the body of David Byrne was returned for burial to his family in Raleigh Square, in Crumlin. Up until that point, his remains had been held at an undertaker's outside the capital amid concerns that the location could be targeted by the Hutch gang. The ERU kept watch as Byrne's coffin was brought into his heavily fortified home.

The following day, gardaí launched 'Operation Hybrid' which would see uniformed cops, backed up by armed units, stage checkpoints close to the homes of all those identified as having associations with the two feuding factions.

The Kinahan brothers, who had fled to the safety of Spain, returned to Dublin on St Valentine's Day for David Byrne's funeral, flying via Faro in the hopes of avoiding detection. It didn't work and the media, who had been tipped off that they were flying into Dublin Airport, were waiting for them.

Christopher Jr is known for his quiet demeanour but it does not mean that he lacks a violent side. While Daniel put his head down and kept walking, amid a barrage of reporters' questions, Junior ran across the road and attempted to assault a photographer before being called off by his clearly exasperated brother.

When asked by the media if the Kinahan gang were responsible for the murder of Eddie Hutch, Daniel replied, 'Please stop chasing us. Thank you.'

Gardaí were not taking any chances on the morning of David Byrne's funeral Mass. The bomb squad was brought in to sweep St Nicholas of Myra Church, in Dublin's Francis Street, for devices. Several cartel members, including Byrne's brother Liam and cousin Liam Roe, wore matching dark suits, sky-blue shirts and dark ties. Cops and the media watched as Byrne's sky-blue, American-style €18,000 casket was brought into the church by his associates, all dressed in the same-coloured suits and ties.

Around a thousand people attended the service, many of them standing in the street outside, as the ceremony was relayed through loudspeakers. As they stood there, a scrawny drug addict shambled between them asking for spare change. 'Have you anything?' he slurred at people, with his hand outstretched. 'Terrible fuckin' sad, terrible fuckin' sad.' The junkie was eventually shooed away angrily, one woman telling him, 'Have some respect.' The next day's *Irish Times* noted the irony – the junkie was quite probably strung out on drugs which David Byrne had helped to import into Dublin.

Mourners heard anecdotes about how Byrne was nicknamed

'Happy Harry', a 'messer' who would walk his pet rabbit, Snowy, on a lead around Crumlin.

Mr A, who was again in fear of his life, was a prominent figure at the funeral. Before the feud, Gary Hutch and Mr A had been best pals, sharing an apartment near Marbella, where they would smoke cannabis together long into the night. After Hutch's murder, however, Mr A knew which side his bread was buttered on and chose to stay with the Kinahans. As a former pal of Gary who was now firmly with the Kinahans, he would be a major target. It was back to the old days for him – each time he was pulled over by gardaí he was found to be wearing a bulletproof vest once again. When he was stopped and searched just two weeks after the Regency attack, he admitted neither he nor the driver of the Mercedes CLK he was travelling in were wearing seat belts. This was to allow them a 'quick getaway' from the vehicle if required.

Afterwards, Mr A stood alongside Daniel Kinahan as mourners were brought in a fleet of eleven limousines to a reception in west Dublin. Just as with the service for Eamon Dunne, there was an unmistakeable air of criminal flashiness. One of the objects on display was a miniature remote-controlled BMW which carried a paper licence plate reading 'Active Car Sales'. The dead man's cortège was led away by bikers from the Chosen Few Motorcycle Club.

Fr Niall Coghlan called for a 'hero' to come forward and put an end to the feud. He said:

> It strikes me that it doesn't take much courage to attack a defenceless person with weapons of destruction. What courage is there to walk into a hotel and blast a man to death when he cannot defend himself, or to walk into a man's

home and do the same thing? It is not courageous. What is courageous is someone willing to put their head above the parapet and call for an end to this despicable destruction of human life.

In the aftermath of the funeral, Fr Coghlan was also forced to appear on RTÉ Radio's *Liveline* current affairs programme following controversy over the lavish funeral service. He told the radio show audience:

I am not responsible for what people put on flowers or how many mourning coaches there are. That's not my job. I'm not responsible for how people conduct their funerals. The only thing I was asked to do was conduct the service and I don't think it's in my remit to refuse that.

Four days after David Byrne was laid to rest, it was the turn of Eddie Hutch's family to say their final goodbyes. In stark contrast to the opulence and wealth on display at Byrne's funeral, the cabbie's service was a modest affair, with floral tributes the only items on display and a taxi plate on top of his coffin. The 'Monk', who wore a grey wig and cap, was one of the hundreds of mourners who packed into Our Lady of Lourdes Church, on Sean McDermott Street Lower, in the north inner city.

In his homily, Fr Richard Ebejer said the Hutch family had pleaded for no retaliation, and he urged both factions to lay down their guns. He told the congregation:

We are all aware of the circumstances of Neddy's death. Circumstances that have spiralled out of control, circumstances that have left families grieving in shock and pain, circumstances that have shocked the nation. All vengeful violence is to be condemned in the strongest terms possible, wherever it comes from. It only degrades the humanity of those who carry it out.

Nobody deserves to die in the way that Neddy died. Neddy was basically a good man, who would, as a taxi driver, wait on elderly ladies as they went to do their errands. He would share a joke and was the life of a party, and he was good company in the pub. He did not deserve to die in this manner. One does not want to seek revenge or to have retaliation. It would be a tragedy if we were to lose that sense of good Dublin values. May Neddy Hutch rest in peace. May God have mercy on his soul, and reward him for his goodness – real Dublin goodness.

This is what the family had asked for, right from the very beginning, that there is no retaliation. This is indeed goodness in the face of evil. They now call on everybody for this cycle of violence to stop – and to stop now.

With the calls for peace falling on deaf ears, however, there would be further bloodshed and more funerals. The gangland feud had only just begun.

16. Vendetta

'Those involved in serious organized crime could be
friends one minute and sworn enemies the next.
There is a lot of paranoia out there.'

Assistant Garda Commissioner
Michael O'Sullivan

Just as with the murder of the journalist Veronica Guerin in
1996, the Regency incident had quickly come to be seen not
just as an attack on the victims, but also upon the State itself.
That much was admitted by one of the gardaí who had first
brought down Christy Kinahan way back in 1986, then
Detective Chief Superintendent Michael O'Sullivan of the
Drugs and Organised Crime Bureau.

In an interview with TV3, the senior cop, now an assistant
commissioner, described what had happened as 'a milestone
in criminal history'. He warned that the feuding gangs 'were
prepared' to turn their guns on gardaí:

The Regency Hotel attack is comparable in magnitude to
the murder of journalist Veronica Guerin. We have a criminal grouping in broad daylight, heavily armed, posing as
guards, carrying out a brutal act with no regard for members of the public. It is more dangerous but we are prepared
for it.

In a subsequent interview with one of the authors, O'Sullivan added:

> None of these criminals are invincible, none of them are indestructible. There are no untouchables out there. Some of them believe their own hype and propaganda. Those involved in serious organized crime could be friends one minute and sworn enemies the next. There is a lot of paranoia out there.
>
> We have had over two hundred prisoners of organized crime groups of various levels. A lot of them are in the higher echelons nationwide. There are criminal gangs who get together that we target, and we will continue with this approach going forward. We have the capacity to disrupt and dismantle the gangs.

In the aftermath of the retaliation attacks, the gardaí were under more pressure than ever to hit back against both the cartel and the Hutch gang. On 23 February, two weeks after the Regency incident, officers from Ballymun Garda Station raided eleven properties across Dublin.

One of them was the modest home of Gerry Hutch, in Clontarf. Unsurprisingly, the 'Monk' himself was not there, but gardaí seized bank statements, travel documents, mobile phones and a laptop.

As the investigations continued, official Garda Information Message (GIM) warnings were still being delivered to both sides in the feud. Gardaí are required to give these out, along with the appropriate advice on increasing personal security, whenever they learn of a credible threat to an individual's life.

David Byrne's brother Liam flew to London for a secret visit with Daniel Kinahan before returning to Ireland, on 28 February 2016. Both men were known to be of the same mind: Byrne wanted quick and bloody vengeance for the death of his brother, and Daniel was still incandescent with rage that a second attempt had been made on his life. Retaliation was inevitable, as the cartel could not be seen to be weak. But for both Byrne and Daniel, this was now very personal.

Just one day later, gardaí had another gangland murder to contend with. Former Real IRA leader Vinnie Ryan, whose 32-year-old brother Alan Ryan had been shot dead on 3 September 2012, was murdered as he sat in his car outside a house on McKee Road, Finglas, in north Dublin.

The dissident republican faction headed up by the Ryans had fallen apart after the assassination of Alan. He had been shot on the orders of a northside drug baron he was extorting, who cannot be named for legal reasons but has been nicknamed 'Mr Big'. It had been three and a half years since Alan Ryan's murder, but his younger brother's killing showed that Christy Kinahan was not the only one with a long memory.

Vinnie Ryan had a criminal history of his own. Gardaí believe he was the gunman who had shot dead Mika Kelly — known as 'the Panda' because of the dark circles around his eyes — with an AK47, in September 2011. 'Mr Big' didn't particularly care about Kelly's death, but he knew killing Vinnie Ryan would eliminate any last threat of retaliation from that faction.

Although gardaí don't believe the incident was linked to the ongoing feud between the cartel and the Hutch gang, Liam Byrne's name did crop up in the investigation when it emerged Ryan had been driving a car from Byrne's business LS Active Car Sales. The Ryan family would later issue a statement denying any links between the murder victim and the cartel member, claiming the Volkswagen Golf was bought legitimately. Gardaí do not believe this was linked in any way to the feud, and the purchase appears to have been a coincidence.

The law's counter-offensive rolled on. On 9 March, the Criminal Assets Bureau (CAB), supported by Revenue, the Drugs and Organised Crime Bureau and detectives from Crumlin Garda Station, who were under the command of senior investigator Detective Superintendent Brian Sutton, began 'Operation Lamb'.

The former head of the CAB, now Assistant Garda Commissioner, Eugene Corcoran, said they would be using the Proceeds of Crime Act, tax legislation and social welfare regulations to target the cartel's assets.

Their first offensive was against LS Active Car Sales. Arriving at the garage in Bluebell, south Dublin, shortly after 6 a.m., the investigators took control of the facility. Cops had obtained a warrant based on intelligence that the garage was being used to launder the cartel's cash.

They seized twenty-three luxury vehicles, including one containing a bulletproof vest in its boot. The cars recovered included a €75,000 Mercedes AMG, a €50,000 Lexus Hybrid, a €70,000 BMW X5 jeep, a €65,000 BMW M Series Sport and a €65,000 BMW M5. They also seized a €13,000 convertible Mercedes, a €30,000 Land Rover Defender and a €40,000 Audi A6. During the day-long search, officers also confiscated six motorbikes, including a €37,000 high-powered Kawasaki. A four-wheel-drive buggy worth €15,000 was also taken.

All the vehicles, which were immobilized and recoded by specialists, were later brought to the Irish Army's base at the Curragh for storage. Investigators also recovered computers, vehicle registration certificates and dozens of documents from the garage. No arrests were made, as owner Liam Byrne did not turn up.

At the same time as investigators were taking control of Byrne's garage, officers had also swooped on his home in Dublin's Raleigh Square, Crumlin. During the raid on the heavily fortified home, investigators seized an engagement ring, Rolex watches, designer shoes and cash. Again, Byrne was not there and the items were seized on suspicion of being the proceeds of crime.

Other homes searched that day included those of Mr A and Sean McGovern, who was still recovering from his bullet wounds from the Regency. A betting slip for €38,500 on a Liverpool football game and signed boots from former Liverpool footballers Steven Gerrard and Luis Suárez were also seized during the raids.

Predictably, the raids dominated the headlines as both the media and the public still tried to come to terms with the Regency attack. Gardaí claimed the raids had been planned before the latest outbreak of violence, but many saw them as the State's response to the wealth displayed at David Byrne's funeral.

That same night, investigators from the Garda's Special Detective Unit (SDU) also made a significant seizure when they recovered a Chinese Type 56 assault rifle, a Romanian PM63 assault rifle and a Zastava M70 machine gun, all variations of the more famous Russian AK47, when they stopped a car at Tuiterath, Balrath, Slane, County Meath. Three magazines, containing seventy-five rounds of ammunition, were also recovered. Shane Rowan, born on 22 May 1976 and from Killygordon, in County Donegal, was subsequently charged with IRA membership and possession of firearms.

Two days later, gardaí launched their second offensive against the cartel. Officers from the South Central Division, under the command of Detective Superintendent Peter O'Boyle, carried out ten raids across the south inner city. Aimed at targeting the cartel's money-laundering activities, detectives hit the homes of mid-level cartel figures, including Liam Roe, and their known associates were searched for drugs, money and documentation. Investigators also uncovered plans by the gang to establish a wedding photo-booth business as a way of cleaning even more drug money.

In other raids on members of the cartel, officers recovered €50,000 in cash hidden behind a cooker, bank statements, a Rolex watch, jewellery and a Breitling watch.

The most surprising part of the haul were four tracking devices discovered at two of the properties. Officers were in no doubt the items were to be used by the cartel to follow the movements of Hutch gang members. It seemed Daniel Kinahan was putting the skills he had learned on his SWAT-style training course into practice.

However, the cartel's next choice of target owed more to spite than any great level of planning. Convicted cigarette smuggler Noel 'Kingsize' Duggan, who had once been saved by Christy from the extortion demands of Eamon Dunne, was to discover Daniel was somewhat less charitable.

Duggan was not involved in the Regency attack and presented no threat to the cartel. He was shot dead on 23 March 2016 as he sat in his Mercedes outside his home in Ratoath, County Meath, simply because he had been a close friend of Gerry Hutch for years.

Unable to find or get close to Hutch gang members, the cartel decided 'Kingsize' would do instead. Choosing this type of 'soft' target was a new departure in the rapidly spiralling feud. It presented gardaí with another major headache. It was clear the cartel saw anyone connected to the Hutches as fair game, not just the gang's main figures.

The following day – Holy Thursday – Archbishop Diarmuid Martin told worshippers at Dublin's Pro-Cathedral:

> We have witnessed horrific, hate-filled violence and retaliation on our streets again last night; when will these people learn that violence and revenge only lead to further viol and revenge? They feel that violence is their strength; yet violence will be their downfall. Will they ever learn?

The Archbishop's words fell on sterile ground.

Senior cartel member Mr A epitomized the attitude of the Kinahan gang when he was pulled over on 25 March. A check of the car showed nothing untoward, but Mr A sneered at gardaí while they searched it, making wisecracks and references to Kingsize cigarettes.

Three days later, he was stopped in another part of the south inner city and told the cops he had been in the zoo with his kids. It was a pointless lie as gardaí knew he had actually been in Tayto Park, out in Ashbourne, County Meath.

The shooting of Noel Duggan had come a day after the owners of the Regency Hotel had taken their insurers to court. It was in an effort to be indemnified for losses of over €217,000 they had suffered in the five weeks since the attack. The hotel would eventually be awarded almost €2 million in compensation, in October 2016.

Slowly but surely, inroads were being made into the cartel's Irish operations. On 7 April 2016, eighty detectives and uniformed gardaí from the South Central Division swooped for a second time on eight properties across the capital. 'Operation Thistle' recovered €112,000 worth of drugs and more than €30,000 in cash. Gardaí also arrested a 73-year-old man who was allegedly forced by the cartel to store drugs at his property.

One of the addresses raided was a luxury apartment on Lower Baggot Street, in Dublin city centre. Inside the property gardaí discovered Moroccan mafia chief Naoufal Fassih. The arrest of the portly 35-year-old highlighted the cartel's links to organized criminals based in Europe.

Fassih was a major player on the Amsterdam gangland scene and had convictions for weapons and explosives offences, as well as extortion. He was clearly not short of a few quid either. The monthly rent for the upmarket residence was €2,500, while €83,000 worth of designer watches, a pair of €800 Valentino trainers and a fake Belgian ID card and bogus Dutch passport were also seized.

During Fassih's first appearance at Dublin District Court, on 15 April, Garda Eoin Kane told Judge Cormac Dunne he was objecting to bail over fears the suspect was a 'flight risk'. He told the court, 'The premises searched were targeting members of the Kinahan Organized Crime Gang. He is a man of means.'

Remanded in custody, Fassih was later jailed on 30 June 2016, after he pleaded guilty to having a false instrument – a forged Belgian ID card – before he was extradited to Holland, to face charges there eight months later.

Gardaí had been given free rein on overtime in the wake of the Regency attack, allowing them both to carry out extra surveillance on the cartel and the Hutch gang, while also increasing armed patrols to prevent more murders. In early April, this overtime allowance was quietly stopped.

The cartel, who were offering up to €10,000 to anyone who

would murder Hutch gangsters, faced no such restrictions. Anyone willing to take the money would be provided with a gun and let loose. Some of those prepared to accept the offer had never held a weapon in their life, but the lure of €10,000 was strong, particularly to people with a heavy addiction to drugs.

Gardaí believe it was an amateur gunman like this who botched the shooting of the next Hutch gang member. Keith Murtagh was a 32-year-old convicted armed robber. He had been shot and severely wounded during an attempted armed hold-up of a cash van, working alongside Gary Hutch's brother 'Del Boy', in 2009. Gardaí had been tipped off about the heist and moved in when two of the four-man gang rushed a security man as he got out to refill an ATM. Murtagh's best pal, Gareth Molloy, had grabbed the security man while holding a shotgun. He was killed by armed officers, who fired five rounds at him, one of which hit Murtagh in the small of his back.

Keith Murtagh got ten years for his role in the affair in 2010, but by 14 April 2016 he had already been released from jail. He was outside Noctor's pub on Sheriff Street, in the north inner city, at 12.30 p.m. that afternoon when a man dressed in black cycled towards him. The cyclist had a scarf wrapped around his face and a gun in his hand.

Standing beside Murtagh was Martin O'Rourke, a 24-year-old homeless man who gardaí believe may have been in the area to buy drugs. Murtagh saw the gunman and began to run. The panicking hitman immediately opened up, firing four shots wildly. One of the rounds hit O'Rourke above the left eye, killing him instantly.

Murtagh, who managed to dive between two parked cars, survived unscathed. The blundering assassin hopped on his bicycle and fled, dumping it down the street and throwing his gun into a nearby wheelie bin.

The feud had claimed its first innocent victim. O'Rourke's pregnant fiancée, Angeline Power, later lost her unborn child. Her dad, Larry, said it was because of the stress brought on by her partner's murder.

Mr A again flaunted his links to the Kinahans when gardaí pulled him over on the night of Martin O'Rourke's murder. 'It's terrible, the young fella got six bullets in the back and two in the face from a nine millimetre,' he declared to cops, as they searched his car. Asked how he could have such information, which was incidentally entirely incorrect, he said he had 'just heard it'.

A month later, Mr A told gardaí at another checkpoint that it was 'tough to stay alive' as they frisked him. He queried whether the Garda TETRA radio system was hooked up to other areas of Dublin and if gardaí would know if there was another shooting in the city that night.

The man for whom Martin O'Rourke had unwittingly taken a bullet, Keith Murtagh, had a serious problem with gardaí. During his sentencing for armed robbery, he had told the court he viewed them as 'murderers' for shooting his close pal, Molloy. However, now gardaí had Murtagh and other serious criminals connected to the Hutch gang, who previously would have given the gardaí two fingers, ringing them up and begging for protection.

The cartel had been targeting Murtagh specifically because they believed he had acted as a 'spotter' on the day of the Regency attack. It was something both Murtagh and his family were adamant was untrue, and his family begged gardaí to release CCTV footage to prove he was not there.

O'Rourke's funeral three days later was attended by the Taoiseach, Enda Kenny. The congregation heard how the victim had been due to attend a drug rehabilitation course and then a FÁS programme in the hope of getting a job. A public appeal for funds to help pay for the service had seen over €5,000 donated by a shocked country.

Gardaí continued to put the squeeze on both sides, and a car and a mobile phone belonging to a close pal of Regency victim Sean McGovern were seized from an address in Crumlin days afterward. The owner subsequently submitted a Police Property Application to have them returned. He failed, with a detective telling Dublin District Court they were 'evidence' from the 'investigation into the murder of Martin O'Rourke'.

The dead man's father-in-law, Larry Power, said O'Rourke's three young children – Angela (aged four), Michael Patrick (three) and Martin Lawrence (one) – had been left traumatized. He said:

> Little Angela has mood swings, and she hates the name Martin being mentioned because it's just too painful for her. She doesn't even want to go to her father's grave. The gangs need to see the destruction they are causing to people's lives on a daily basis. They also just need to look at my three beautiful grandkids and see the pain they're in.

Eleven days later, there was another assassination.

Dissident republican Michael Barr was working as a barman at the Sunset House pub in the Hutch stronghold of Ballybough, in north inner-city Dublin, when a gunman walked in and shot him dead. Originally from County Tyrone, the 35-year-old had been living in Dublin since 2014, and was considered by gardaí to be one of the Hutch gang's main suppliers of weapons.

A man was arrested over the killing and his trial is pending. Speaking after the killing, local independent councillor

Nial Ring said a man with special needs, who was in the pub at the time, had to be carried away from the scene after he went into severe shock.

Assistant Garda Commissioner John O'Mahony also revealed how the shooting had taken place despite the presence of an armed Garda unit in a nearby street. 'I think it's indicative of the challenge we are facing that people are willing to go and commit a crime of this nature despite the presence or close presence of armed gardaí,' explained the senior officer.

Michael Barr was later revealed to be a member of the dissident New IRA. It is the largest dissident group in Northern Ireland and is composed of a motley hotchpotch of former Provos, some of whom are confusingly also members of another dissident group, the Real IRA, and of the Direct Action Against Drugs organization, which carries out 'punishment shootings' of alleged dealers. It has claimed responsibility for the murder of two prison officers in the North, David Black and Adrian Ismay, along with that of Catholic PSNI officer Ronan Kerr.

The hearse at Barr's funeral in Strabane, County Tyrone, was flanked by over a dozen men wearing paramilitary uniforms, black berets and sunglasses. The PSNI arrested fifteen men over the display.

The dissident republican's death came on the same day as members of the Garda Representative Association (GRA) laid part of the blame for the Regency Hotel attack on the lack of State support to the force. The union's thirty-eighth annual conference in Killarney, County Kerry, heard how the first officer to respond to the Regency Hotel attack was unarmed and could not get there any faster as he was banned from breaking the speed limit. Garda Colin Morgan told delegates:

The driver of the first marked Garda car to respond to the Regency was not qualified to drive either at speed or with his blue light or siren on. He couldn't break the speed limit, and he would not have been able to break any lights on the way. It all boils down to the fact that we need more armed cover.

The events at the Regency have opened our eyes to what sort of criminals gardaí deal with in order to keep the peace in this country. Whitehall Garda Station is situated one kilometre from the hotel and I have no doubt it being closed was taken into account by these criminals when planning their attack. While I welcome the expansion of the Emergency Response Unit and the introduction of the Regional Support Unit in Dublin on a 24-hour basis, our local first responders are not equipped to deal with situations like they faced at the Regency Hotel.

Under force regulations, gardaí have to be specially trained to be allowed to drive above the speed limit. But due to cutbacks, many of those who should have had such training have yet to receive it.

The views were shared by new GRA President Ciaran O'Neill, who said, 'There is a concern about the nature of the threat. It's not just a city problem. We don't have a 24/7 armed cover around the country. The Regional Support Units need to be beefed up.'

Garda Commissioner Nóirín O'Sullivan assured delegates at the conference that tackling organized crime was her 'number one priority'. Garda management, however, came in for further criticism, on 26 April 2016, when independent Dublin councillors Christy Burke and Nial Ring claimed they had been told Garda numbers had dropped from 600 to 500 in the north inner city.

At a community meeting held two days later, Marie Metcalfe, co-ordinator of the Community Policing Forum, said the area was now 'smothering and living in fear of the next attack'. She explained:

> We as a community feel we need to step up and do something for the safety of our community. The Kinahan gang won't stop, why would they? They feel badly hurt and they want to hurt this community really hard. It's completely out of hand.

Gardaí continued to swamp areas of the capital with armed checkpoints in a bid to prevent further bloodshed. On 9 May 2016, two men with close links to the cartel were arrested by detectives investigating the Eddie Hutch murder, before being released without charge.

The following day, investigators in Store Street Garda Station believed they foiled another murder attempt when two men, again with links to the cartel, were caught with a stolen motorbike on Sheriff Street. Although unarmed, detectives suspect the men were on their way to collect a firearm before targeting a member of the Hutch gang.

The incident would be one of ten planned murder bids foiled by gardaí after the attack on Daniel Kinahan at the Regency Hotel.

Three days later, armed officers were back in action again when two men were stopped on Dublin's Malahide Road after a high-speed chase. One man was released without charge. The other man was Patrick Hutch, who is the brother of Gary Hutch.

Patrick Hutch later appeared in court, on 18 May 2016, charged with the murder of David Byrne at the Regency Hotel the previous February. He was remanded in custody, where he remains awaiting trial.

The day before Patrick's appearance in court, Gary Hutch's father, Patsy, would also be arrested in connection with the incident at the Regency Hotel, but he was subsequently released without charge. Another father and son were also arrested over the hotel attack but were later freed.

Investigators from Operation Thistle were back in action on 18 May 2016, when they seized €300,000 worth of heroin, cocaine and cannabis resin from five raids in the south inner-city area. It was another strike against the cartel's cash cow, but the Kinahans' desire for more blood was relentless.

Three days later, Keith Murtagh was in the living room of a house in Ballyfermot, in west Dublin, when nine shots were fired through the window. Both Murtagh and the woman who was with him had a lucky escape, as one bullet grazed his arm and she suffered minor leg injuries.

The respite was temporary, however. On 26 May 2016, the feud claimed its sixth victim when Gareth Hutch, a nephew of the 'Monk', was shot dead. He was the son of the 'Monk's' brother John, and had also been charged over the same armed robbery in which Gareth Molloy was killed by gardaí, in 2009. Gareth had fled the country, but was recaptured and extradited home from Holland. He was later acquitted.

Gareth Hutch knew he was a marked man but his primary concern was for his young son. He had been warned by gardaí that his life was under threat and had planned to deliver a letter to Dublin City Council asking to be rehoused because of fears for the safety of his seven-year-old boy. The letter read:

This situation is a cause of worry, concern and anxiety for me and, more importantly, is possibly putting my child at risk. This is the most important issue for me and for this reason I am asking for a welfare priority and transfer from the flat. You should be aware of the background issues surrounding my family and I have been advised by the gardaí about my personal safety. Indeed, the house number is with the Emergency Response Unit in case of any incident.

Gareth Hutch's death was captured on the CCTV cameras covering the car park outside the Avondale House complex, on North Cumberland Street, in Dublin's north inner city. It showed 35-year-old Hutch walk down towards his car and open the back door to put his jacket inside, before opening the driver's door. In the background, two hooded men appear and run down towards the vehicle which was parked beside the railings separating the car park from the street outside.

Hutch was completely oblivious to the men's presence until one of them fired a shot into the back of his head and he slumped backwards. On the CCTV footage, detectives could then see the lead gunman firing another shot into his prone victim before the pair ran out of view.

The same day, Taoiseach Enda Kenny was heavily criticized when he told the Dáil (Irish parliament) he was powerless to stop the cycle of violence. Addressing fellow TDs, he said, 'This is a dispute between two families and it's a vicious, murderous dispute and I don't think that I can stop that.'

Hours after the killing, a 29-year-old man handed himself in to gardaí and has since been charged with Gareth Hutch's murder. A 44-year-old woman was charged with withholding information from gardaí investigating the killing but these charges were subsequently dropped.

The man suspected of killing Hutch remains on the run. His name was widely known around the local community within hours of the shooting, but when gardaí went to his flat to arrest him, he had already fled the city. He has close links to the INLA and is from the same north inner-city area as the man he shot. He is not a member of the cartel, but gardaí believe he decided to carry out the hit on Gareth Hutch, who he knew personally, because of the money on offer.

By now, the extent of Gerry Hutch's involvement in the feud was becoming apparent to gardaí. It had emerged that the 'Monk' had been recorded in an incriminating phone call relating to the ongoing feud in the aftermath of the Regency Hotel attack. Following the assault, the veteran criminal had disappeared to Holland, as he was an obvious target for the cartel's revenge scenario. Fifty-three-year-old Hutch remained on the run on the Continent, with Europol unable to locate him.

Gardaí believe the Hutch patriarch was using the same encrypted PGP phones favoured by his adversary to stay in contact with relatives back in Dublin. Tensions remained high in his absence.

On the night of the Belgium vs Ireland Euro 2016 soccer clash, on 18 June, Keith Murtagh was watching the match in a pub in Dublin's city centre. Unbeknownst to him, another attempt on his life was being lined up. It was foiled by officers from the Drugs and Organised Crime Bureau, and a man has since been charged with possession of a weapon.

The cops continued to chip away at both gangs' infrastructure on the ground and, by the end of June 2016, another man was arrested for the Regency Hotel attack, and later released without charge.

By this point, the freelance hitmen employed by the cartel were having trouble finding any targets. Most members of the Hutch family were under Garda protection, while others had fled Dublin. The assassins realized they would have to cast their net even wider.

On 1 July, former IRA man David 'Dotty' Douglas was standing in the doorway of Shoestown, a children's clothing store he ran with his Chinese wife, Yumei. He was approached by a lone gunman, who shot him four times in the head and body. The hit team fled in a stolen €60,000 Mercedes, which was found burnt out less than a mile away.

Douglas was a 55-year-old ex-Provo who had been given the boot from the movement in 2008 after he was caught in a taxi containing 8kg of cocaine, with three other men. An attempt had already been made on his life as he walked his dog, in Cabra, the previous November.

Initially, Garda intelligence indicated that his death was due to an outstanding drug debt, but it later emerged that the Kinahans believed Douglas had taken part in the attempted hit outside the Red Cow Moran Hotel, in November 2015, in which a gun aimed at Liam 'Imelda Marcos' Roe had jammed.

Gardaí were not even sure if Douglas was there that night, but in June 2016 they had given him an official warning that his life was in danger. The ex-Provo also had somewhat tenuous links to the 'Monk'. That was enough to damn him in cartel eyes, and his death was sanctioned. A man has been charged with his murder and is awaiting trial.

The incident at the Red Cow had cast a long shadow. It had also come to light that another murder, which had taken place on 30 December 2015, in Dublin, was most probably linked to the same event. Darren Kearns was fatally shot as he sat in the passenger seat of his car beside his wife in a pub car park. His wife miraculously escaped injury, though witnesses reported hearing 'seven or eight shots' being fired.

Gardaí had originally attributed the shooting to a row over a drug debt. Kearns had been jailed for six years, in 2012, after being caught with cannabis worth €1.7 million. His trial heard he was spending up to €1,000 a day on cocaine and had been kidnapped and tortured by dealers to whom he owed €180,000.

But it subsequently emerged that Kearns' death was more likely caused by that same incident outside the Red Cow Moran Hotel, almost two months beforehand. There had been two men in the car which pulled up alongside Liam Roe and, rightly or wrongly, the cartel believed Kearns was one of them and Douglas was the other.

This information brought the number of fatalities linked to the feud to eight so far. Douglas's death would be the last that July, but more were on the way, even though the high-profile feud went against everything for which the cartel had previously stood.

17. A One-sided War

'I'm broken. My life is over and I've nowhere to go.
I don't know what I'm going to do now.'

Gary Hutch's father, Patsy

Keeping a low profile has always been a priority for Christy Kinahan. Like other intelligent men in his business, he is well aware there is no such thing as good publicity, as it inevitably brings closer scrutiny from law enforcement with it.

Even in the aftermath of the media feeding frenzy which followed the Operation Shovel raids, in May 2010, the Dapper Don believed that if he kept his head down and continued his activities out of sight, he would soon drift out of the public mind.

It took his elder son Daniel just six months to obliterate the fruits of a strategy which Christy had successfully followed for decades. Gardaí believe Daniel took the decision to renege on the peace deal with the Hutch family and have Gary Hutch killed in Estepona, in Spain, in September 2015. Based on intelligence from informants, this is one theory being explored by Irish detectives and their colleagues in Spain, as part of their ongoing investigations into the reasons behind Gary Hutch's murder.

Christy's elder son is also considered the main force behind the current Kinahan campaign to have anyone connected with the Hutch family murdered in revenge for the attempt to kill him at the Regency Hotel. The vindictive selection of easy targets like Noel 'Kingsize' Duggan is simply not Christy's style. Even allowing for the grudge murder of the man he blamed for his first ever drugs conviction, the Dapper Don has always erred on the side of pragmatism and caution.

Daniel does not seem to have shown such restraint. The psychotic vendetta he has embarked on against the Hutch family, and anyone connected to them, in the wake of the Regency Hotel attack seems to have established this beyond doubt.

Thanks to his activities, the Kinahan gang became front-page news, on a daily basis. Their activities and how to curb them were even being raised regularly in the Dáil question time by Sinn Féin and Independent TDs. Such attention could not be good for the cartel's illicit activities, yet the killings continued unabated.

The Hutch family had gone from living in peace in the north inner city to having the threat of death hanging over them. All their lives had changed, but the problem for them was that the north inner city was the only place they knew. It was where they spent their lives. They had nowhere else to go.

While the surviving Hutch family members may have been safe, life as they knew it had come to an end. When Gary Hutch's father, Patsy, had been questioned after the Regency shooting and then released without charge, in theory he was a free man. Except he wasn't.

On his release, Patsy had been escorted back to his home on Champions Avenue, in the north inner city, by the Armed Support Unit. En route, he had confessed to gardaí who were protecting him how lost he had felt since the cartel murder campaign had begun. Once he was safely inside the house, the 'Monk's' older brother had met with officers from the nearby Store Street Garda Station to discuss his security arrangements.

Patsy was just one of sixty-six members of the extended Hutch family who had been warned their lives were in danger after the Regency Hotel incident, with forty-one people on the Kinahan side also advised on their safety. The gardaí would continue to give out GIMs as new intelligence came through.

In the following months, the father-of-five, who had already lost one of his sons to an assassin's bullet, was under no illusions – with the 'Monk' safely out of the country, Patsy would be the number one target for the Kinahans. But unlike his brother Gerry, Patsy did not have the financial resources or a network of international contacts established after a life of crime that would allow him to relocate abroad. His only option was to remain in Dublin.

Throughout the next six months, Patsy Hutch effectively became a prisoner in his own home, and he rarely ventured outside. When he did, it was to stay in different safe houses supplied by a close circle of family and friends who were risking their lives by putting him up.

During the months of June and July 2016, gardaí mounted fifty checkpoints per day close to his and other Hutch family members' homes, as part of ongoing efforts to prevent more killings. Uniformed officers also undertook more patrols close to these properties, and a Garda liaison officer was appointed to deal directly with the Hutch family.

By mid-July, the Garda's new Special Crime Task Force was also officially up and running. It was under the Drugs and Organised Crime Bureau and was made up of forty officers. The task force's remit was to target senior members of the feuding gangs, and other gangs involved in the distribution of drugs and firearms. Justice Minister Frances Fitzgerald insisted this offensive would prove neither side was 'untouchable'. She said:

> There are hitmen, both nationally and internationally, who are willing to be paid a certain amount to do the dirty business for others and we have to watch that as well. No effort is being spared in bringing these people to justice, and they aren't above the law.
>
> I can see how corrosive organized crime and drugs are. This has been very hard on the community, for children and their families. I appreciate it's difficult for communities when they see armed officers, but we have to do this to prevent further murders.

Gardaí released statistics showing how 6,221 checkpoints had been held in the capital since the attack in the Regency, under Operation Hybrid. With the Garda budget to tackle the feuding gangs set at €90 million, twenty firearms, including AK47 assault rifles, had been recovered, thirty-seven arrests made and five people charged since the outbreak of violence between the warring factions.

The checkpoints were not just for show. On 14 July, gardaí learned a gunman on a bike had abandoned plans to kill Patsy Hutch because of intense police activity in the area.

Fourteen days later, gardaí received intelligence that a contract killer had sourced a weapon and was en route to kill Patsy Hutch. Officers in Store Street immediately increased patrols in the streets surrounding his house on Champions Avenue, and raced to the property to inform him of the imminent threat. Fearing for his life, Patsy fled, returning eight days later to find a permanent Garda checkpoint outside his home.

Unsurprisingly, the tension was affecting neighbours too. One resident, who did not want to be named, told one of the authors:

> It looks like the Kinahans are never going to stop. Patsy used to have many people calling at his home but this is no longer the case. People feel sorry for him and his family but they just don't want to be caught up in the feud. Anyone who's even remotely associated with the Hutch family could be a target. People are getting fed up with the whole thing and just want to get their lives back.

Keith Murtagh, who by the end of June 2016 had survived three attempts on his life, was also suffering the same fate. His family reiterated their claims that CCTV footage would prove he wasn't acting as a 'spotter' on the day of the Regency Hotel attack. A family spokesman said:

> His life is in turmoil at the moment and he keeps moving around because they've tried to kill him three times He just wants his life back. It's up to the gardaí to prove that he was nowhere near the Regency – we don't want them to wait until it's too late.

No target was considered too obscure for the cartel's thirst for vengeance. Protection was given to carers providing home help to a Hutch family member with special needs. Across the city, in west Dublin, armed officers also patrolled outside a facility where a young disabled relative of the Hutch family was receiving treatment.

Gardaí asked the Hutches to inform them of any future plans for birthdays, christenings, weddings or other family events in public places. Simply being near a Hutch, or anyone connected to the clan, inspired a real fear for people, terrified of becoming collateral damage.

One city councillor, Mannix Flynn, described how parents with children in the same classes as relatives of the 'Monk' were deliberately dropping them off late in the mornings, to avoid potential shootings at the school gates.

As August 2016 arrived, it had been over a month since the last feud killing and there was a feeling the cartel would strike again soon.

When they did, it was in a place where the Irish authorities could offer no protection and in a way which illustrated how the cartel's money was buying them all the information they required.

Jonathan Hutch was another member of the family whose life had been drastically affected by the Kinahan vendetta. He had seen his brother Gareth die outside his home and was one of the sixty-six members of his family to receive the GIM about the threat to his life.

The 37-year-old had installed bulletproof windows and a new state-of-the-art CCTV system at his family home in Drumalee, north Dublin. Like his Uncle Patsy, Jonathan had become a virtual pariah, with old friends afraid to associate with him in case they too were attacked.

One neighbour, who didn't want to be named, explained how the family had even struggled to get a furniture removal van to bring home a bed:

> They managed to get the bed transported in the end, after Patsy got the loan of a van; people were afraid to help them.

When they got the bed it was too big, and they also found it difficult to get a tradesman to alter it.

A local tradesman had continued to visit the house, refusing to let the Kinahans deny him his friendship with the family. On one occasion, the man was coming on a visit and pulled up nearby in his car. When he got out, he was immediately surrounded by armed gardaí who thought he might be a contract killer about to carry out a further murder.

Jonathan, who was not a member of his Uncle Gerry's criminal organization, had required an armed escort to safely get to a family confirmation, in the south inner city, in June. Detectives kept guard at the rear and front of the church, before also keeping watch at a reception later that evening.

It was with a degree of relief that he and his young family headed off on a two-week holiday to Majorca in early August. As Jonathan Hutch and his family relaxed in the Costa de la Calma resort, he ran into a fellow Dubliner, Trevor O'Neill. He was staying at the same spot with his partner, Suzanne Power, and their three children, aged eleven, six and four.

Suzanne and Hutch's partner had been in school together and the two families exchanged greetings and chatted to each other over the next few days, as they met around the pool. O'Neill and his partner had initially planned to holiday in Turkey in the early part of 2016. The council worker had written on his Facebook page in March: 'Looks like we're heading to Turkey for the summer holiday. 2000 for 5 all inclusive. Not bad. First 2 weeks in August, I'm not paying 5k for Spain.'

However, bloody suicide attacks by ISIS on Istanbul

city centre and on the city's airport made the couple change their mind. It was a decision which would have tragic consequences.

On 17 August, the family were coming towards the end of their holiday when they went out for an evening meal. On the way to the restaurant, they met Jonathan Hutch and his family. Suzanne told RTÉ the next day:

> We went out the front of the hotel, and Trevor was walking in front with the chap we met on holidays. I was walking behind, pushing the buggy. I saw a man walking up wearing a hoodie. I thought it was strange because it was roasting, and I saw him pull out a gun.

One local described how there had been 'pandemonium' as people in nearby cafes and terraces initially thought it was a jihadi attack. He said:

> People were screaming and running in all directions. The wife of the man that was shot had one of their children in a pushchair that she was wheeling along when the victim was shot. He was walking slightly in front of them on his own. That child and another with her must have seen what had happened.
>
> Another two children were behind them and wouldn't have seen it and the woman turned round and screamed at them as it happened, and that gave them time to run for cover in a side street. I know that lady was married to the victim because when we ran out to tend to the injured man she kept on repeating the word 'wife, wife'.
>
> We took her to one side and I got some water for her and held the man's hand to try to encourage him to keep his eyes open while we waited for the ambulance to arrive. He

had a bullet wound in his lower back and I couldn't see any other wounds.

He couldn't talk and his eyes started to close and go yellow and then white and his mouth changed colour. Another neighbour was trying to stem the flow of blood from the wound. The ambulance took about twenty-five minutes to arrive and by the time they did he was in agony.

Although witnesses had reported hearing four shots, O'Neill, who was of a similar build to Jonathan Hutch, was shot once in the lower back and died in hospital. His partner, Suzanne, had been taken to a safe house in Palma shortly after the shooting and only found out he was dead when she was contacted by family back home in Ireland.

The following day, a female relative of the murder victim contacted the *Irish Sun* to outline the family's concerns. She said:

> Please, please let people know that he had nothing to do with the Hutches or the Kinahans or gangland, or any of that. Trevor was never in his life in trouble with gardaí. We can't bear to think that people would associate him with them. This was mistaken identity. Trevor was only over on a holiday with his three children. This is the result of this feud. This is what happens; innocent people get killed.

Majorcan newspaper *Ultima Hora* reported the next day that Interpol had warned the Guardia Civil of the arrival of two dangerous Irish criminals on the island the day before, but failed to mention they were connected to the Kinahan cartel. It said cops had placed the pair under surveillance at their hotel, but this was later withdrawn. The two cartel members were also reported to have left Majorca shortly after the killing.

The Guardia Civil would not comment on the report, but made no arrests in the aftermath of the murder. No detentions are expected any time soon either. No forensic evidence or shell casings were collected from the murder scene. While the gunman was caught running from the scene on CCTV from a nearby shop, he had his hood up and was recorded only fleetingly. Effectively, the Spanish authorities had no leads and their main suspects had, most likely, already fled the island.

Back in Ireland, gardaí continued to try to take guns off the streets. A raid in the middle-class suburb of Castleknock saw 3kg of high-purity cocaine, worth around €300,000, seized, along with a Mac-10 sub-machine gun, a favoured weapon of the SAS, the British special forces unit. A man was later charged and is awaiting trial in connection with the seizure.

Cops were confident they were making a difference, though it was coming at a high price. Figures released by the Department of Justice under Freedom of Information legislation revealed that the Garda overtime bill had soared by 62 per cent, to €18.5 million, in the first six months of 2016. Assistant Commissioner O'Sullivan insisted:

> When you look at costings, it's very difficult to say what is the cost of a human life, but lives are being saved. In the last few months we have certainly foiled quite a number, probably as high as ten, eleven, assassination attempts.

One of those failed plots was an attempt to kill Jonathan Hutch's father, John. On 2 September 2016, the 63-year-old grandfather, who had already seen his other son Gareth die at the cartel's hands, had just dropped his daughter home. He was in the street outside his house in Drumalee Park, off the North Circular Road, when a hooded gunman ran towards him.

A passer-by, who saw what was about to happen, bravely threw a brick at the hitman. The distraction allowed Hutch to slip into an enclosed yard, behind a steel door he had recently fitted to the property. The gunman fired five shots, which hit the wall at the front of the house, and then turned and fled.

He escaped in a car driven by a second man, but a third member of the hit team, who was acting as a spotter, was stopped and arrested by the Emergency Response Unit nearby. The lookout had an extensive history with the cartel. He had been the gunman in Christy's attempted hit on Martin 'the Viper' Foley, back in 2008.

Before he could be cuffed, he pulled the SIM card out of his phone and swallowed it. Arrested and brought to Store Street Garda Station, he spent the entirety of his seventy-two hours in custody refusing to eat or defecate, so he could avoid passing the incriminating chip before being released without charge.

The shooting was the third murder bid on the one branch of the Hutch family in four months. A few days later, John Hutch could be seen outside his house adding extra bricks to the wall which had saved his life.

Despite it all, some cartel members such as Mr A have retained their sense of the ridiculous. When stopped in late summer 2016 by gardaí in the south inner city, they discovered the gangster was dressed in drag and had completed his outfit by painting his toenails pink.

Mr A has since informed detectives he is 'home for good' from Spain, though it appears this was not a decision he came to himself. Senior officers believe Daniel Kinahan wants him on the ground pulling the strings in his attempts to wipe out the Hutch gang because of his years of experience with the long-running Crumlin-Drimnagh vendetta.

In the midst of the feud, Christy was, as ever, focusing on business. He was still exploiting the same old law enforcement problems of lack of co-ordination between different jurisdictions, which enabled him to move out of reach and surveillance of the authorities by flitting off abroad. He was spotted in Hong Kong at one stage and in the United Arab Emirates' city of Dubai soon afterwards.

By 2016 the cartel was operating a drug-trafficking route across Ireland, the UK, Spain and Dubai. Gardaí had received intelligence from Spain that Christy Kinahan had also been looking into the property market in Dubai as a way of laundering cash and seeking new business opportunities, because of the increased attention from the Spanish authorities. Garda and Spanish police intelligence had been informed that the cartel was moving some of its operations to Dubai, though Spain would remain its primary base. Several key members were spotted in the emirates over the summer of 2016 and it appeared the gang felt its money-laundering operation would be less traceable there.

Calls have been made by former *Irish Times* editor Conor Brady for a European FBI to be established to combat the cartel – an unlikely prospect. There were signs that co-operation was improving at international level, though. On the day John Hutch began further strengthening his already fortified home, a man appeared in court in Belfast on foot of a European Arrest Warrant. Kevin Murray stood accused of being 'Flat Cap', one of the alleged gunmen photographed outside the Regency Hotel on the day of the attack.

Bail was refused, despite Murray's legal team producing evidence to show he was suffering from multiple sclerosis, and 46-year-old Murray was later described in court as dying in hospital.

Extensive co-operation between the gardaí and the PSNI had long been established because of the Troubles. The feud, however, was forcing gardaí to break new ground with the Spanish police forces, with which they traditionally only had limited dealings.

Relations between gardaí and both the Policía Nacional and the Guardia Civil were good, and a Spanish-speaking garda liaison officer had been based in Madrid for several years. The ongoing activities of the cartel in both jurisdictions meant collaboration would have to be ramped up. An extra garda liaison officer was assigned to Spain, and both cops now began spending much of their time in the Kinahan heartland on the Costa del Sol. To avoid them being recognized, and potentially targeted, the Irish detectives were rotated at intervals.

On 10 September 2016, five days after Murray's appearance in court in Belfast, kickboxing cartel member James Quinn was stopped and arrested over the killing of Gary Hutch, as he prepared to board a plane at Barajas Airport, in Madrid. Undercover Guardia Civil agents had been tailing Quinn for several days and moved in at the airport, fearful he was about to skip the country for good.

Quinn, a south inner-city native and nephew of Martin 'the Viper' Foley, was a career criminal with over seventy convictions to his name. He was kept in custody for four days under anti-gangland legislation, while a series of simultaneous raids were launched by gardaí in Dublin and the Guardia Civil around Marbella.

For the first time ever, gardaí took part as observers in Spain, while their counterparts did likewise in Ireland. At 6.30 a.m., around sixty cops began searching six different properties around Dublin connected to the Kinahans. The properties included three in the south inner city and one each in Clondalkin, Lucan and Baldonnel, in south Dublin.

At one of the properties linked to James Quinn, €23,000 in cash was found hidden in garden flowerpots and the hot press. An identity card bearing the photo of a known cartel member, but with a different name, was also discovered. The ID had been used to open a foreign bank account outside the EU.

Another of the properties belonged to an electrician suspected of assisting the cartel in its money-laundering activities. Gardaí also took away phones, laptops and other documents for analysis.

Detective Superintendent Tony Howard of the Drugs and Organised Crime Bureau gave a press conference in Dublin that afternoon, flanked by a female Guardia Civil captain. She was not introduced, even though her face was broadcast on television, as Spanish law forbids the identification of police because of the threat posed by the Basque separatist group ETA.

Detective Superintendent Howard commented that the operation had been aimed at tackling the cartel's money-laundering activities in Ireland. He said:

> Criminals who are operating here in Ireland do seem to have, on the face of it, access to a lot of money. Over the last number of weeks, we have seized substantial cash, close to €1 million here in Dublin, as a result of the operations.

As gardaí battered down the doors of homes in Dublin, the Guardia Civil were also busy in Marbella. Officers from the force's Special Intervention Unit (UEI), which investigates terrorists and top-level organized crime, broke into the MGM gym at sunrise on the same day. Tens of thousands in euros were found in a safe inside, though the gym was otherwise empty.

Other officers were busy combing through Quinn's rented Spanish home. It was a luxury chalet located on the road between Marbella and Ronda, in a scenic mountain village which was Ernest Hemingway's favourite place in Spain. The chalet was part of a plush complex which had an indoor and an outdoor swimming pool and its own gym. The chalet itself came equipped with a sauna, cinema room and even a lift.

At a third property linked to the cartel, cops were videoed as they took an angle grinder to another safe. At the same time Quinn was brought to Puerto Banús Harbour in handcuffs, and made to watch while police searched an Irish-flagged yacht.

The final haul included the yacht, which was impounded, a Bentley, and a handgun found at one of the properties. Thirty-four-year-old Quinn was brought before an investigating judge in Fuengirola, who remanded him in custody. He had been arrested for Hutch's manslaughter, but after hearing the evidence against him during a closed session, the female judge upgraded the inquiry from *homicidio*, which roughly equates to manslaughter, to *asesinato*, or murder.

This was significant, as it not only increased the sentence range against him – from ten to fifteen years, up to fifteen to twenty years – but it also made the chances of him getting bail less likely.

Fittingly, the Spanish operation which resulted in Quinn's arrest had been codenamed *Geraneo*, or 'Geranium', after the street name of the apartment block at which Hutch had been shot dead.

Sources close to the investigation later revealed Quinn's arrest had been a direct result of the DNA and phone evidence recovered from the getaway car used in the Gary Hutch murder. The actions of the public-spirited Marbella local had been crucial – once the Guardia Civil were actually able to retrieve the partially burnt-out vehicle from their Policía Nacional colleagues.

In a strange twist, Quinn's DNA was also matched to evidence found by forensic detectives sweeping the scene of the shooting of boxer Jamie Moore outside Daniel's home, in Estepona, back in August 2014. The sample was recovered from a car parked close to the scene. Investigators do not believe Quinn was involved in the apparent bid on Daniel's life which led to Gary Hutch's murder, but the development is considered further proof of Quinn's links to the cartel.

Ironically, he and Gary Hutch, the man he is under investigation for murdering, were once so close they shared prostitutes and bottles of wine. A transcript of a call from Hutch to his then pal, in January 2010, read:

> Gary says he's going to buy a bottle of wine and a hooker from the other side of the street [where they normally go]. James Quinn says he'll be around shortly and Gary says he'll get two hookers to bring back.

Quinn's kickboxing background had seen him used as an enforcer by the gang, and Gary Hutch had on more than one occasion called upon his friend to sort out trouble. In one incident, on 19 April 2010, Hutch had rung Quinn and asked him to get to the Auld Dubliner pub immediately. Two men had been causing trouble in the bar and Quinn's martial arts skills were required to sort them out. Luckily for the trouble-makers, they had left before he arrived.

Quinn, nicknamed 'Frizzy' due to his wiry hair, can expect to spend years on remand in Spain while the judge-led inquiry continues. Gardaí also want to question him over an alleged threat to murder another Dublin gangster, Michael Frazier, who has so far survived four attempts on his life.

Back in Ireland, the situation on the ground in the cartel's and the Hutches' inner-city strongholds remained as difficult as ever. The threat of intimidation prevented locals, who were disgusted at the drug peddling taking place in their areas, from speaking out.

The days of concerned citizens' groups, back-boned by republican groups, marching on the homes of dealers like Raymond Salinger and taking them on physically were long gone. A Public Forum on Crime, held at Dublin City Hall, at the end of September 2016 heard that many residents felt powerless to do anything about the problems in their areas.

'A lot of people here would know people who are selling drugs, but they're afraid to say anything,' one inner-city resident, identified only as Noel, told the gathering. He added that, following an anti-drugs march a week beforehand, two of his friends who participated had been threatened by teenagers who had been watching it:

> They heard two young fellas aged fourteen or fifteen saying, 'They're not going to effin' well stop us. They come near us, we'll shoot them.' Everybody knows these are not the big fellas any more. The young fellas, kids are selling the drugs.

He called for gardaí to implement a 'stop and frisk' policy. Another local youth worker, based in the north inner city, also criticized community gardaí for not interacting with the area's kids enough, but conceded cuts to numbers are a major factor. He said:

> It did happen ten years ago, five years ago, before the previous government got in and slashed their way through inner-city life, and we're reaping the rewards now. We're coming into situations where children are re-enacting the Regency Hotel. Ten-year-old boys are having pool cues in their hands and saying, 'You take the Glock, you take the AK47 and I'm waiting in the car.' A long-term solution is required.

Marie Metcalfe of the North-East Inner-City Community Policing Forum said, while armed checkpoints were helping to prevent more bloodshed, there were just not enough gardaí on the ground. She said:

> We don't have enough gardaí to make my community feel safe. There's drug dealing going on at every corner and there's nobody there to police this because the resources aren't there to give to us. We can't get kids into the training centre because they're earning too much money off of drugs.

Though with the cartel offering upwards of €10,000 for the killing of anyone connected to the Hutches, drug dealing was not the only way for ambitious young criminals to earn themselves some cash.

18. No End in Sight

'The informant is perhaps law enforcement's
most important tool.'

Former FBI director, William H. Webster

For four months, since the murder of Trevor O'Neill in August 2016, there had not been another killing in the feud. That was primarily because gardaí had intercepted at least eighteen attempts to kill people in that time. The hiatus ended just before Christmas.

On 22 December, Noel 'Duck Egg' Kirwan was returning from a meal with his partner, Bernadette, to her home in Clondalkin, in west Dublin. With them were Bernadette's daughter and three-month-old granddaughter. As they travelled a relative of Bernadette's called to say he had mislaid his house key. Bernadette's daughter had a copy so Kirwan dropped her and the baby off at the relative's house. As he pulled into the driveway of Bernadette's house a lone assassin carrying a silenced weapon ran up to the car and fired several shots through the side window.

Kirwan turned in shock to Bernadette and said, 'I'm only after being shot.' She had avoided injury and, despite her frantic state, managed to summon the emergency services. However, they were unable to save the 62-year-old grandfather from his injuries.

'Duck Egg' (he inherited the nickname from his father) had been in school with Gerry Hutch and happened to be photographed alongside the 'Monk' at the funeral of his brother Eddie. Kirwan was a lifelong republican and had been active in the anti-drug vigilante groups that had marched on drug dealers like Raymond Salinger and driven them out of inner-city communities in the eighties and nineties. However, he was not a member of the Hutch gang and his murder was more reminiscent of the killing of Noel Duggan – an attempt to get at the Monk by any means possible.

There were reports in the following days that Kirwan had been warned of a threat against him, but these were later confirmed to be incorrect. On the face of it, it appeared Kirwan had been killed simply because he had been seen with the Monk at Eddie Hutch's funeral. His daughter Donna said:

> Gardaí have confirmed to us that there was no threat on his life, he didn't sign any forms. He had no reason to look over his shoulder. If his life was in danger he would have told us because he told us everything.
>
> He went to Eddie Hutch's funeral because they went to school together and that's the reason they killed him. What are these people going to do now – murder everyone including the priest who was at the service?

The Kirwan murder underlined the cartel's determination to continue its counterproductive killing spree.

By the time he was killed it had transpired that a man found in a car in Leixlip, County Kildare in early December, shot through the right eye, might have been one of the Kinahans' hitmen, on his way to carry out a job. He had died in hospital the next day.

Glen Clarke, aged twenty-six, a father of two with no serious convictions, was discovered unconscious in a car that had been stolen in Blanchardstown in October and fitted with false number plates. The *Sunday Times* reported he was wearing a boiler suit when he was found and had earlier bought a container of petrol. The handgun used to kill him was under the driver's seat.

At the time of writing, gardaí are unsure how Clarke was killed. His family is adamant that he was not working for the cartel and was murdered. However, Clarke has been linked to the shooting of Martin O'Rourke on Sheriff Street over seven months previously. Clarke's DNA was found on the murder weapon that was dumped a short distance from the scene so, while he may not have carried out the killing, he had certainly handled the gun.

Meanwhile, gardaí were recording some significant successes against the cartel. On 20 January 2017, they stopped one of the biggest hauls of cannabis ever found in the State. The drugs had been hidden amongst machinery parts being brought in through Dublin Port. The 1.8 tonne load was valued at €37.5 million.

It is believed the drugs had been purchased by a number of cooperating mobs, the Kinahans amongst them, and would have been broken up and sent onwards to the UK. The seizure would put a massive hole in all their finances.

For over four months members of the National Surveillance Unit had been trailing a number of members of the gang. The objective was to find where and when they were storing both the weapons being used for attacks on the Hutches and the drugs being used to pay for them.

On 23 January, gardaí watched as a man entered a

nondescript warehouse in the Greenogue industrial estate in Baldonnel, west Dublin. Two other men waited in a Ford Transit van nearby. The gardaí followed the man inside the warehouse and a search revealed 15 weapons of various grades, ranging from handguns to an assault rifle to a sub-machine gun, together with 1,300 rounds of ammunition. Some of the guns were loaded and appeared to be awaiting collection.

The Ford Transit was found to have a custom-made storage compartment in a false ceiling, which could be opened using a hydraulic switch hidden under the driver's seat. The level of technical sophistication harked back to the Kinahans' English counter-surveillance expert in Spain.

All three men were arrested and documentation was seized. A fourth was detained during a follow-up search of a house, where €300,000 in cash was found vacuum-packed in the attic. At the time of writing, three men are facing charges over the find.

As part of their operation, the cops had also learned that one low-ranking cartel figure was suspected of renting a house in County Kildare, informing the owners of the property he was a haulier to explain any potential queries about lengthy absences. On the night of Saturday, 28 January, detectives obtained a search warrant and went inside. Packed tightly into the base of a sofa and an armchair was €3m worth of cocaine and heroin.

The cumulative efforts meant that more drugs – €44m worth – had been seized in January 2017 than in the entirety of 2016 (the total includes the value of all drug seizures in January, not just the two mentioned). The Baldonnel and Kildare hauls had been considerable and, along with the €300,000 in vacuum-packed cash in the attic, gardaí were able to freeze a further €180,000 in bank accounts linked to the cartel.

The surveillance had also allowed gardaí to identify the man working as the cartel's feud logistics 'fixer' in the absence of Mr A. This man – nicknamed 'Mr Nobody' by the *Irish Independent* – stored the guns, organized getaway cars and generally oiled the cogs of the cartel's killing machine.

Gardaí had been aware of Mr Nobody's links to the cartel and his involvement in money laundering on their behalf, but not of the status to which he had risen within their operations. This new intelligence, coupled with the arms and cash seizures, represented a major dent in the Kinahans' capabilities.

They would suffer another setback a month later when enforcer Gareth Chubb, a convicted cocaine dealer who had taken over Mr A's drug-dealing operations, was arrested and charged with attempted manslaughter after allegedly pulling a gun on a man in an Amsterdam bar. The gun had jammed when he tried to fire it. Chubb's stupidity meant the cartel would have to find someone to replace him.

In the aftermath of the Regency attack, gardaí recovered AK47 assault rifles, Smith & Wesson handguns, MP9 machine guns and other weapons. They made several arrests, including one man being charged with the murder of Michael Barr, two people charged in connection with the killing of Gareth Hutch, two men charged with possession of weapons during a Euro 2016 game, and Patrick Hutch charged with the murder of David Byrne.

In the twelve months since the attack, 456 guns have been taken off the streets, a total of €6 million has either been seized in cash or frozen in bank accounts, and a dedicated

Dublin Garda Armed Support Unit has been established. But while these successes are seriously hampering Daniel Kinahan's efforts to continue the killing spree, they are not guaranteed to end it.

Garda Commissioner Nóirín O'Sullivan has admitted as much. At a briefing to publicize these statistics at the end of January 2017, she said: 'In terms of retribution the fact and the unfortunate reality is that individuals who are determined on retribution will continue that determination.'

It was an unusually frank concession and was echoed by Detective Superintendent Tony Howard, the head of the Drugs and Organised Crime Bureau:

> Many of these individuals are lifelong friends so the feud has become very personalized and it has split down along two families. It makes that feud all the more difficult to tackle when you are actually family-on-family. Communities have been torn apart.
>
> Historically feuds have been northside/southside or east or west. The problem is that people in these communities have supported people on the opposite side of the fence so it does make it significantly more difficult. But we have made huge inroads.

Despite the gardaí's successes, the problem of how to bring down the cartel's top tier remains. Since the Operation Shovel raids in May 2010 senior gang members have made it very difficult to monitor their electronic communications, so increasingly police forces rely on informants to obtain details of their inner workings. Finding those high enough up the chain to supply accurate information is a difficult business, but some former and serving officers feel An Garda Síochána's own regulations have made it even more so.

The Covert Human Intelligence Sources (CHIS) set-up was introduced by force chiefs following embarrassing revelations into serious abuses of authority by some officers in Donegal. The Morris Tribunal into complaints about some gardaí in the Donegal Division heard that a woman, Adrienne McGlinchey, was being blackmailed by a local Superintendent, Kevin Lennon, and a detective, Noel McMahon, into posing as an IRA informant in order to explain a series of large explosives finds. In reality, the pair were planting the explosives themselves and ordering McGlinchey – who had no connection with the terror group – to grind up fertilizer into the powder used by the IRA to build its home-made bombs. The situation became so farcical; McGlinchey was regularly crossing the border into Northern Ireland, buying up every coffee grinder she could find in the local Argos, as the machines were not built for such a purpose and would quickly burn out. (The tribunal found it unlikely she supplied more than a fraction of the ground powder in the fake explosives 'finds'.)

The Donegal affair and the subsequent tribunal were hugely embarrassing for the force, which sacked several cops and disciplined over a dozen others. Reforms were inevitable and CHIS was a major plank of these. A controversy involving Louth drug trafficker Kieran Boylan, who was arrested and charged by the former Garda National Drug Unit over a €1.7 million drug haul while claiming to be working as an informant for a separate special national unit, seemed to reinforce its necessity.

But gardaí who regularly handle informants say the system presents serious practical difficulties. CHIS requires cops to pass on their informants to a centralized management system and forbids them to directly handle them themselves. This interferes in a crucial element of the garda–informant relationship: personal trust. One senior investigator who has worked within the CHIS system says:

> In the past, gardaí would have had detectives from different districts dealing directly with informants in their districts. However, this all changed after 2006.
>
> This posed problems, because informants might not have felt safe dealing with an 'outsider', compared to someone they might have known from their district. Everything should be properly monitored, but there's no reason why detectives in a Garda district shouldn't manage informants rather than handlers from outside their area. At present, there is no flexibility and there are too many layers that obstruct the aim of getting as much intelligence as possible.

Another issue is that experienced on-the-ground detectives had a better grasp of the goings-on in their areas than CHIS handlers coming in from outside. That put them in a much better position to instantly assess the importance and accuracy of what they were hearing.

But perhaps the most crucial element is that CHIS decrees those registered as informants cannot be involved in crime. It is a logical rule, but one which acts as a catch-22 situation. Anyone in a position high enough within the cartel to provide information significant enough to convict the top tier will almost certainly be an experienced criminal. If they suddenly refrain from engaging in crime they will immediately draw suspicion upon themselves. Yet gardaí risk compromising the legality and status of their investigation if they take information from someone who is committing criminal acts.

'Participating informants', as they are known, are widely

used in other jurisdictions such as the UK and Canada, where they are allowed to engage in limited lawbreaking to maintain their cover. The introduction of legislation governing their use here was recommended by a 2013 Garda Ombudsman report which declared that while it would 'clearly require extraordinarily careful monitoring to execute . . . it is not beyond us to draft such a process.'

At the time of writing, no moves have been made to act upon this by the current government. Former Detective Superintendent Gabriel O'Gara, who led Operation Goldeneye, believes this has been a major mistake:

> If the fight is to be won against organized crime there has to be a loosening up of the current system. There have to be exceptions when you are dealing with murderous, feuding organized crime gangs. The process can surely be overseen by a senior Garda member of chief superintendent rank, and in cases of significant importance like the current feud.
>
> In reality the registered informant cannot be actively involved in crime. All things, aside from the name of the informant, are also available to defence counsels.

This latter point is hugely important. The murder of Gary Hutch highlighted what can happen to those identified as 'rats' or even perceived as being too 'mouthy'.

Ironically, the gang's ruthlessness may well prove to be the biggest recruitment aid for gardaí and other police forces. Chief Superintendent Pat Leahy, who commands the Dublin North Central Division covering much of the feud territory, said the increasingly paranoid Kinahans could decide to eliminate some of the contract killers who have been doing their dirty work, to avoid them turning supergrass in future:

We have seen this before where those in the inner sanctums of criminal gangs feel exposed once a serious crime has been committed by someone they have recruited. They realize there's a weak link and the only way to deal with it is by killing someone – this is how they do business.

When they do start to clean house, you have other people recruited by them thinking, 'I could be next.' They could end up chasing people into the arms of the gardaí because they have no other way of staying alive or anyone else to turn to.

At the time of writing – early March 2017 – the main prospect of putting away the cartel's principal players lies with the accusations dating from Operation Shovel. As explained in chapter 11, under the Spanish system, an initial police investigation will gather enough evidence to see if an individual can be named an *investigado* and then remanded in custody or bailed so that a judge-led probe can continue. A trial date can be set, but the suspect will not officially be charged until they appear in court.

In many ways, Operation Shovel has been a failure. Julio Martínez Carazo, chief prosecutor for the Marbella area, admitted as much in an interview with *El País* in March 2016. 'The expectations were very high, but the results were not all as satisfactory as had been hoped,' he conceded.

The 20,000-page Policía Nacional file, seen by the authors, is replete with officers' observations that the gang's activities are 'indicative' or 'typical' of criminal activity, but contains little in the way of proof.

Had Gary Hutch and Mr A been stopped returning from Portugal with a drugs and arms haul that night in February 2010, police might have been able to directly link Christy and

Cunningham to its transportation. But that never came to pass. And while cops can legitimately question the lavish lifestyles of the Kinahans and John Cunningham, despite having no apparent means of financial support, this does not prove they have been making their money from drugs or arms trafficking.

Now that the police phase of the investigation is over the matter is in the hands of prosecutors, who are responsible for presenting the case against the cartel in court. In Spain the process of coming to trial regularly takes between two and four years. Yet almost seven years on from the spectacular Shovel raids, there are no signs of any charges being brought against the Kinahans or John Cunningham. 'Judicial delays are normal here on the Costa del Sol,' a court source told *El País* in November 2016, 'but this is unprecedented.'

The dropping of the court-led probe into drugs and arms running in 2013 was a major blow to police hopes of a significant conviction. They must now pin their hopes on prosecutions for money laundering and criminal association.

Some of the delay is down to the financial crisis which has afflicted Spain since Shovel was launched. As in Ireland, court budgets have been slashed, resulting in a logjam in the judicial process and a halving of resources.

Shovel was launched out of the investigative court in Estepona because it is where Paddy Doyle was shot dead, back in 2008. But as the probe grew into an international inquiry involving several European police forces, the lack of resources available to magistrates became apparent. The files that contained potential evidence for a prosecution of the Kinahans sat piled high with others in corridors prone to mould and flooding and under ceilings that had partially collapsed. A judge told a local paper how the court had been contacted by an FBI agent seeking assistance in a separate international investigation, but had been unable to call back because there was no phone that would allow officials to make outgoing calls.

However, much more of the delay is down to the old failing that has continually been exploited by international criminals such as the Kinahans – cock-ups and poor cross-border cooperation. Many of the cartel's assets, and many of the crimes they have ordered, took place in different countries. This required Spanish authorities to send out rogatory commissions – a request by one country for another to gather evidence on its behalf. In 2011, Spain sent rogatory commissions seeking information on the cartel's assets in Brazil and Cyprus and on its activities and holdings in Ireland and the UK. Ireland appears to have responded well, but Brazil took five years to get back to the Spanish, and Cyprus only returned the requested documentation towards the end of 2016. At the time of going to press, the UK – despite four separate queries – has yet to respond. At least some of the delay is at the Spanish end, as they sent the documents without having translated them into English.

The lack of cooperation is finally being tackled. European governments realize it is in all their interests to work together. The joint An Garda Síochána-Guardia Civil raids in September 2016 were the first of their kind and, during an official visit to Madrid by Taoiseach Enda Kenny in mid-January, his counterpart Mariano Rajoy promised 'even more in the future' to 'make sure there is no impunity for these criminal gangs'. Europol director Rob Wainwright has said the agency regards the Kinahan cartel as one of the most active

criminal outfits within the EU and it is now being prior-
itized as a target:

> Drug trafficking remains the number one criminal activity
> across Europe – and the Kinahan gang are at the centre of
> it. This has become more than a problem affecting Ireland.
> The amount of intelligence that we are sharing has grown
> in two years; this is a huge increase.

However, even if the Kinahans and Cunningham are convicted of money laundering – a far more serious offence than
criminal association – Spanish sentencing precedents would
indicate they are not likely to face much jail time.

The Financial Action Task Force (FATF) is an international anti-money laundering body founded in 1989 by the
G7, the representative body of some of the world's most
economically powerful nations – the USA, UK, France,
Germany, Japan, Canada and Italy. (It used to be the G8
until Russia was kicked out for invading Ukraine.) A
December 2014 FATF evaluation report on Spain's anti-
money laundering and counter-terrorist financing declared
the country's sentencing regime to be a 'weak spot'. The
report reads:

> The majority of natural persons generally convicted for ML
> [money laundering] in the most complex cases are sanctioned
> within the lower range of the scale and receive sentences
> ranging from six months to two years imprisonment.
>
> Even professional money launderers who have laundered
> millions of euros rarely receive the maximum of six years
> imprisonment. However, it should be noted that normal
> judicial practice in Spain is to apply a sentence at the lower
> end of the range of penalties set out for the offence.

Higher penalties may be applied, but in practice are only used in exceptional circumstances. It is hard to understand why the upper range of sentences is not being imposed in more serious cases.

The report found that in 2011, the average jail term upon conviction for money laundering in Spain was one year, eight months and twenty days. By 2012, that had increased to just shy of two years. All of which will be music to the ears of the cartel.

A much heavier blow would be the confiscation of the property in which the gang has invested in Brazil, Cyprus and Spain, worth millions of euros, all of which is currently frozen. The seizure and sale of his Antwerp casino, villa and apartment by the Belgian courts were a massive setback to Christy Kinahan. Carving up and flogging off the estimated €750m global investment portfolio he has built up would force the Dapper Don to start all over again, not an appetising prospect for a man approaching his sixties.

It is perhaps a measure of Christy Kinahan's confidence that he will again escape justice that the apartment whose door had been battered down by police during the early morning Shovel raids in May 2010 appeared for sale on a private website in November 2015, with Kinahan's Dutch wife listed as the contact person. Like all of the other assets linked to him, it had been frozen by court order and could not legally be sold. The asking price was €600,000. While a sale could technically be agreed, there could be no transfer of title until the embargo was lifted. The advert was later taken down, and the embargo remains in place.

On 5 February 2017, members of the cartel gathered at the grave of David Byrne at Mount Jerome cemetery in Dublin's

Harold's Cross on the first anniversary of his death. Brother Liam and father James 'Jaws' Byrne – himself a convicted armed robber – were there, as was cousin Liam Roe. Also present were enforcer Paul Rice and Sean McGovern, who had been injured at the Regency attack. As expected, there was no sign of the Kinahans themselves.

The gang was only too happy to take advantage of the State's determination to avoid further bloodshed and informed gardaí of their plans in advance. Gardaí took no chances and ahead of the ceremony they carried out sweeps of the graveyard with sniffer dogs. An armed unit maintained a visible presence throughout and watched as those attending released balloons bearing a picture of the dead man and laid floral tributes.

Among the messages on the wreaths was one that was obviously intended to be read by gardaí and the media: 'If there had've been proper protection there or police you wouldn't have been innocently murdered.'

It continued – incorrectly, perhaps deliberately so – 'And still no one charged. Why, why, oh why? All we want is justice.'

Three days later, gardaí found an example of the kind of 'justice' the gang had in mind. Two beat cops patrolling the North Strand area, not far from the home of the late Eddie Hutch, became suspicious of two cars parked on Newcomen Avenue, a small residential street off the North Strand Road. The cars seemed out of place on the narrow roadway, so they decided to force the doors. The cops' hunch proved correct. They found a loaded revolver, ammunition and a can of petrol, all apparently ready for use in another murder. Word was sent out to keep an eye out for similar vehicles hidden in plain sight across the city.

In late January veteran crime journalist Paul Williams

reported that the Kinahans had placed a €1m bounty on the head of Gerry Hutch, should he be taken alive. He reported that they wanted to torture him to death.

Garda intelligence has revealed that their ongoing operations have caused fractures within the top echelons of the cartel. It is known that Christy and Cunningham are deeply unhappy about the heat the feud is continuing to bring down on them. Both his father and the 'Old Man' have asked Daniel to scale back his actions for the time being, but he is refusing to do so.

Daniel has the support of Liam Byrne, who wants vengeance for his brother's death, and is determined not to let the issue lie. The pair's stubbornness is not only drawing unnecessary attention to their drug-trafficking business but is affecting themselves as much as anyone else. Though not confined to their own homes, like members of the Hutch families, they are unable to move about openly, even on the Continent. Byrne has also installed a panic room in his Crumlin property, to add to the existing armoured doors.

Daniel Kinahan and Liam Byrne's entrenched position, and the 'Monk's' inability to trust them, means gardaí do not expect the extermination campaign to end. Senior sources say the rate of killing may slow down, but is unlikely to stop entirely, barring another 'spectacular' hit, where either the 'Monk' or Daniel are eliminated.

Chief Superintendent Pat Leahy, though, is confident that, in the end, the cartel will tumble:

> When someone challenges the authority of the State, there is a realignment of resources at all levels, not just policing. All arms of the justice system will focus on a single

problem, because there's no alternative, we can't put up the white flag to these people.

When any criminal organization has experienced the full wrath of the State, they have not survived, and the Kinahan cartel won't survive it either. None of these gangs have survived the long haul. There is a long way to go yet, but I've no doubt all of them will go down. Whether it's through jail or a shallow grave, they will fall.

Acknowledgements

We offer our sincere thanks to those who can't be named for sharing their insight into and knowledge of the Kinahan Organised Crime Group. We would particularly like to thank members of An Garda Siochána who took time to provide us with advice on the contents of the book. Special thanks to former Assistant Commissioner Michael O'Sullivan for taking the time to look over the material.

We are extremely grateful to those in Ireland and abroad who shared their expertise. Their contributions were invaluable. A special note of thanks to 'The Jedi' for his friendship, guidance and advice.

We are most grateful to the families of Martin O'Rourke and Noel Kirwan for sharing their stories of the devastation caused by the loss of their loved ones during the feud. They welcomed us into their homes during a period of immense grief for their families.

The authors received valuable guidance and advice on this project from Stephen's former colleague at *Sunday Life* in Belfast – and one of Ireland's finest sub-editors – Damien McArdle. Credit must go to Barry Cummins from RTÉ for his support.

Praise is due to our editor at Penguin, Patricia Deevy, for all her advice, hard work, guidance and her countless emails on this project. We also owe much to editor Aoife Barrett for reshaping and improving our original raw efforts. Thanks also to Michael McLoughlin, MD of Penguin Ireland, for his support and enthusiastic response to the project and to libel expert Kieran Kelly for his direction.

This book would not have been possible without the support of *Irish Sun* editor, Kieran McDaid, Neil Cotter, head of news, Chris Doyle, picture editor, and all our colleagues at the *Irish Sun* for their support. Special thanks to fellow reporters Eavan Murray and Niall O'Connor for their help when covering this subject.

Thanks to the team on the *Irish Sun* picture desk for their assistance in compiling the images for the picture inset. Huge thanks to Jon Lee for burning the midnight oil when tracking down the images and special thanks to photographer Crispin Rodwell for taking many of the photographs. All pictures in the inset – apart from those specified next – are used courtesy of the *Irish Sun*. Additional copyright as follows: 17, 18, 36, 37, 38, 45, 57 – photojournalist, Padraig O'Reilly; 10, 58, 62 – Collins Picture Agency; 44 – Reuters; 55 – Policia Nacional España. Thanks to all the photographers for allowing us to use their images.

And on a personal note . . .

Stephen: I would like to thank my wife Chrissie and our son Tom for all their love and for putting up with me during the writing process. Thanks also to Chrissie's parents, Hilary and Dennis (particularly for allowing me to use their home when working on the book), to my mum Lorraine and her partner Brendan, and to my brother Paul and sister-in-law Toni for their huge support.

Owen: I would like to thank my partner Maria for helping massively during the lengthy writing and editing of this work. Love also to my family for the understanding and backing they offered throughout.